BBQ Bash

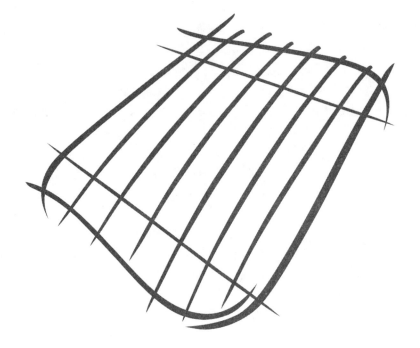

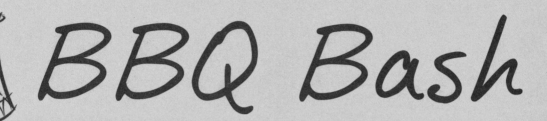

BBQ Bash

The Be-All, End-All Party Guide, from Barefoot to Black Tie

Karen Adler and Judith Fertig

The Harvard Common Press
Boston, Massachusetts

The Harvard Common Press
535 Albany Street
Boston, Massachusetts 02118
www.harvardcommonpress.com

Printed in the United States of America
Printed on acid-free paper

Library of Congress Cataloging-in-Publication Data
Adler, Karen.
  BBQ bash : the be-all, end-all party guide, from barefoot to black tie / Karen Adler
and Judith Fertig.
      p. cm.
  Includes index.
  ISBN-13: 978-1-55832-348-3 (hardcover)
  ISBN-13: 978-1-55832-349-0 (pbk.)
  1. Barbecue cookery. 2. Cookery, International. 3. Entertaining. 4. Parties. I. Fertig, Judith M.
II. Title. III. Title: Barbecue bash. IV. Title: Barbeque bash.
  TX840.B3A318 2008
  641.7′6—dc22

                                                            2007046209

Special bulk-order discounts are available on this and other Harvard Common Press books.
Companies and organizations may purchase books for premiums or resale, or may arrange
a custom edition, by contacting the Marketing Director at the address above.

Cover and photo insert design by Night & Day Design
Interior design by Edward Miller
Photographs by Becky Luigart-Stayner
Food styling by Judy Feagin; prop styling by Fonda Shaia
Illustrations by Heather Holbrook

10 9 8 7 6 5 4 3 2 1

To R., G. K., and L.,
and everyone else who thinks life
is just one great big party!

Contents

Acknowledgments

Special thanks go to Remus Powers, Ph.B., aka Ardie Davis, founder of Greasehouse University; the Baron of Barbecue, Paul Kirk; John Ross, the Barbecue Professor; and Carolyn Wells, executive director of the Kansas City Barbeque Society, for bestowing the coveted Doctorate of Barbecue upon us BBQ Queens. So along with Karen's Masters of Barbecue and Judith's membership in the Magic Order of the Mop, we both proudly add Ph.B. to the end of our names!

Both our families include many fine cooks, grillers, barbecuers, and connoisseurs of wine and spirits. They are our most frequent guests in the kitchen and around the grill and include Judith's mom, Jean Merkle (indoor cook and baker extraordinaire); dad Jack Merkle (the family butcher and all-around meat man); sister Julie Fox (the entertainer who shares her fabulous recipes); and Julie's husband, John (who pours the drinks and quizzes us on rock & roll trivia). Karen's mom, Denise Conde (the dessert queen), has everyone making a beeline for her cakes, pies, and cookies. Her sister Linda Yeates bakes great pies and prepares perfect deviled eggs, but, most important, she's the sparkling-wine expert. Sister Nancy McKay creates the perfect ambience and settings along with fabulous casseroles and the best salads. Baby sister Betsy Peterson is very accomplished, since she worked as a caterer—she makes great appetizers and has that innate baking expertise that runs in the family, too. Karen's husband, Dick, pours the cocktails, including his famous Da Das (page 40) and intoxicating martinis, plus he shares grill time with her.

Our children are all grown and they have developed their own styles of cooking. Judith's daughter, Sarah Fertig, likes to cook with an international flavor and flair. Son Nick Fertig makes Famous Cheesy Elk Dip, among other things, and owns his

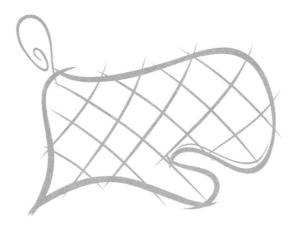

own smoker, too, so we are expecting competition from him. Karen and Dick's eldest daughter, Ellen Young, doesn't love to cook, but she can whip up a great spaghetti, and she doesn't have to cook anyway, because her husband, Brian, loves to be the man in the kitchen and the dude at the smoker. Brian doesn't spin sugar, but he can make a mouthwatering salmon soufflé. Daughter Jill and her husband, Jimmy Donnici, share the duties indoors with lots of wonderful Italian-style meals, but Jimmy grills up a storm outside on his gas grill and makes some awesome barbecue in his smoker, too.

Other friends who have shared their recipes or entertaining tips with us include Diane Phillips, Rebecca Miller, Dennis Horner, Judy and Joe Evans, Roxi and Ralph Steinheimer, Rose Kallas, Susan Howard, Angie and John Stout, Ron and Barb Martin, Doug and Lisa Youngblood, Janet and Don Coffey, Jack and Janine Joslin, Jack and Susan Helm, A. J. Rathbun, chef Jasper Mirabile, *Culinary Travels* guy Dave Eckert, Chef Karen Putman, Jean Tamburello, Kathy Pelz, Andrea Benjamina, and Judi Moritz. The members of our monthly cookbook club are a wonderful source of inspiration and support. These fine ladies include Dee Barwick, Liz Benson, Vicki Johnson, Gayle Parnow, Mary Pfeifer, Kathy Smith, and Roxanne Wyss.

We are especially fond of all the foodies with whom we work and play, including members of Les Dames d'Escoffier, the American Institute of Wine and Food, and our Slow Food Convivium in Kansas City.

We both thank Mary Ann Duckers, who runs the show at Pig Out Publications and keeps our lives as neat and tidy as possible. Our agent, Lisa Ekus, and her wonderful associates are a pleasure to work with. The Harvard Common Press has been part of our lives for more than a decade, and we thank everyone there for their good work. Plus, we are so appreciative of their unending support for all of our books, including Judith's *Prairie Home Cooking*, *Prairie Home Breads*, and *All-American Desserts*, and our collaborative titles, which are *Fish & Shellfish, Grilled & Smoked*; *The BBQ Queens' Big Book of Barbecue*; *Weeknight Grilling with the BBQ Queens*; and, now, *BBQ Bash*!

How to Throw a Be-All, End-All Barbecue Party

What's a barbecue bash?

It's a gathering with equal parts food, drink, and fun. It's the old-style dinner party loosened up and taken outside under the stars. It's a kick-off-your-shoes good time—even if you're dressed to the nines.

When you take a sip of something bubbly on a moonlit night, or just under some twinkling lights—whether it's beer, vintage Champagne, or even sparkling water—life is good. And no matter what food you serve, if it's sizzled on a grill, you know it's going to taste great. But there's more to a barbecue bash than food and drink.

Although a barbecue doesn't have to mean weeks of planning and a cast of thousands, a be-all, end-all bash does require some forethought. In our previous books *The BBQ Queens' Big Book of Barbecue* and *Weeknight Grilling with the BBQ Queens*, we urged you to think about the whole meal, not just the hunk of meat over the flames. In *BBQ Bash*, we want you to think about the whole party. Sure, you can pretty easily throw an outdoor barbecue with hot dogs and hamburgers, mismatched paper plates and napkins, deli potato salad, chips and salsa, a few citronella candles, and a cooler full of beer and soft drinks. But you don't need any advice from us on that, now, do you?

A successful bash, on the other hand, calls for a little style. And, as you'll see, it's not hard to get it.

It's Your Party!

It's your party, so decide how you want to entertain and what ambience you want to create. You're going for a holistic approach to entertaining in your outdoor (or indoor) space—food, drink, music, table setting, serving pieces, and lighting. Does this mean a shopping spree to your favorite kitchenware or tabletop store? If you've got the dough, go! But all of this doesn't have to be expensive, either. We're big fans of using colorful bed sheets for tablecloths, pots of inexpensive plants from those big-box stores, serving pieces from discount stores, and goodies from our own gardens.

Decide on the "feel" you want your bash to have, then go with it. Is your style

• **Urban Chic?** Then bring out the martinis, grilled hors d'oeuvres served on white platters, white tablecloths and candles, and stainless-steel or chrome accessories.

Decorate with architectural plants like bamboo or ornamental grasses. For music, think jazz or alternative rock, Norah Jones or Corinne Bailey Rae. This style is perfect for a rooftop or patio party outside your urban loft.

• **South Seas?** Then pour margaritas or a rum-based punch. Use tropical prints for tablecloths and disposable (and renewable) bamboo plates and leaf-shaped platters for serving. Grill foods on skewers or wrapped in tropical leaves, and set out pots of tropical plants like bougainvillea and rubber trees. Get funky with Hawaiian music (Go, Don Ho!), reggae, or the soundtrack of *South Pacific*. This style is great for poolside entertaining. Don't have a proper pool? Buy an inflatable wading pool and see what happens.

• **Farmhouse?** Throw old quilts over the tables. Serve grilled entrées on speckled tinware platters and pass the spiked lemonade. Pile geraniums or Queen Anne's lace and wildflowers into rustic baskets. Crank up the bluegrass music, let the fiddler do some pickin', and your guests will start grinnin'. You, too, can be out standing in your field, a park, or under the trees in your backyard.

• **All-American?** Bring out the red (geraniums), white (bistro-style serveware), and blue (checked tablecloths). Grill up a great steak and offer a big salad with blue cheese dressing, along with plenty of cold beer. Go for Willie Nelson, Bruce Springsteen, or an Evening at Pops. Light up the cake or cupcakes with sparklers. Hit the deck.

• **Tuscan Villa?** Turn your outdoor space into a villa courtyard. Use earth-toned colors for tablecloths and napkins, and terracotta or glazed earthenware for serving pieces offering grilled pizzas, vegetables, and Italian-style entrées. Strew lots of vines and grapes or flowers in burnished colors. Quaff your favorite Italian wines as you listen to Dean Martin warble "That's Amore" or Andrea Bocelli sing anything.

Now that you get the big picture, let's get that party organized.

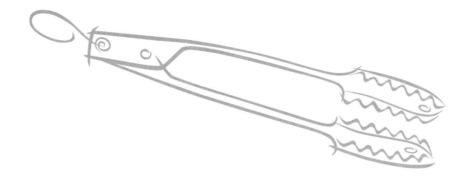

BBQ Bash 101

Attending to details early on will let you relax and enjoy your own party.

Lighting

Set the mood with soft lighting that flatters guests. If you're going to be outside, string clear or white lights on backyard trees, and consider hanging colorful paper or Chinese lanterns as well. Set out lots of votives and pillar candles with hurricane shades. Use mirrors behind or underneath candles for reflection. And if you're using a charcoal grill, enjoy the fire, or set up a separate enclosed outdoor firepit so that guests can gather around the firelight.

If you're going to be indoors, set out plenty of candles as well. Maybe consider stringing tiny white lights around your ceiling molding or doorways, to add a bit more sparkle. If you have a fireplace, enjoy the crackle and flickering flames of a wood fire, or set lots of candles inside the fireplace.

Setting Up the Bar

A bar area can be as simple and casual as glasses set out on a table and bottles iced down in tubs outdoors for guests to help themselves, or as formal as a full-service bar area, complete with a tuxedoed bartender. Whatever your choice, arrange for an area where guests can circulate easily and not create a bottleneck. You can even have several bar stations—one for wine, one for beer, one for nonalcoholic drinks—or a couple of different stations each serving everything. Here are some basic pointers.

- Have plenty of glasses. Figure three per person (one old-fashioned glass, one wine or beer glass, one water glass) for a cocktail or appetizer party, and four per person (one old-fashioned, two wine or beer, one water) for a dinner party.
- Keep cold drinks cold. For informal backyard barbecues, we like to use galvanized metal tubs purchased at hardware or home improvement stores. Fill the tubs with ice and add the beer and soft drinks. For a black-tie barbecue, buy lightweight garden urns that have the look of stone or terracotta. Line these discreetly with plastic trash bags if the urns have drainage holes, then fill with ice and drinks—or bottles of bubbly! Also, clear acrylic ice buckets go with everything.

- Hire help, if necessary. This can be a professional, or it can be your grad-student neighbor who's looking for some extra cash. If you have more than 12 guests, you'll need extra help in the way of bartending and/or cleanup.

Setting the Tables

According to style setter Carolyne Roehm, "Plain white china and clear glass plates are the equivalent of the little black dress." We wholeheartedly agree. Like that little black frock, you can dress them up or down, depending on your gathering. Start with these basics, and then add color and theme with linens and flowers.

Have enough plain white or clear glass plates on hand, at least two to three per person for a cocktail party, and at least a five-piece place setting (bread, appetizer, dinner, salad, and dessert plates) for a dinner party. You can buy inexpensive plain white and clear glass plates at restaurant supply or discount stores.

Banish plastic cutlery. Either go with finger food for which you don't need silverware, or bring out the real stuff—or a decent-quality stainless set. You can't cut much of anything with a plastic knife, and plastic forks tend to snap in half at the most inconvenient times. Figure on two knives, forks, and spoons per person for a cocktail party, and one place setting per person for a dinner party.

Think beyond the tablecloth. We use sheets, quilts, matelassé bedspreads, and lengths of fabric to cover tables. The common denominator for us is that they're all washable. And speaking of tablecloths, it's always nice to have enough tables and seating for everyone, too. Count how many chairs and seats are available throughout your house, patio, and/or backyard, then add the number of card tables and chairs that you need. You can borrow, buy, or rent these. It's inexpensive and convenient to go for sturdy card tables, which you can set up in strategic locations that won't block traffic flow.

Go for height on a buffet table. The biggest mistake that people make is to keep the buffet table flat, flat, flat. Stack boxes underneath the cloth(s) covering the table to give you raised areas. Invest in a tiered stand or two to serve appetizers or bite-size desserts.

Believe in flower power. With "rustic" as our byword, we like to go the easy and natural route with floral accents. Judith likes to fill big, rustic baskets with pots of whatever single-color flowers are in season—white poinsettias or cyclamen in winter; yellow daffodils, blue hyacinth, or purple hydrangeas in spring; orange zinnias or salmon geraniums in summer; or golden chrysanthemums in fall. In the summer, Karen goes out to her herb garden and picks branches of herbs in flower for fragrant bouquets. We also like to put just one stem of a flower in individual vases, one above each plate, for occasions like sit-down family birthday dinners. In the fall, hollow out a pumpkin, place a plastic container inside for water, and then add dahlias, mums, sprays of bittersweet, and wild grapevines. Remember: As with the food, "rustic" and "simple" are good guidelines. Please don't fuss for hours getting the perfectly shaped arrangement—that's what florists are for! And if perfectly shaped is what you want, by all means give your florist a call.

Music

Music provides another layer of interest and energy, like a wonderful perfume or aftershave that becomes an invisible but alluring accessory. If you're having a black-tie barbecue and you can afford it, provide live music: a string quartet, a bluegrass trio, a jazz singer and pianist, a hip-hop deejay—you get the picture. Or simply set up the CD player with your favorites. The only mistake you can really make is having the music too loud. You don't want the music dominating the party and drowning out conversation. In our Party Menus found throughout the book, we have made some suggestions to help you set the scene.

BBQ Bash Checklist

You want to enjoy the party, too, right? So take a peek at this checklist and get organized, as organization is the key ingredient to a successful barbecue bash.

- Make up a guest list. Will you send out invitations or call your guests?
- Plan a menu with the interchangeable components you are most comfortable executing.
- Always choose recipes and foods that are in season.
- Perfect two or three recipes and make them your signature dishes.
- Practice whipping up great sauces that are quick to assemble.
- Do a rehearsal of the menu several days or weeks ahead of time, then make any changes needed to help you pull it off on the big day.
- Make a list of all the foods and garnishes you need and check them off when they're purchased, then again when they're prepped.
- Embrace high-style, low-fuss grilling (choose items that can be grilled ahead and served at room temperature, or easy-to-grill items for the evening).
- Have extra charcoal or an extra tank of propane on hand.
- Think *mise en place* (everything in its place) for when you begin to cook.
- Set out your serving utensils, plates, and bowls ahead of time (place little notes on each serving vessel so you know what goes where).
- Check out your supply of dinner plates and silverware to make sure you have enough.
- Do the same with your tablecloths, basket liners, and kitchen and guest-bath towels.
- Have more than enough paper or cloth napkins, both cocktail and dinner size.
- Round up extra tables and chairs if necessary.
- If you can, hire some help for serving and/or cleanup.
- Set out mirrors and candles, flowers and vases the day before, mark where they go, then put them in place the day of the party.
- Plan to have enough music so that you don't end up repeating any selections.
- Serve a special apéritif, like Lillet with a French-themed meal or fino sherry with a Spanish-themed party.
- Reseat your guests for dessert so that everyone gets a new dining partner.
- Think of a small gift for your guests to take home: potted plants or herbs, handwritten or nicely typed menus of the dinner, fireworks (like sparklers) for each person, fortune cookies with handwritten fortunes, a small bottle of your special homemade barbecue sauce, or a small glass jar of your special barbecue spice.
- Imagine being a guest at your own party, and then fine-tune the details according to what you see.

How to Use the Barefoot to Black-Tie Party Menus

For each of the dozen themed bashes we've put together for you, which you will find in boxes throughout the book, we offer easy, foolproof ways to suggest a mood or theme at your gathering, from dishware to linens to flowers and music. For each party menu we've also suggested the foods, wines, special drinks, and other beverages that go together well. We offer an array of possible dishes that you can mix and match for your party. We certainly don't think you'll make them all, but you might choose a few to serve—along with your own favorite dishes. We're just trying to help take the guesswork out of entertaining, so you've got even more time to relax and put your feet up beforehand.

Pairing Wine and Grilled Food

Many people think of beer when they think of barbecue, but one of the great things about grilled foods for a party is how well wine goes with them. Writes wine authority Karen MacNeil in *The Wine Bible* (Workman Publishing, 2001), "Grilling is also one of the best things that can happen to wine, especially red wine. . . . The sweet, charred flavor and slightly crusty texture grilling imparts make any food more red-wine willing."

You can go one of two ways: comparable flavors or contrasting flavors. Smoky, toasty, slightly oaky, and woody flavors in wines compare well to the flavors foods pick up from the grill and smoker. Slightly sweeter and fruitier wines will offer a contrast with foods that have a little zing and spice, and dry, crisp wines will give any natural sweetness in foods a run for its money. When you're at the wine shop, cultivate a relationship with a knowledgeable employee, or simply read the description of the wine and you'll have a good idea if it will match your dish.

Or take a tip from our friend Dave Eckert, the host of *Culinary Travels with Dave Eckert* on PBS. An avid barbecuer, Eckert likes to host parties for which guests are asked to bring a bottle of wine they *think* will go with a certain dish, for whatever reason. You go through the buffet line, then head to another table where all the bottles have been uncorked. There, you pour just a bit of one wine in your glass. Nibble a bit of the entrée in question, sip your first wine, and consider. Pour another wine, nibble, and consider again; and so on. This is a great way to get your guests involved, and it's also a great conversation starter.

For a casual outdoor meal, you won't want to pour your costliest wine, but when you set the table with your finest china and bring that celebratory smoked rib roast to the table, it's time to uncork the good stuff. In the end, of course, it's all about what you and your guests like, so experiment in advance to get a sense of what works best for your tastes. For more on pairing wine with grilled and smoked food, see page 88.

Sizzle and Smoke

Once you've decided on your style and have gotten organized, you can start thinking about the food. On the weekend, when we expect most of you will be hosting your barbecue bashes, you're guided more by pleasure and less by the clock—you have time to be a little experimental, to kick back and relax, and to entertain in a fun, casual way. To that end, in our recipes, you'll find:

- A seasonal approach. It's less stressful to grill and entertain when you don't have to search for blood oranges in July or fresh strawberries in January. For some recipes, we even give "four seasons" options so that you can adapt them according to when you plan to serve them.
- Foods that look and taste great right off the grill, without being too time-consuming or fiddly. That's what we mean by "rustic."
- Colorful, tasty, easy appetizers that look great on platters.
- Entrées with big, bold flavors and great rustic looks.
- Delicious desserts that often can be made ahead.
- Cocktail, mocktail, wine, and beer suggestions with the appetizers, entrées, and party menus.

Now that you're ready to go outside and fire up the grill, it's time to take you through the basics of grilling and smoking, with some side trips into specialty techniques such as skewering, stir-grilling, planking, and rotisserie cooking.

Utensils for Grilling and Smoking

Several basic tools make grilling and smoking easier. A kitchen shop or a barbecue and grill store will be a good source for finding the items listed. Choose professional utensils that are heavier and are superior in quality and durability. Long handles are preferable on everything, to keep you at a safe distance from the fire. Remember to oil your utensils, grill racks, and gadgets on both sides to prevent sticking and for easier cleanup.

- A **stiff wire brush** with a scraper makes cleaning the grill a simple job (tackle this while the grill is still warm).
- A **natural-bristle basting brush** for applying oil to the grill grates and a separate brush to baste food during grilling or smoking.
- **Perforated grill racks** are grates placed on top of the grill to accommodate small or delicate items, such as chicken wings, fish fillets, scallops, shrimp, and vegetables.
- **Hinged grill baskets** hold foods in place and make turning an easy process.
- **Grill woks** are punched with holes to let in smoky flavor. You can use them to stir-grill pieces of fish, chicken, shellfish, other tender cubes of meat, and vegetables by tossing with wooden paddles.
- **Heat-resistant oven or grill mitts** offer the best hand protection.
- Long-handled **spring-loaded tongs** are easier to use than the scissors type. They are great for turning most food and skewers.
- A **spray bottle** filled with water will douse any flare-ups.
- **Charcoal chimneys or electric fire starters** are great for starting charcoal fires.
- **Wooden skewers** should be soaked for about 30 minutes before using. Double-skewer foods for more control and to prevent the food from spinning on the skewer. **Flat metal skewers** are also great.
- A **long-handled offset fish spatula** with a 5- to 6-inch blade makes for easy turning of fish fillets.
- Two **long-handled spatulas** are also welcome utensils, especially when turning a large fish fillet. Position the spatulas at each end of the fillet and roll quickly to turn.
- **Disposable aluminum pans** hold liquid during the smoking process. Or use the pans as tents to cover thick steaks that need a bit more cooking time on the indirect side of the grill.
- We like **instant-read thermometers** for a quick read when cooking meat and poultry.
- Aromatic **wood planks** (cedar is our favorite) impart a lovely wood flavor to fish, shellfish, poultry, and vegetables. Planks make for a cool presentation, too.
- Metal **smoker boxes** are very useful for holding soaked wood chips that are placed over a gas grill fire to create smoke. Their perforations allow smoke to escape but keep chips from falling out.

Grilling 101

Light My Fire!

Most of our food is grilled directly over a medium-hot to hot fire, though sometimes we grill over indirect heat. There are a number of different ways to achieve that fire.

CHARCOAL GRILLS

Charcoal fires can be started in any of several safe, ecologically sound ways. We like using hardwood charcoal because it is natural and gives a better wood flavor, but we also use charcoal briquets or a combination of hardwood charcoal and briquets. If you like, mix them together, as many of our barbecue competition buddies do. Hardwood charcoal is available at some grocery stores, as well as at hardware, barbecue, and home improvement stores. Briquets are more readily available at grocery stores, convenience shops, and hardware and home improvement stores.

Choices for lighting a charcoal fire include using a charcoal chimney, an electric fire starter, or lighter fluid. The charcoal chimney is an upright cylindrical metal canister, like a large metal coffee can with a handle. Fill the top of the chimney with hardwood lump charcoal and/or briquets. Place the chimney on a nonflammable surface, such as concrete or the grill rack. Slightly tip the chimney over and stuff one to two sheets of crumpled newspaper in the convex-shaped bottom. Light the paper with a match. After 5 minutes, check to make sure that the fire is still going. If not, stuff with paper and light again. The coals should be red hot and starting to ash over in 15 to 20 minutes. Carefully dump the coals onto the bottom of the grill grate, and add more charcoal if needed. You will also use the charcoal chimney to add coals if you're grilling something over a low fire for a longer time.

To use an electric fire starter, place it on the bottom grill grate. Mound the charcoal on top and plug it in. The coals will take about 15 minutes to ignite. Carefully remove the starter and set it in a safe place to cool.

Lighter fluid has gotten a bad rap from improper use. Used correctly, it's just fine and will not impart any off taste to your food. Douse the charcoal with lighter fluid and light with a match. Don't start to grill until the coals have burned down to an ashen coating over glowing embers. That way, any petroleum residue will have burned off.

GAS GRILLS

Follow your manufacturer's directions for starting your gas grill. This will include attaching the propane tank to the grill, turning on the propane valve, then lighting the burners of the gas grill. About 40,000 combined BTUs (British Thermal Units, which measure the maximum heat output of a burner) are optimum. Many grills have thermometers attached to the grill lid, so close the lid and let it heat up to the desired temperature.

Fueling the Fire

Now that you've got your fire, you need to maintain and manage it for cooking over direct or indirect heat. Here's how.

CHARCOAL GRILLS

Direct fire: After you have started the fire according to your method of choice, wait until the charcoal is red hot and beginning to ash over before putting on the grill grate. Place food on the grill grate directly over the hot coals. Leave the grill lid open or closed, depending on which method you like. If you need to add more coals, ignite them in the charcoal chimney first.

Indirect fire: Prepare a direct fire first. Once you have your hot coals on the fire grate, push the coals over to the side of the grill. One side of the grill will have hot coals—that is the direct-heat cooking side. The other side will not have hot coals—that is the indirect-heat cooking side. Carefully place a disposable aluminum pan filled with water on the indirect side, next to the hot coals on the bottom of the grill or smoker. (Smoking is longer and slower, so you need the extra moisture from the water in the water pan.) Place water-soaked wood chunks or chips or dry wood pellets in an aluminum foil packet poked with holes (for wood smoke flavoring) on top of the coals. Replace the grill grate. To cook this way, you must close the grill lid.

GAS GRILLS

Direct fire: Turn the burners on. Place the food on the grill grate directly over the hot burner; that is direct heat. To cook this way, you can either leave the grill lid up or down.

Indirect fire: Light the burners on one half of the grill only. The side of the grill without the burners on is the indirect-heat side. Add water-soaked or dry wood chips to a smoker box, or wrap the chips in a foil packet poked with holes and place directly over the lava rock. Place a disposable aluminum pan filled with water over direct heat. To cook this way, you must close the grill lid.

The Hand Method for Judging a Grill's Temperature

Hold your hand 5 inches above the heat source. If you can only hold it there for about 2 seconds, your fire is hot (500°F or more) and perfect for grilling; 3 seconds is a medium-hot fire (about 400°F) for grilling; 4 seconds is a medium fire (about 350°F) for grilling or higher-heat indirect cooking; and 5 to 6 seconds is a low fire (225° to 250°F), the ideal temperature for slow smoking.

ADJUSTING YOUR GRILL'S TEMPERATURE

On a charcoal grill, you can lower the temperature by slightly closing the side vents, or by closing the lid. Don't close the vents and the lid at the same time, or the fire will go out. You can raise the temperature by opening the side vents or by adding more charcoal to the fire.

On a gas grill, you adjust the heat by turning the heat control knobs to the desired level. It's pretty simple!

How to Wood-Grill or Grill with a Kiss of Smoke

On a charcoal grill, add water-soaked wood chunks or chips directly to the charcoal fire. Place dry wood pellets in a packet made from heavy-duty aluminum foil (poke holes in the packet) or in a metal smoker box and place directly over the charcoal.

To get wood-smoke flavor on a gas grill, place dry wood pellets or wood chips in a packet made from heavy-duty aluminum foil (poke holes in the packet) or in a metal smoker box and place directly over the lava rock. Do not put unwrapped wood chips or pellets directly on the lava rock or ceramic plates in the bottom of the grill, as the residue could block the holes in the gas burners. Properly contained, the wood chips or wood pellets will smolder rather than burn, and give an added wood-smoke flavor.

Getting Ready to Grill

The grill should be clean and the grill rack(s) lightly oiled with vegetable oil or Grate Chef Grill Wipes, pre-oiled towelettes for the grill. Have all of your equipment handy.

Cook with the grill lid open or closed. If your grill has less than 40,000 BTUs, closing the lid allows the heat to build up in the grill, making a hotter fire.

How to Grill

When ready to grill, place the food over the hot fire. Grill food for half the cooking time on one side, allowing for good searing and grill marks. Turn once and finish cooking. Do not make the mistake of flipping the food several times. Be patient.

Grilling Times

Estimated grilling times are just that: estimates, not hard and fast "set your watch by it" times. In every recipe, we give you an estimate of how long something will take to grill. We also guide you with a recommended internal temperature or a description of the look of a food when that food is done. When you cook outdoors, the weather is always a factor. On hot days, things grill faster; on cold days, things grill more slowly.

People in our cooking classes always seem to worry that their foods won't get done on the grill. We're here to tell you that undercooking food on the grill is not something to worry about. If you want to worry about something, worry about overcooking it, which is far more likely to happen.

Of course, while our goal is always to grill and smoke perfectly, we would rather undercook than overcook foods on the grill. You can always finish cooking the food by zapping it for a few seconds in the microwave or putting it back on the grill. If food is undercooked, you can always rescue it. If your food is overcooked, there's nothing you can do about it.

We recommend that, if you're just starting out, you use an instant-read thermometer to test the doneness of most grilled foods. Just insert the thermometer into the thickest part and read the temperature. After some experience, you'll be able to tell the doneness of grilled foods by touch alone. When you hold a pork tenderloin with tongs and it's charred on the outside but still soft and wiggly, that's rare. If the tenderloin offers some resistance, it's medium. When it feels solid, it's well done.

DONENESS CHART FOR GRILLING

Because foods continue to cook for a few minutes after they're taken off the grill, we recommend pulling them off the heat at the temperatures listed below, such as 145°F for pork loin. If you pull off a pork loin at that point, it will go up to 150° to 155°F on its own. If you leave the pork loin on the grill or smoker to reach 155°F, the meat will end up well done, dry, and less appetizing. Although burgers can be made from beef, chicken, lamb, pork, or even tuna, because they're all ground and have a similar texture and volume, they follow the same doneness guidelines.

Burgers	130°F for rare, 145° to 150°F for medium, 160°F for well done
Beef steak	130°F for rare, 145° to 150°F for medium, 160°F for well done
Chicken breast	155° to 160°F for done
Chicken legs, thighs	160° to 165°F for done
Fish fillets or steaks	Begin to flake when tested with a fork in thickest part
Shellfish	Opaque and somewhat firm to the touch
Lamb chops	130°F for rare, 145° to 150°F for medium, 160°F for well done
Pork loin or rib chops	145° to 150°F for medium, 160°F for well done
Pork tenderloin	130° to 135°F for rare, 145° to 150°F for medium, 160°F for well done
Veal chops	130° to 135°F for rare, 145° to 150°F for medium, 160°F for well done
Vegetables	Done to your liking

Smoking 101

With most types of grills—including gas grills—you can slow-smoke almost any food for delicious barbecue in your own backyard. Most grills can be set up to function as smokers. However, smokers are usually set up just to smoke, not grill.

Preparing the "Pit" and Equipment

The grill or smoker should be clean and the rack(s) lightly oiled with vegetable oil or pre-oiled Grate Chef Grill Wipes. Have all of your equipment and fuel handy, and relax and enjoy the smoking experience.

Preparing an Indirect Fire for Smoking

CHARCOAL GRILL

Use hardwood charcoal and/or briquets to start a fire. When the coals have ashed over, use a long grill spatula to push them over to one side of the grill. Place a metal or disposable aluminum pan of water on the bottom of the grill next to the coals. Place the grill rack over the top. The side with the coals is direct heat; the side with the pan of water is indirect heat. Use grill thermometers to monitor the temperature on both sides of the grill. Ideally, smoking is done at a temperature (measured on the indirect side) of 225° to 250°F.

GAS GRILL

To prepare an indirect fire on a gas grill, you need the type of grill that has two separate burners. Turn one burner on, and leave the other one off. The side with the burner on is direct heat; the side with the burner off is indirect heat. You can place a water pan in the back of the grill on the direct side. To get more wood-smoke flavor, place dry wood chips or wood pellets in a packet made from heavy duty aluminum foil (poke holes in the packet) or in a metal smoker box and place directly over the lava rock. The wood chips or wood pellets will smolder rather than burn, and give an added wood-smoke flavor. Some gas or electric grills also have a smoker box, to which you can add wood chips or dry wood pellets. Do not put these directly on the lava rock, as the residue could block the holes in the burners.

How to Add Wood for Wood-Smoke Flavor

When you're slow-smoking at a low temperature, the flavor comes from smoldering aromatic woods—such as hickory, cherry, oak, mesquite, or pecan—that are placed on or near the fire. Depending on the type of smoking equipment you have, there are several types of woods to use and ways to use them.

Fine wood chips: A little bigger in size than sawdust, these are used in the stovetop smoker. You use them dry and in small amounts—1 to 2 tablespoons placed in the middle of the bottom of the stovetop smoker. When you place the stovetop smoker over a heat source, these fine chips smolder and burn, giving off aromatic smoke.

Wood chips: These can be used dry or moistened. Try them both ways to see how they work best on your grill or smoker. They should smolder, not burn up. Use about 1 cup at a time, and replenish every 45 minutes for 2 hours of wood smoking. Make an aluminum foil packet to enclose the chips (poke holes in the packet) or place in a metal smoker box, and place on the grill rack over the heat (in a gas grill) or around the electric coil (in an electric smoker).

Wood pellets: These are pellet-shaped bits of compressed sawdust. The wood-pellet grill uses these for both fuel and wood-smoke flavor. The pellets can also be used with other grills and with smokers, too. Wood pellets must be used dry; if you moisten them, they turn into mushy sawdust. For smoking, use ⅓ cup at a time. Make an aluminum foil packet to enclose the dry pellets (poke holes in the packet) or place in a metal smoker box. Place directly on the coals in a charcoal grill, on the grill rack over the heat in a gas grill, or around the electric coil in an electric bullet smoker. Wood pellets must be replenished about every hour.

Wood chunks: Bigger pieces of aromatic wood, chunks are 2 to 3 inches long and wide. Soak them for at least 30 minutes before using them. Wood chunks are most often placed directly on hot coals or around but not touching an electric coil on an electric bullet smoker. We don't recommend using wood chunks with a gas grill; they're not as effective as wood pellets or chips. Begin with two or three water-soaked wood chunks on a charcoal fire and replenish with two or three more in about 30 minutes. Three wood chunks will last for about 2 hours in an electric smoker and may be all the wood flavor you need.

Wood "sticks" or "logs": Even bigger pieces of wood, these are cut to fit the diameter of the firebox on a competition-style rig, and placed right on the hot coals. You generally use three sticks to start with and replenish them as necessary.

Varieties of Hardwood Flavors

Whether you use logs, sticks, chunks, pellets, shreds, or chips, hardwoods can infuse foods with great smoke flavor. You can find all kinds of unusual woods, from mulberry to sassafras, but here are the most common hardwoods available for smoking. Mix and match for your own custom smoke blend. Buy them at a grilling store, or make sure you buy untreated food-safe wood.

- **Alder** gives a light, aromatic flavor that's perfect with seafood.
- **Apple** provides a sweeter, aromatic flavor that is good with poultry or pork.
- **Cherry** lends a deeper, sweeter note to smoked foods and is delicious with beef tenderloin, pork, poultry, or lamb.
- **Hickory** gives a stronger, hearty smoke flavor to beef, pork, or poultry.
- **Mesquite** provides the strongest, smokiest flavor and is well suited to beef, especially brisket. It's also good with poultry and pork.
- **Oak** provides a medium smoke flavor without being bitter and pairs well with any food.
- **Pecan** creates a medium smoke flavor, less pronounced than hickory but more so than oak. Pecan is great to use for grilling with a kiss of smoke.

Getting Ready to Smoke

The smoker should be clean and the rack(s) lightly oiled with vegetable oil or Grate Chef Grill Wipes. Have all of your equipment handy. Place the wood of your choice on or near the heat source on your smoker. Smoke with the lid or hood closed as much as possible. This will trap the heat, allowing it to circulate. With the hood down, the smoke will be more concentrated and will permeate the food better.

The Hand Method for Judging a Smoker's Temperature

Hold your hand 5 inches above the indirect side of a grill or over the rack on a smoker. If you can hold it there for 5 to 6 seconds, then you have a low fire (225° to 250°F), the ideal temperature for slow smoking.

ADJUSTING YOUR SMOKER'S TEMPERATURE

On a charcoal grill, lower the temperature by slightly closing the side vents. Raise the temperature by opening the side vents or by adding more charcoal. Keep the grill lid closed while smoking for a steady temperature and more smoke.

On a gas grill, you adjust the heat by turning the heat control knobs to the desired level. For smoking, adjust the heat control on one burner while leaving the other burner off.

How to Smoke

When the smoker is at the proper temperature for the recipe you want to make, place the food in a disposable aluminum pan or directly on the grate of the smoker, on the indirect side. Let it cook for 45 minutes to 1 hour before checking it. The more you open the smoker, the more the temperature will drop and the longer your food will take to get done.

Check periodically—about once every hour—to make sure your water pan has enough liquid and that you have enough fuel and wood.

Smoking Times

Estimating smoking times will be a challenge, because the time required to cook a food varies due to the heat of the fire, the temperature outdoors, and whether the day is windy, sunny, overcast, or rainy. The better you can control the heat and the temperature of your smoker, the better barbecue you'll produce. With smoking, it is less crucial to be exact than with grilling, as smoking is a gentler cooking process that takes longer. But smoking food too long will give it a bitter, acrid flavor. We recommend smoking with wood for the first 1 to 2 hours of the cooking process.

Use the suggested cooking times we provide in each recipe, but also watch your food while it's smoking—use an internal meat or an instant-read thermometer to gauge its doneness. We always recommend allowing extra time—an hour or two perhaps—as a cushion when smoking any kind of food.

DONENESS CHART FOR SMOKING

Knowing at what temperature your smoked food is done is crucial. You want succulent, moist, tender barbecue, not dried-out jerky. For ribs, the doneness test is visual—when the rib meat has pulled back about an inch from the ends of the bones. We use both heat-safe meat thermometers inserted in brisket or pork butt, left in during smoking, and instant-read thermometers quickly inserted in foods and then removed.

Pork ribs

Baby back	1½ lbs.	Meat pulls back from bone
Baby back	1¾ to 2¼ lbs.	Meat pulls back from bone
Spareribs	2½ to 3-plus lbs.	Meat pulls back from bone
Pork butt (Boston)	6 to 8 lbs.	160°F
Pork loin	8 to 10 lbs.	150° to 155°F
Pork sausage	1½- to 2½-inch diameter	150° to 155°F
Beef brisket	8 to 12 lbs. trimmed	160°F
Poultry (whole)	2½ to 3 lbs.	165°F
	3½ to 4½ lbs.	165°F
Poultry (breast)	5 to 8 oz.	155°F
Lamb (leg)	7 to 9 lbs.	130°F (rare)

Specialty Grilling and Smoking Techniques

When you've got basic grilling and smoking techniques down pat, try venturing into new territory. With the right equipment and grill gadgets, you can skewer, stir-grill, plank, rotisserie cook, and even smoke foods in a stovetop smoker.

Skewering 101

The first choice is the basic skewer itself, and you've got lots of options here. The old standby is the inexpensive wooden skewer, which comes in packages at the grocery store. These skewers need to be soaked in cold water for at least 30 minutes before threading them with food and grilling. After grilling, you just throw the charred skewers away.

Reusable metal skewers, some with prongs on both ends, or the new metal coil skewers, can be easily cleaned after grilling with soapy water, then towel dried so they don't get water spots.

Kabob baskets are also an option. They are great time-savers, as you simply place the cubed food in the basket rather than threading the chunks onto skewers. You will need to spray or brush the baskets with oil before grilling so that the food doesn't stick.

And finally, natural skewers, such as fresh rosemary and lavender branches, bamboo, lemongrass, sugarcane, maple twigs from the yard—are all safe for food to touch. Avoid pine and other resinous woods, as they will give an off flavor to your food. And before branching out into unknown territory, check to make sure the branch you want to use is safe for consumption.

We've found that the best way to make sure all food gets done at the same time is to avoid those '50s-style kabobs with meat or chicken and vegetables all on one stick. Put all the meat pieces on their own skewers and all the vegetables on their own skewers. Leave about ⅛ inch of space between each piece of food on a skewer. If the pieces of chicken or fish are squashed together, that inside part where the pieces touch will not get done as fast. You don't want chicken sushi on a stick.

To make sure foods don't twirl around on the skewers—so annoying!—you can try a couple of things. Use flat metal or bamboo skewers rather than the rounded kind. Or run two skewers through food to keep it more stable while grilling.

Stir-Grilling 101

To stir-grill, you need a metal grill wok with perforations and wooden spoons, paddles, or long-handled spatulas. The perforations in the grill wok allow for more of the wood and charcoal fire aromas to penetrate the foods.

The technique is easy: Marinate the food in a zipper-top plastic bag in the refrigerator. Prepare a hot fire in the grill. Spray both sides of the grill wok with nonstick cooking spray. Then place the prepared wok in the sink and dump the bag of marinated food into the wok. The excess marinade will drain away. Place the wok on a doubled baking sheet and take it outside to the grill. Place the wok over direct heat and, using wooden paddles, long-handled spoons, or metal grill spatulas, stir-grill the food until done. Place the wok on the clean (bottom) baking sheet to carry back to the kitchen.

Planking 101

Plank cooking is easy, too. You can buy untreated hardwood planks at a lumberyard or barbecue shop. The most common planks come in 16 x 8 x $\frac{3}{8}$-inch, 12 x 10 x 1-inch, and 15 x 6½ x $\frac{3}{8}$-inch sizes. Use whatever size best fits in your grill. We also use 2- to 3-inch-thick reinforced cedar planks (made for oven use, but also great on the grill), available at kitchen or barbecue and grill shops. Food cooks in about the same time on thinner or thicker planks, but thicker planks last longer. Planks can be reused until they're either too charred or too brittle to hold food.

Although planking on cedar is the universal favorite because that wood gives the best aromatic flavor, any regional hardwood—such as alder, hickory, maple, oak, or pecan—will produce great-tasting planked food.

To use the plank, submerge it in water for at least an hour. A deep sink or a large rectangular plastic container that you can fill with water both work. Use a couple of large cans to weigh down the plank so that it stays under the surface. A water-soaked plank produces maximum smoke flavor and is more resistant to charring on the grill.

Prepare an indirect or dual-heat fire (high or medium-high on one side, low on the other) in a grill. You can do this with a gas grill with dual burners, or in a charcoal grill by massing two thirds of the hot coals on the "hot" side and moving one third of the hot coals to the "medium" side.

Now, here's a case of dueling BBQ Queens, where Karen and Judith agree to disagree: Judith prefers to season the presoaked plank over hot coals. She places the plank over high heat for about 5 minutes. When the plank starts to char and pop, she turns it over so the charred side is up, then arranges the food in one layer on the charred side of the plank. Karen, on the other hand, doesn't like to season her planks.

We can agree that both ways produce great-tasting food, but we recommend you experiment to decide which method you prefer.

Food touching the wood takes on more flavor, so don't crowd the food onto the plank. Use two planks, if necessary. Then close the grill lid and cook according to the time specified in the recipe. Stay close by, though, in case of flare-ups. Keep a spray bottle filled with water handy, just in case.

For a rustic restaurant-style effect, serve the food right on the plank, like a platter. After you've cooked and served on the plank, clean it up with a little hot, soapy water and a good rinse. Eighty-grit sandpaper may be used to help clean the plank, too.

Hardwood Flavors for Planking

- **Alder** gives a light, aromatic flavor and is great paired with fish.
- **Cedar** is probably the most aromatic of the woods, lending a deep but gentle woodsy flavor to planked foods of all kinds.
- **Hickory** lends a stronger, hearty wood flavor to beef, pork, or poultry.
- **Maple** smolders to a sweeter, milder flavor that pairs well with poultry, vegetables, or fish.
- **Oak** gives a medium, woodsy aroma without being bitter. It also pairs well with any food.

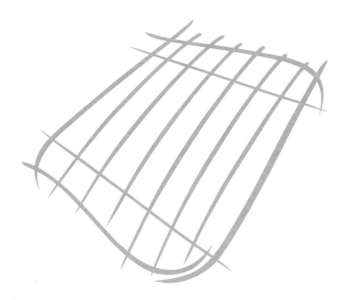

Rotisserie Cooking 101

To spit-roast or rotisserie cook, first set up your rotisserie on the grill. Every gas grill has a different way to set up a rotisserie, so we're just giving you an overview here. Please refer to your manufacturer's directions for the best way to set up the rotisserie on your grill. The drip pan should contain 2 or 3 inches of liquid—marinade, vinegar, juice, beer, wine, or just plain water—whatever you would like for aroma. The liquid will steam up into the food, adding moisture and a wonderful aroma as the food turns and cooks. Replenish with additional liquid as necessary.

Run through your setup first. Do not skewer the food and place it on a lit grill until you are certain that everything is set properly. With the grill off or unlit, measure the food over the drip pan. The pan will prevent flare-ups, so make sure the meat, chicken, or fish is not larger than the drip pan you are planning to use. If it is, use either a larger pan or an additional drip pan. For easy cleanup, we recommend using a disposable aluminum pan.

Trim the meat, poultry, or fish, then season it. If you're using the rotisserie basket (great for fish or other delicate foods), spray it with nonstick cooking spray, place the food inside the basket, and close firmly. Slide one of the pronged attachments or spit forks onto the rotisserie rod. Position the attachment and clamp to tighten. Slide the rod through the center of the meat, fish, or fowl. Slide the second prong attachment so that the tines are touching the food. Holding a prong attachment in each hand, press both attachments into the food so that the food is held firmly in place. Secure and tighten the clamps for the pronged attachments. Use pliers to tighten the thumbscrews on the spit forks to prevent loosening during the rotisserie process.

BALANCING THE FOOD ON THE SPIT

It's very important to balance the meat on the spit so it can turn easily. If the meat is not balanced, it could shorten the life of your rotisserie. To balance the rod, hold it so each end lies across the palms of your hands; the heavy side of the food will rotate down. Position the food on the rod so that there is no heavy side.

Tie any loose bits to the body of the meat with kitchen twine. Insert a meat thermometer in the thickest part of the meat, away from the bone. Make sure that the thermometer is positioned so that you can read it and also so that it will turn freely as the meat turns.

Place the spit on the rotisserie. Start the rotisserie, watching it rotate until you're sure the meat turns easily. Place the drip pan under the food. Add liquid to the drip pan until it is 2 to 3 inches full. This helps keep the food moist and prevents the drippings from burning.

Check to make sure the grill's lid will close while the rotisserie is on. If necessary, you can prop the grill lid open a bit with bricks or metal cans.

Prepare a medium-hot fire in your grill. Check with a grill thermometer to make sure you have achieved a temperature of close to 350°F. Cover and cook, checking the meat, the fire, and the drip pan at least every hour. You may need to add liquid to the drip pan during cooking. Sometimes the thumbscrews can loosen, or the meat may shrink and the forks may need to be adjusted, so keep a clean pair of pliers handy just in case you need to make some adjustments. When the food is done, lift the rotisserie and food off the grill. Place the whole thing on a baking sheet, then remove the rod and proceed to retrieve your food.

Stovetop Smoking 101

Made of stainless steel, the stovetop smoker is designed to trap and smolder tiny wood particles away from the food so that the resulting smoke permeates the food but doesn't make your kitchen smoke alarm go crazy.

To use a stovetop smoker, place 1 to 2 tablespoons of very fine wood chips in the center of the base of the smoker. These fine wood chips are available in many different varieties, from alder and apple to cherry, corn cob, hickory, oak, maple, mesquite, and pecan. Make sure the wood chips are dry when you put them in the base of the smoker, so that they smolder effectively.

A metal drip tray fits snugly on top of the wood chips; then a coated, footed wire rack is placed on the tray. Coat or brush whatever food you're smoking with olive oil, then season with salt and pepper. Arrange the food in a single layer on the rack, so that the most surface area is exposed to the smoke—the same idea as in planking. (If you want to double the recipes, smoke the foods in two separate batches.) Slide the metal lid almost closed.

Extend the handles and place the stovetop smoker over one burner. Flat ceramic burners will need 20 percent more cooking time than gas or electric coil burners.

Turn the burner on medium (375°F), medium-high (400°F), or high (450°F or more). Although the instructions (enclosed with the stovetop smoker) say to keep the heat on medium, we don't. We mainly use medium-high heat for maximum smoke. The food gets done faster and doesn't dry out. Your stovetop smoker won't be in perfect alignment anymore after placing it over medium-high heat, but who cares? We are far more concerned with how our food tastes that with how our smoker looks! We each have one and have used them many times over medium-high to high heat, and they still work just fine.

Start counting the cooking time when you see the first hint of smoke escaping from the smoker. Then close the lid tightly.

It's easy to tell when your food is done. Fish and shellfish should have a golden-bronze cast and be opaque all the way through. Poultry, beef, and pork will also have a golden-bronze look but can be checked for doneness with an instant-read thermometer. Vegetables and cheeses are done when they have the amount of smoke flavor you desire.

For meats like pork or beef tenderloin, we prefer to use a grill or an indoor grill pan to get grill marks on the meat first—for taste and aesthetic reasons—then finish the cooking in the stovetop smoker. That way, you get a slight caramelization and grill marks on the exterior, with a smoky and juicy interior. Perfect!

After you've finished smoking, remove the smoker from the heat. Be careful, because the smoker will be very hot. Let the smoker sit for a minute or two so the smoke can dissipate before opening the lid. Open and remove the food and let the smoker cool before handling it. Discard the ashes by rinsing them with cold water and washing them down the drain. We do not recommend discarding them in your wastebasket, as they could be a fire hazard.

The stovetop smoker can be cleaned with hot, soapy water by hand or can go in the dishwasher. The bottom of the smoker will become discolored after the first use because of the direct heat, but then, you didn't want to display your smoker in the china cabinet anyway, did you?

Now, get ready to party with the BBQ Queens!

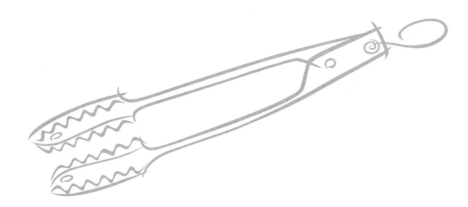

Appetizers and Little Foods to Set the Mood

We adore little foods, whether you call them tapas, meze, antipasti, hors d'oeuvres, or just, well, little foods! What we don't like are tedious or fiddly little bites that take you hours to make or, at the opposite extreme, a humdrum bag of chips and jar of salsa. So here we've thought beyond the toothpick and come up with lots of creative, great-tasting tidbits that assemble quickly, look fabulous on a platter, and are easy to grill or smoke.

Here's a quick guide to our favorite varieties of little foods, examples of which you will find in this chapter.

- **Dippers:** Smoke-roasted fingerling potatoes, wood-grilled shrimp, slices of grilled pork tenderloin, or grilled baby lamb chops taste wonderful with a savory dollop on top, such as Horseradish Crème Fraîche (page 78), Smoky Cocktail Sauce (page 76), or Thai Chili-Peanut Dipping Sauce (page 53).
- **Poppers:** Why fry when you can grill or smoke? Bite into a Pecan-Smoked Goat Cheese–Stuffed Peppadew (page 36), a Wood-Roasted Oyster (page 76), or a piece of Thai Grilled Flank Steak (page 50) nestled in a little lettuce cup, and you'll taste a big burst of flavor.
- **Wood-grilled pizzas, flatbreads, and sandwiches:** You can change the ingredients and flavors as you please with each season.
- **Mini burgers:** Grilled tuna or lamb mini burgers make irresistible bite-size sandwiches that won't ruin your appetite for the rest of the meal.
- **Bundles:** Several ingredients are rolled together and wrapped with prosciutto or pancetta. You can assemble them hours ahead of time, then grill and serve whenever you're ready.
- **Parcels:** Our favorite parcels feature grilled lobster wrapped in phyllo pastry, then brushed with butter and baked.

Now, get out there and sizzle!

Grilled Farmers' Market Antipasto Platter

We love appetizers served on platters in a rustic style so that the food looks great without us having to do much to it. We also love finger-food appetizers that fully occupy our guests so we can get last-minute things done before everyone sits down to dinner. The freshest, most beautiful vegetables of the season become the star attraction on this platter, surrounded by appropriate artisanal cheeses, olives, and prosciutto or salami. How easy is that?

Makes 6 to 8 servings

- **2 pounds best-quality seasonal garden vegetables, such as whole baby zucchini and/or yellow summer squash, cherry tomatoes still on the vine, whole baby stem-on peppers of all kinds, or whole baby Japanese eggplant**
- **Olive oil for brushing**
- **Sea salt and freshly ground black pepper to taste**
- **1 pound artisanal cheese of your choice, such as Pecorino, goat cheese, or fontina, cut into bite-size pieces**
- **1 pound prosciutto or artisanal salami, very thinly sliced**
- **1 pound brine-cured black olives**

1. Prepare a hot fire in your grill.
2. Brush whatever vegetables you are using with olive oil, then season with salt and pepper and place on a baking sheet to take outside.
3. Grill the vegetables for 2 to 4 minutes per side, turning once, until the vegetables have blistered but are still crisp. Arrange the vegetables on a platter and surround with the cheese, prosciutto, and olives.

Change It Up

In the springtime, try fresh fava beans in their pods, brushing each pod with olive oil and seasoning with sea salt and pepper, then grilling the whole pods over a hot fire for 3 to 4 minutes per side, or until black blisters form. Turn the pods and grill for another 2 to 4 minutes. To serve, pry open the pods, then slip each fava bean out of its skin and pop it in your mouth, along with bites of fresh Pecorino and prosciutto. You'll feel like you're in Italy!

Smoke-Roasted Fingerlings with Crème Fraîche and Caviar

Break out the bubbly—or the beer or vodka—for this finger-food appetizer that is as delicious in front of the fireplace or at a tailgate bash as it is at a fancy New Year's Eve party. If your budget doesn't stretch to include caviar, use a good-quality prepared tapenade instead. The crème fraîche can be left out on the kitchen counter to ripen and thicken the day before, but it also tastes fine when made the same day. The fingerlings can be kept warm in the oven until serving time. Smoke-roasted potatoes will stay hot for hours in a beverage cooler, so you can take them to the big game.

Makes 8 servings

Suggested wood: Hickory or pecan

- **2 pounds fingerling potatoes**
- **Olive oil**
- **Sea salt and freshly ground black pepper to taste**

Crème Fraîche:
- **1 cup sour cream**
- **1 cup heavy cream**

4 ounces caviar or tapenade

1. Prepare a fire in your smoker.
2. In a disposable aluminum pan, toss the potatoes with olive oil until well coated, and season with salt and pepper. Smoke at 225° to 250°F for 1 hour.
3. While the potatoes are smoking, preheat the oven to 400°F.
4. Stir the potatoes in the pan, then transfer to the oven and continue roasting until tender and crispy, about 30 minutes more. Meanwhile, combine the sour cream and heavy cream in a bowl until well blended; set aside.
5. To serve, arrange the potatoes on a platter, and offer small plates. Guests place a potato on the plate, then a dollop of crème fraîche and a spoonful of caviar on top.

Deck It Out

Use yellow fingerling and red baby potatoes for a two-tone look. Arrange the potatoes on a silver platter around a crystal bowl of crème fraîche and a crystal bowl of caviar, with the appropriate horn spoon for dolloping this delicacy.

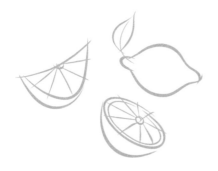

Smoke the potatoes, in batches, in a
stovetop smoker for 15 minutes, then finish
in a 400°F oven for 15 to 20 minutes,
or until tender. Or melt ½ cup (1 stick)
unsalted butter and blend with 1 teaspoon
liquid smoke, toss the raw potatoes in this
mixture, and oven-roast at 400°F until the
potatoes are tender, about 45 minutes.

Grilled Polenta with Caramelized Onions and Gorgonzola

Here's another do-ahead appetizer that's great for weekend grilling. Make the polenta
and caramelized onions the day before, then enjoy these goodies hot off the grill the
next day. Or have the appetizers done and ready to reheat before your guests arrive, if
you wish. Polenta offers a blank canvas that can be "painted" with the seasonal foods of
your choice. Cream cheese provides a mellow flavor and helps the polenta stay together
while grilling.

Makes 8 servings

- **3 cups chicken or vegetable broth**
- **1 cup uncooked polenta or corn grits**
- **2 tablespoons fresh thyme leaves**
- **2 tablespoons fresh rosemary leaves, chopped**
- **8 ounces cream cheese, cut into cubes**
- **Sea salt and freshly ground white pepper to taste**

1. Spray a baking sheet with nonstick cooking
   spray and set aside. In a large pot over
   medium-high heat, bring the broth to a
   boil. Sprinkle the polenta into the broth in a
   steady stream, whisking constantly. Continue
   whisking for 5 minutes. When the polenta has
   bubbled into a thick mass, whisk in the thyme,
   rosemary, and cream cheese until the cheese
   has melted. Season with salt and pepper.
2. Spread the hot polenta on the baking sheet and
   smooth with a spatula to a ½-inch thickness.
   Let cool to room temperature. (At this point,
   you may cover the polenta with plastic wrap
   and refrigerate for up to 24 hours.)

Caramelized Onions:

- **4 tablespoons (½ stick) unsalted butter**
- **1 tablespoon olive oil, plus more for brushing**
- **2 large yellow onions, thinly sliced**
- **1 to 2 teaspoons sugar**
- **1 tablespoon port, sherry, or other fortified wine**

- **4 ounces Gorgonzola or other blue cheese, crumbled**
- **Sprigs of watercress or fresh Italian parsley for garnish**

3. To caramelize the onions, heat the butter and oil in a large skillet over medium-high heat. Add the onions and stir to coat. Cook for several minutes, until the onions begin to wilt. Turn the heat down to medium-low and continue cooking and stirring occasionally until the onions have started to turn a golden brown, about 10 minutes. Add the sugar and the port and keep cooking and stirring until the onions have turned a medium brown, 10 to 15 minutes longer. Let cool to room temperature. (At this point, you may cover and refrigerate the onions for up to 24 hours.)

4. Prepare a hot fire in your grill.

5. With a sharp knife or a pizza wheel, cut the polenta into triangles or other shapes (anywhere from 16 to 24 pieces). Brush both sides with olive oil and place the shapes on a baking sheet to take out to the grill. Grill the polenta shapes, turning once, until they have good grill marks on both sides, 2 to 3 minutes per side. Place back on the baking sheet. Top each wedge with a bit of crumbled Gorgonzola, a tangle of caramelized onions, and a sprig of watercress. Serve warm or at room temperature.

Take It Easy

Caramelizing onions is so easy. It does take a little time and patience, but the depth of flavor is worth every minute. But hey—why not caramelize a quadruple batch while you're at it? Place the extras in three zipper-top plastic bags and freeze. The next time you make this recipe, you'll say *Voilà!* as you pull a package from the freezer.

Tiny Bubbles: Champagne and Sparkling Wine

Champagne is so festive, from the pop of the cork to the tingle of bubbles on your nose and the taste of that first crisp sip. If you want to have a lighthearted gathering from the moment your guests arrive, pour bubbly. As proof, just look at the twinkle in their eyes when you offer a flute of something sparkling.

We associate sparkling wines with happy memories. When our cookbook club read *French Women Don't Get Fat* by Mireille Guiliano, we sipped Veuve Clicquot, *bien sûr*. On our group trip to Château du Feÿ in the Burgundy countryside, Anne Willan invited us for cocktails and gougères and she served crémant (a sparkling wine from the Loire Valley) with a splash of peach, or *pêche*, liqueur.

True Champagne comes only from the French region of the same name, which is about 90 miles northeast of Paris. Popular makers include Moët et Chandon, Taittinger, Mumm, Veuve Clicquot-Ponsardin, and Perrier-Jouët. When purchasing Champagne, it is most important to know the level of sweetness. *Brut* is bone dry, *extra sec* or extra dry is slightly sweeter, *sec* is medium sweet, *demi-sec* is sweet, and *doux* is very sweet.

We refer to bottled bubblies from anywhere other than the Champagne region as sparkling wine. There are many delicious and affordable varieties of sparkling wine in the $10 to $15 price range, including Spanish cava and Italian spumante. The popular Freixenet is an inexpensive cava (less than $10), great for mixing in cocktails. Barefoot Bubbly is another less-than-$10 bottle that is fun to mix with fruit juices and liqueurs. Italian Prosecco, a dry, gently fizzy wine, is generally priced in the teens.

California produces many fine sparkling wines, including Domaine Carneros, Domaine Chandon, Gloria Ferrer, Iron Horse, Roederer Estate, and Schramsberg. These pricier bottles are first-rate bubblies, and we prefer them icy cold, sans embellishment.

And of course, bubbly is great with grilled and smoked foods. (Isn't it good with just about anything?) Here are several simple chilled concoctions to make with inexpensive sparkling wine served in a Champagne flute:

- Mimosa: half orange juice, half sparkling wine
- Kir Royale: splash of crème de cassis topped with sparkling wine
- Bellini: splash of peach nectar, peach schnapps, or peach brandy topped with sparkling wine
- Pomegranate and Bubbly: splash of pomegranate juice topped with sparkling wine and a sprinkle of pomegranate seeds
- Aloha Fizz: half pineapple juice, half sparkling wine
- Gold and Silver Champagne Cocktail: Rub rim of glass with orange peel to moisten, dip in Edible Glitter (page 47), pour in the Champagne, and sip away.

Grilled Figs on Rosemary Skewers

We love rosemary skewers and have many favorite recipes that use them. The branches need to be sturdy and are best presoaked in water so that they don't burn up on the grill. These lovely figs could be served as dessert, too, minus the pâté.

Makes 12 servings

- **Twelve 6- to 8-inch fresh rosemary branches**
- **6 large, firm, ripe figs**
- **½ cup honey**
- **Zest and juice of 1 lime**
- **Coarse kosher salt and freshly ground black pepper to taste**
- **Lime wedges for squeezing and garnish**
- **6-ounce wheel or wedge double-cream Brie cheese**
- **6 ounces pâté de foie gras**
- **French baguette, sliced, for serving**

1. Strip the leaves from the bottom of the rosemary branches, leaving 2 to 3 inches of leaves at the tip. Place the branches in a bowl of water and soak for at least 30 minutes. Finely chop 2 tablespoons of the stripped rosemary leaves and set aside.
2. Prepare a medium-hot fire in your grill.
3. Halve the figs lengthwise. Skewer each fig half crosswise on a rosemary branch. Set the skewered figs on a baking pan, cut side up. In a small bowl, combine the honey, lime zest, and lime juice. Brush the cut side of the figs with the honey mixture. Grill the figs 1 to 2 minutes per side, or until lightly browned and soft.
4. On a large platter, attractively arrange the skewered figs and the lime wedges. Lightly sprinkle the figs with the chopped rosemary, salt, pepper, and a squeeze of lime. Place the Brie, a wedge of pâté, and the baguette slices on the platter. Serve while the figs are still warm.

Sangria!

Sangria is great to serve with Spanish tapas or Southwestern or Mexican appetizers, or any time you want a festive twist on plain old wine. Here are a couple of wonderful sangria recipes, one with white wine and one with red wine.

Red Wine Sangria

Makes 8 to 10 servings

- **1 medium-size orange**
- **¼ cup superfine sugar**
- **2 cups orange juice**
- **One 750-milliliter bottle fruity red wine, such as red Rioja or Merlot**
- **½ cup Cointreau**
- **Crushed ice**

1. Cut the peel from the orange and place the peel in a small bowl. Mash the sugar into the peel until the sugar is absorbed.
2. Combine the orange juice, wine, and Cointreau in a large pitcher or punch bowl, add the sugared peel, and chill for several hours or overnight. Just before serving, thinly slice the orange and place a slice in each glass, along with some crushed ice. Pour in the sangria and serve.

White Wine Sangria

Makes 8 to 10 servings

- **One 750-milliliter bottle dry white wine, such as white Rioja or Sauvignon Blanc, or 4 to 5 cups extra-dry vermouth, to your taste**
- **1 cup triple sec**
- **8 teaspoons superfine sugar**
- **Juice of 3 oranges**
- **Juice of 2 limes**
- **Juice of 2 lemons**
- **1 orange, halved and thinly sliced**
- **1 lemon, halved and thinly sliced**
- **1 lime, halved and thinly sliced**
- **1 cup sparkling water**
- **Ice cubes**

Combine all of the ingredients, except for the sparkling water and ice cubes, in a large pitcher or punch bowl. Stir well and chill for several hours or overnight. Add the sparkling water and ice cubes just before serving.

Pecan-Smoked Goat Cheese–Stuffed Peppadews

Peppadews are tiny red bell peppers that have been seeded, cored, and preserved in brine. These slightly hot, slightly sweet peppers are perfect for stuffing with fresh goat cheese, then smoking, for a new take on the jalapeño popper. Just make sure you get your peppadews from an olive bar where you can select them yourself or in a jar where you can see them, so you get well-formed peppers that are good for stuffing. Put these on the smoker when you're already smoking something else, or do these indoors in a stovetop smoker. This recipe can be doubled, tripled, etc., if necessary.

Makes 4 to 6 servings

Suggested wood: Pecan

- **16 brined peppadews, drained**
- **4 ounces goat cheese**
- **Olive oil for brushing**
- **Sea or kosher salt and freshly ground black pepper to taste**

1. Pat the peppadews dry. Using a spoon or a small spatula, stuff the peppadews with the goat cheese. Brush the top of each stuffed pepper with olive oil and season with salt and pepper. Place the peppadews in a small disposable aluminum pan (if they're going on the smoker) or, if using the stovetop smoker, make a small tray with raised sides out of a sheet of aluminum foil and place the stuffed peppadews in the tray.

2. To smoke the stuffed peppers in an outdoor smoker, prepare a fire in your smoker. Place the pan of stuffed peppers on the smoker rack, close the lid, and smoke for 45 minutes to 1 hour at 225° to 250°F, or until bronzed and aromatically smoky. To smoke the stuffed peppers in a stovetop smoker, place the tray of stuffed peppers on the smoker pan rack and close the smoker pan lid. Place the smoker pan over high heat on the stove over one burner. After the first wisp of smoke escapes from the smoker, cook for another 8 minutes. Slide open the lid to check for doneness. When the stuffed peppers have a bronzed look and are redolent of smoke, remove the smoker from the heat, but keep the lid closed for another minute. Serve hot, at room temperature, or cold.

Deck It Out

Serve this appetizer on a white platter lined with fresh greenery for the holidays, or lined with sprigs of fresh herbs at other times of the year. The branches of greenery or herbs also help prop up these miniature stuffed peppers.

Change It Up

Use plain or herbed cream cheese in place of the goat cheese.

Raise a Glass

These are great served with Vienna-style lager, pilsner, or martinis.

Razzle-Dazzle: Open-Faced Bruschetta

Here's a quick-as-a-wink appetizer that will gain you a lot of goodwill while the main course cooks. Start with the bread of your choice—English muffins, rye, pumpernickel, sourdough, Boboli, flatbread, ciabatta, baguette, etc. Lightly brush with olive oil and grill on one side. Turn and top with a garden-fresh slice of tomato, a bit of crumbled cheese of your choice, and a sprinkle of coarse kosher salt and freshly ground black pepper. So simple, yet so good.

A Martini Party
with a French Accent

Karen's high school friend Judy Evans is known for her martini parties. We've taken that concept and run it around the grill for a black-tie barbecue that offers rustic flavors in a sophisticated way.

"A couple of years ago, I bought 60 martini glasses with ball stems when they were on sale at Crate & Barrel," says Judy, who is co-owner of With a French Accent in Liberty, Missouri (816-792-8320), a store the BBQ Queens find irresistible. "Then, we found these great martini-shaped vases in graduated sizes for the shop. I brought a set of three home with me. Then I thought, I've got all of this fabulous stuff, I should use it! So I started doing martini parties for 40 to 50 people. It's really easy to have a party if you already have the theme and the serving pieces. Now, I just repeat the theme. The menu and colors depend on the season."

Setting the Scene
Says Judy, "What I've learned about the French is that attention to detail is of utmost importance. It influences the way I do everything now. So for this party, I have flowers everywhere. I like to use large white porcelain serving pieces, glass plates, and real silverware, but I do use good paper napkins for a large party. And I have plenty of candles for atmosphere. We set each type of martini off with a different garnish: an apple slice, fresh flower, lemon peel, or chocolate pastille."

Making Beautiful Music
Try soft jazz; vintage Edith Piaf, Maurice Chevalier, or Josephine Baker; or modern French pop. The soundtrack from *Something's Gotta Give* is also a great choice.

Perfect Partners

Judy's husband, Joe, makes up large pitchers of the four types of martinis they usually offer: Apple, French (with Cointreau and Chambord), Cosmo (with cranberry juice), and Chocolate. You can find recipes for these types of martinis online at www.martiniart.com or www.stirrings.com, or simply buy bottled martini mixtures to which you add vodka or gin, according to the instructions on the bottles. Make as much ahead as you can so that you can enjoy your party, too.

With the Apple Martinis

Brie, Boursin, and Port-Salut cheese platter served with sliced green apples and pears and lavash bread

Grilled Lobster Parcels (page 80)

Thai Grilled Flank Steak in Lettuce Cups (page 50)

With the French Martinis

Brandy-soaked cherries stuffed with goat cheese

Grilled Prosciutto-Wrapped Asparagus with Fig Balsamic Vinegar and Shaved Parmesan (page 62)

Wood-Grilled Duck Breast Paillards with Raspberry-Thyme Sauce (page 143), sliced and served at room temperature in endive leaves

With the Cosmo Martinis

Grilled Figs on Rosemary Skewers (page 34)

Wood-Grilled Shrimp Cocktail with Horseradish Crème Fraîche (page 78), served in martini glasses

Big Easy Grilled Beef Tenderloin (page 96), served chilled on rounds of French bread

With the Chocolate Martinis

Grilled Chocolate Crostini (page 216)

Vanilla Cupcakes with White Chocolate–Cream Cheese Frosting (page 218), made in mini muffin tins

Golden Raspberry Meringues with Pistachios (page 233)

Spritzers

As refreshing as they sound, spritzers include wine or fruit juices with a splash of something bubbly like sparkling water, club soda, or sparkling wine. They are party perfect and easy to assemble. Our Chicago friend Rose Kallas served lemonade spritzers to our cookbook club one summer evening. The frozen lemonade mixed with sparkling water instead of plain water was so simple and so good. The same can be done with frozen limeade or orange juice.

Here are a few other festive spritzer ideas to get your barbecue bash started.

Limoncello Spritzers

We were introduced to the Italian liqueur limoncello by our Slow Food Convivium leader, Italian restaurant owner Jasper Mirabile. We're sure he'll dub these spritzers a winner. Prosecco is an Italian sparkling wine, but you can use any sparkling wine here.

Makes 4 servings

- **8 tablespoons (½ cup) limoncello**
- **2⅔ cups lemonade**
- **1⅓ cups Prosecco**
- **4 lemon wedges, for garnish**
- **4 sprigs fresh mint or lemon balm, for garnish**

Fill four highball glasses with ice. Add 2 tablespoons limoncello, ⅔ cup lemonade, and ⅓ cup Prosecco to each glass. Stir to blend. Garnish each glass with a wedge of lemon and a sprig of mint.

Da Das

These are named for the way they make you talk if you drink too many, as in "Da da, da da, da da!" Karen's husband, Dick, is a master at making them, and they are a tradition with brunch on New Year's Day. The apricot brandy adds a smoothness that makes these Da Das much tastier than a mimosa.

Makes 4 servings

- **8 tablespoons (½ cup) apricot brandy**
- **2⅔ cups orange juice**
- **1⅓ cups sparkling wine**

Fill four highball glasses with ice. Add 2 tablespoons apricot brandy, ⅔ cup orange juice, and ⅓ cup sparkling wine to each glass. Stir to blend and serve.

Cranberry-Orange Sparklers

Festive, colorful, sparkling, and nonalcoholic, this drink is welcome all year round. The frozen juice cubes add just that extra touch. The fresh mint sprigs are deliciously fragrant, too. You may substitute a sparkling wine for the water, if you like.

Makes 8 servings

- **5 cups freshly squeezed orange juice, chilled**
- **5 cups cranberry juice cocktail, chilled**
- **2 cups sparkling water, chilled**
- **8 fresh mint springs, for garnish**

1. To make the ice cubes, pour 1 cup of the orange juice into an ice cube tray. Pour 1 cup of the cranberry juice into another ice cube tray. Freeze until solid.
2. When ready to serve, combine the remaining 4 cups orange juice, 4 cups cranberry juice, and the sparkling water in a large glass pitcher. Stir and pour into eight tall glasses. Add frozen juice cubes to each glass and garnish with mint sprigs.

Monte Carlo Imperials

This is a Chandon recipe for a drink that they say "is as sexy as the Riviera, but available in your own backyard."

Makes 4 servings

- **3 cups Chandon Brut Classic**
- **2 ounces (¼ cup) white crème de cacao**
- **6 ounces (¾ cup) gin**
- **4 dashes of freshly squeezed lemon juice**
- **4 lemon peel twists, for garnish**

Fill four highball glasses with ice. Add ¾ cup Chandon Brut Classic, ½ ounce crème de cacao, 1½ ounces gin, and a dash of lemon juice to each glass. Stir to blend. Garnish each glass with a lemon peel twist.

Wood-Grilled Pizza with Two Toppings

Individual grilled pizzas are great to cut into wedges and serve as appetizers or as a casual entrée. The wood chips or pellets will give them a touch of smoky outdoor flavor. Just make sure you don't load up the pizzas with too much topping. These are meant to be thin and crispy, with enough topping to be flavorful, but not heavy. Each topping makes enough to top all four pizzas.

Makes four 8-inch pizzas to serve 8 as an appetizer or 4 as an entrée

Suggested wood: 1 cup chips or ⅓ cup pellets (apple, cherry, mesquite, oak, or pecan)

- **3¼ cups unbleached all-purpose flour, plus more for kneading and sprinkling**
- **¼ cup semolina or finely ground cornmeal**
- **2 tablespoons instant yeast**
- **1 tablespoon honey**
- **5 tablespoons olive oil**
- **½ teaspoon salt**
- **1 cup warm (110°F) water**
- **Topping of choice (see page 44)**

1. Combine the flour, semolina, and yeast in the bowl of a food processor or electric mixer. Combine the honey, 3 tablespoons of the olive oil, salt, and water in a cup and stir to blend. Turn on the food processor or mixer and pour the liquid mixture through the feed tube or into the mixing bowl in a steady stream. Process or mix until the dough forms a mass and cleans the sides of the bowl.

2. Turn the dough out onto a floured surface and knead by hand for 5 minutes, or until smooth and elastic. Place in a large oiled bowl and turn to coat. Cover with plastic wrap. (At this point, you may refrigerate the pizza dough for up to 3 days. Let the dough come to room temperature before letting it rise.) Let rise in a warm place until doubled in bulk, 1 to 1½ hours.

3. Prepare an indirect fire in your grill, meaning a medium-hot fire on one side and no fire on the other. If using a charcoal grill, place moistened wood chips (or a foil packet of dry wood pellets with holes poked in the top) directly on the coals right before you want to grill. If using a gas grill, enclose dry wood chips or pellets in a foil packet with holes poked in the top; place the packet on the grill grate over the heat source. You're ready to grill when you see the smoke from the smoldering wood and the fire is hot.

4. Divide the dough into four equal parts and press or roll each piece into an 8-inch circle. Sprinkle flour on two large baking sheets and place two rounds of dough on each sheet. Have olive oil and the toppings ready and bring everything out to the grill.

5. To grill using a pizza stone, place the pizza stone on the grill rack over medium-high heat. Cover the grill and let the stone preheat for 10 minutes. Slide two rounds of pizza dough onto the preheated stone. Arrange the topping on the pizzas, cover, and grill until the dough is golden brown and the topping is bubbly, about 10 to 15 minutes. To grill directly on the grill grate, brush one side of the pizza dough with olive oil and place, oiled side down, on the direct heat side of the grill grate. Grill for 1 to 2 minutes, or until you see the dough starting to bubble. Brush the top side with olive oil and flip the pizza, using tongs, onto a baking sheet. Quickly spoon the topping of your choice over the pizza. Use a grill spatula to place the pizza on the indirect side of the fire. Cover and grill for 5 minutes or until the topping is bubbly.

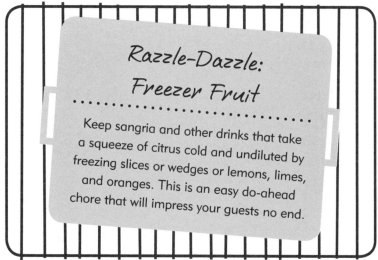

Razzle-Dazzle: Freezer Fruit

Keep sangria and other drinks that take a squeeze of citrus cold and undiluted by freezing slices or wedges or lemons, limes, and oranges. This is an easy do-ahead chore that will impress your guests no end.

Stir-Grilled Italian Sausage, Peppers, and Onions

Before you grill the pizza dough, stir-grill this classic topping.

- **8 ounces Italian sausage, cut into thin slices**
- **2 cups bell pepper slices, including red, yellow, and green**
- **1 large red onion, cut into 8 wedges**
- **2 tablespoons olive oil**
- **Shaved Parmesan cheese**

1. Oil the interior and exterior of a grill wok and place on a baking sheet. In a zipper-top plastic bag, combine the sausage, peppers, and onion. Drizzle with the olive oil and toss to coat.

2. Place the grill wok on the grill grate over the heat. Dump the contents of the bag into the prepared grill wok and stir-grill, tossing with wooden paddles every 2 minutes or so, for 15 minutes, or until the vegetables have browned and softened and the sausage is done. Remove the wok to the baking sheet before topping the pizza dough with the mixture. Sprinkle the Parmesan over the top and grill according to the instructions above.

Caramelized Onion, Brie, and Kalamata Olives

The onions can be made ahead for this super-easy topping combo.

- **1 recipe Caramelized Onions (page 32)**
- **1 pound Brie cheese, cut into small pieces**
- **1 cup brine- or oil-cured kalamata olives, drained, pitted, and coarsely chopped**

Top the pizzas with the caramelized onions, Brie, and kalamata olives, and grill according to the instructions above.

Take It Easy

Use prepared refrigerated pizza dough from better grocery stores or Italian delis, or even packaged bread roll mix made according to the package directions but with 2 tablespoons semolina added to the dry ingredients. Then form the dough into your own individual pizza crusts.

Wood-Grilled Country Bread with Four Seasons Toppings

This is a simple appetizer that can be elevated to star status by the great flavor it gets from the grill and the wood smoke. Depending on the season and how much time you have, you can vary the toppings in any number of ways. If you wish, you can serve the bread in a basket, with bowls of topping alongside so that your guests can help themselves (and the bread won't get soggy that way).

Makes 6 servings

Suggested wood: 1 cup chips or ⅓ cup pellets (apple, cherry, mesquite, oak, or pecan)

- **Six ½-inch-thick slices of artisanal or country bread, such as sourdough, Italian, or French boule**
- **Olive oil for brushing**
- **1 large clove garlic, peeled and cut in half**
- **Topping of choice (see pages 46 and 47)**

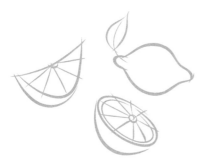

1. Prepare a hot fire in your grill. If using a charcoal grill, place moistened wood chips (or a foil packet of dry wood pellets with holes poked in the top) directly on the coals right before you want to grill. If using a gas grill, enclose dry wood chips or pellets in a foil packet with holes poked in the top; place the packet on the grill grate over the heat source. You're ready to grill when you see the smoke from the smoldering wood and the fire is hot.
2. Brush both sides of the bread with olive oil, then rub the garlic clove halves over one side of the bread. Place the bread slices on a baking sheet and take out to the grill.
3. Grill the bread, turning once, for 3 to 5 minutes total, or until the bread has turned golden and has good grill marks. Place the bread on a platter and spoon over the topping of your choice. Serve immediately.

Take It Easy

Buy prepared bruschetta toppings of your choice as a complement to or instead of the homemade toppings.

Goat Cheese with Garlic and Herb Topping for Spring

Makes about 1 cup

- **6 ounces fresh goat cheese, at room temperature**
- **1 clove garlic, minced**
- **½ cup finely chopped mixed fresh herbs, such as tarragon, Italian parsley, and chives**
- **Kosher or sea salt and freshly ground black pepper to taste**

Mash all the ingredients together in a small bowl. (You can prepare this up to 1 day in advance and store it, covered, in the refrigerator.) Serve at room temperature.

Smoky Tomato Fondue for Summer

Makes about 2 cups

- **2 large tomatoes, peeled, seeded, and chopped**
- **2 tablespoons unsalted butter, melted**
- **1 teaspoon liquid smoke flavoring**
- **Kosher or sea salt to taste**

Whisk all the ingredients together in a small bowl. (You can prepare this up to 1 day in advance and store it, covered, in the refrigerator.) Serve at room temperature.

Grilled Pear and Gorgonzola Topping for Fall

Makes enough to serve 6

- **2 large pears, peeled, cored, and cut in half lengthwise**
- **Olive oil for brushing**
- **1 cup crumbled Gorgonzola cheese**

Brush the pear halves with olive oil and, at the same time you grill the bread, grill the pears over the fire, turning once, until the pears are golden and have good grill marks. Slice the pears and serve on the grilled bread, topped with the crumbled Gorgonzola.

Feta and Pink Peppercorn Topping for Winter

Makes about 1½ cups

- **1 cup crumbled feta cheese**
- **1 clove garlic, minced**
- **2 teaspoons cracked pink peppercorns**
- **½ teaspoon dried dill weed**
- **¼ cup extra-virgin olive oil**

Mash all the ingredients together in a small bowl. (You can prepare this up to 1 day in advance and store it, covered, in the refrigerator.) Serve at room temperature.

Razzle-Dazzle: Edible Glitter

To lend even more black tie to a black-tie barbecue, employ edible gold and silver powder, petals, and leaves, with shimmering results. The products from Easy Leaf Products (www.easyleafproducts.com) include Oro Fino, the gold line, and Argento Fino, the silver collection. Combine equal amounts of the gold and silver powders with superfine sugar to create edible glitter for the glass rims of fruity martinis or spritzers and Champagne cocktails.

Frozen Assets, Cocktail Style

What could be better in the heat of the summer than an ice-cold drink? We BBQ Queens say, "Ice-cold frozen drinks that are make-aheads!" Here's a trio of them: a frozen margarita that you serve without blending, a frozen version of the popular Cosmopolitan martini, and a grown-up "slushy." These recipes each make a fairly large batch, but remember: you can keep them in the freezer and then pull them out to serve at a moment's notice. They will keep in the freezer for up to 3 months.

The World's Best Frozen Margarita

The more we're out and about, the more we realize it's a small world. At a BBQ Queens event at Books & Co. in Dayton, Ohio, Judith met Susan Howard and, after talking together, realized their families knew each other. Susan sent Judith her famous recipe for The World's Best Frozen Margarita, perfect for entertaining, along with some advice. Says Susan, "It's a good idea to use a Nalgene or Lexan container to store the margarita mix in, as these materials do not absorb flavors from other foods you may have stored in them. I use 1-liter bottles of both materials and keep a couple liters of mix in the freezer at all times. I also usually juice limes in quantity (I buy bags when the price is good) and freeze the juice in small, round deli containers that hold just about 250 milliliters. That way, I always have plenty on hand to turn into margaritas."

Makes 6 to 8 servings

- **1 cup freshly squeezed lime juice**
- **1 cup triple sec**
- **2 cups tequila**

Pour the lime juice, triple sec, and tequila into a plastic 1-liter container. Close tightly and shake to blend. Serve right away over crushed ice for a regular margarita, or freeze for at least 8 hours. When ready to serve the frozen version, thaw the mixture until just slushy, about 30 minutes.

Variation
Replace half of the lime juice with bottled pomegranate juice for a festive jewel-toned margarita for the colder months.

Frozen Cosmopolitans

Sweetened cranberry juice with its tart tang hits the spot on a hot summer day. A sprig of mint from the garden is a nice touch for this grown-up martini.

Makes 16 to 18 servings

- 1¾ quarts cranberry juice cocktail
- 1½ cups vodka
- ½ cup triple sec
- ¼ cup grenadine
- Lime wedges for garnish

1. Combine the cranberry juice, vodka, triple sec, and grenadine in a metal bowl. Place in the freezer until it has a slushy consistency (stirring occasionally), at least several hours.
2. When ready to serve, thaw the mixture until just slushy (or scoop into a blender and blend until just slushy). Spoon or pour into your favorite martini glasses. Garnish with lime wedges and serve immediately.

BBQ Queens' Royal Slush

This is a lemony iced tea with a smooth finish of apricot brandy.

Makes 22 to 24 servings

- 1¾ quarts water
- 1½ cups sugar
- 5 green tea bags
- One 12-ounce can frozen orange juice concentrate, thawed
- One 12-ounce can frozen lemonade concentrate, thawed
- 2 cups apricot brandy
- Lemon wedges for garnish

1. In a large saucepan, boil the water. Remove from the heat and add the sugar, stirring to dissolve. Add the tea bags and steep for 2 hours.
2. Remove the tea bags and stir in the orange juice concentrate, lemonade concentrate, and brandy. Pour into a large metal bowl. Place in the freezer until it has a slushy consistency (stirring occasionally), at least several hours.
3. When ready to serve, thaw the mixture until just slushy (or scoop into a blender and blend until just slushy). Spoon or pour into your favorite stemmed glasses. Garnish with lemon wedges and serve immediately.

Thai Grilled Flank Steak in Lettuce Cups

"Bring an appetizer" is a hostess request that can send chills down your spine. Visions of fiddly food that takes hours to make, but minutes to eat, can also send us BBQ Queens into a tizzy. But happily, we have appetizer recipes like this one, which is simple but impressive looking. Grill the steak, which takes minutes, a day or two ahead of time if you wish. Then set up an assembly line and you're done. While you're at the market, ask the butcher to run the flank steak through the cuber for you and you'll have an extra-tender result. You will have leftover steak and marinade, but the good thing is that you can use both to make a great Thai beef salad the next day.

Makes 12 to 16 servings

- 2 cups regular or light canned coconut milk
- 2 tablespoons green curry paste
- ¼ cup seasoned rice wine vinegar
- One 1½ -pound flank steak
- 36 Bibb lettuce leaves, from about 6 heads of Bibb (or other small, cup-shaped, and tender lettuce leaves like Little Gem or Sweet Gem)
- Fresh cilantro leaves for garnish

1. Mix the coconut milk, curry paste, and rice wine vinegar together in a bowl. Pour half in a zipper-top plastic bag and add the steak. Reserve the remaining marinade in the refrigerator. Seal the bag and massage to coat the steak with the marinade, then refrigerate for at least 3 to 4 hours, or preferably overnight.
2. Prepare a hot fire in your grill.
3. Remove the steak from the marinade, discard the marinade, and pat dry. Grill the steak for 2½ to 3 minutes per side for medium-rare. Let the steak cool to room temperature. (At this point, you may refrigerate the steak for up to 2 days.)
4. Slice the steak—perpendicular to the grain of the meat and on the diagonal—into very thin slices. Cut each slice into bite-size pieces. Place a bite-size piece in the center of each cupped lettuce leaf. Drizzle each piece with ½ teaspoon of the reserved marinade and garnish with a small cilantro leaf. Serve at room temperature.

Deck It Out

Add ½ teaspoon of finely chopped cucumber to each lettuce cup as an additional garnish, or serve this appetizer on cucumber rounds instead of inside lettuce leaves.

Change It Up

You can substitute boneless, skinless chicken breasts (flattened with a meat mallet into ½-inch-thick paillards) or pork tenderloin in this dish. Grill the flattened chicken breasts for 2½ minutes per side, and the pork tenderloin for 8 to 10 minutes per side for medium.

Raise a Glass

A Thai beer would be delicious here.

Razzle-Dazzle: Cabbages and Kings

Serve dips and sauces in veggie vessels. Hollow out a beautiful cabbage and place a small glass bowl in the hole, then fill with dip or sauce. Bell peppers and winter squash are also great containers. Even citrus fruits can be hollowed out to hold a sweet yogurt dip or a scoop of sherbet or sorbet.

Grilled Veal Bundles with Fontina, Sage, and Prosciutto

Here we have adapted and reconstructed the Roman dish of saltimbocca. The classic version features the same ingredients, but pan fried. We go for the grill instead and put the prosciutto on the outside as a way to keep the veal juicier and more tender. And we sauté the fresh sage leaves to tone down their flavor and improve their texture.

Makes 6 to 8 appetizer servings or 4 main course servings

- 1 tablespoon olive oil, plus more for brushing
- 12 fresh sage leaves
- 12 veal scaloppine (about 2 ounces each)
- Kosher or sea salt and freshly ground white pepper to taste
- 12 thin slices fontina cheese (6 to 8 ounces)
- 12 thin slices prosciutto

1. Prepare a medium-hot fire in your grill.
2. In a saucepan or small skillet, heat the olive oil over medium-high heat. Add the sage leaves and sauté for 1 to 2 minutes, or until the leaves have curled and turned slightly golden. Set aside to cool slightly.
3. Place the scaloppine on a flat surface and season with salt and white pepper. Top each scaloppine with 1 slice of fontina and 1 sautéed sage leaf. Roll each piece of veal, starting from a long side, into a bundle. Wrap each bundle with 1 slice of prosciutto and secure with a toothpick. Brush each bundle with olive oil and place on a baking sheet to take out to the grill.
4. Grill the bundles until golden brown on the outside and cooked all the way though, turning to cook evenly, 4 to 5 minutes total. Serve hot, removing the toothpicks first.

Deck It Out

Serve the bundles on an attractive platter, garnished with lots of fresh lemon wedges and sprigs of fresh herbs.

Change It Up

Use boneless, skinless chicken breasts pounded to a ¼-inch thickness instead of the veal.

Raise a Glass ·

Serve these bundles with a crisp, chilled dry white Italian wine like a Pinot Grigio, Vernaccia, or Orvieto.

Grilled Lamb Chops with Thai Chili-Peanut Dipping Sauce

With this easy appetizer, you get so much flavor with so little effort. Whip up the easy dipping sauce a day or two ahead, using Thai sweet chili sauce from the Asian section of the grocery store. That leaves plenty of time for last-minute primping. These chops get done so quickly that you'll want to have everything else prepared and ready to go. Serve them rustic style, on a platter surrounding a bowl of the dipping sauce. You can double or triple this recipe for a bigger party.

Makes 4 servings

Thai Chili-Peanut Dipping Sauce:
- ½ cup chunky peanut butter
- ½ cup Thai sweet chili sauce
- ¼ cup chopped fresh cilantro leaves

- ¼ cup vegetable oil
- 2 teaspoons red curry paste
- 12 thin lamb chops, cut from the shoulder or loin, pounded to ½-inch thickness
- Coarse kosher or sea salt and coarsely ground black pepper to taste
- Cucumber slices or spears for serving

1. To make the dipping sauce, whisk the peanut butter and Thai chili sauce together in a bowl, stir in the cilantro, and set aside. (At this point, you may cover and refrigerate the dipping sauce for up to 2 days. Let it come to room temperature before serving.)
2. In a small bowl, combine the vegetable oil and red curry paste. Place the lamb chops in 1 layer in a baking dish or on a baking tray. Brush each side with the curry paste mixture, then leave to marinate for 15 to 30 minutes at room temperature.
3. Meanwhile, prepare a hot fire in your grill.
4. When the coals are their hottest, season the chops with salt and pepper and place on the grill rack. As the oil drips on the coals, you will have flare-ups, but that is good. The flames will rise up for several seconds, then die down, giving your chops a bit of char. (Keep a spray bottle of water nearby, just in case things get

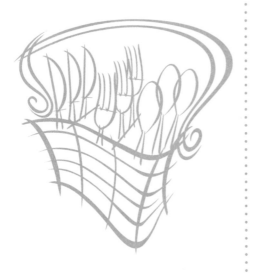

out of hand.) Let the chops cook for 1 to 2 minutes per side, or until definite grill marks appear. Then turn the chops with long-handled tongs and cook on the other side for 1 to 2 minutes more for medium-rare. Serve on a platter accompanied by cucumber slices and the bowl of dipping sauce.

Change It Up

Instead of the cucumber slices, serve this dish with steamed green beans and strips of raw red bell pepper.

Raise a Glass

Pour plenty of cold Singha beer to enjoy with these chops.

Spanish Sherry

From serving a simple glass of sherry, supposedly, the tradition of tapas began. A small plate was traditionally placed on top of the glass, some say to keep bugs away. In fact, *tapa* is Spanish for "lid." Eventually something to nibble on was placed on the plate— olives, or thinly sliced ham on a piece of bread. So a truly authentic drink to serve with tapas is Spanish sherry.

Southern Spain's Andalusia region is the most prolific winemaking area of that country, and most of its output is wonderful sherry. This fortified wine has a high alcohol content and is meant to be served chilled. Fino and manzanilla sherries are pale, light, dry wines. Amontillado is a medium-bodied dry sherry. Dry oloroso is a fuller-bodied sherry. All are meant to be drunk as an apéritif along with tapas. Some sherries, such as moscatel, sweet oloroso, and cream sherries, are darker in color and syrupy, making them perfect dessert wines. With so many delicious choices, it's no wonder that the Andalusians possess a zesty "joy of life." So celebrate the Spanish and include some sherry selections at your Spanish tapas party.

Razzle-Dazzle: Good Things from a Jar or a Can

Fancy bruschetta toppings can be purchased at upscale gourmet shops and specialty grocery stores. Artichoke relish, tapenade (olive spread), sun-dried tomato spread, roasted red peppers or pepper spread, and hummus are all nice to have on hand. With a tiny bit of effort, canned beans can become extraordinary with this recipe from our friend Jasper Mirabile, owner of Jasper's Restaurant in Kansas City. He prepared this for a Slow Food event. It knocked our tiaras off because it was so good, yet so simple. It makes a great side salad, too.

Rustic White Bean Spread

Makes 10 to 12 servings, about 20 to 24 bruschetta on sliced baguette

- One 15-ounce can cannellini beans, rinsed and drained
- 3 cloves garlic, chopped
- Juice of 1 lemon
- ½ cup freshly torn basil leaves, or more to your taste
- ¼ cup extra-virgin olive oil, or more to your taste
- Freshly ground black pepper to taste

In a large bowl, combine all of the ingredients and toss to blend. Spoon onto toasted pieces of bread (bruschetta) and serve at room temperature.

Up at the Villa, Out in the Courtyard: An Autumn Dinner in Tuscany

When Judith's family went to Italy for her parents' golden anniversary, they rented a hilltop villa near La Foce, in Tuscany. On a memorable Fourth of July, they brought tables and chairs outdoors to the graveled courtyard overlooking wheat fields lined with cypress trees. On those tables set with colorful cotton prints in the vivid colors of Italian pottery, they served a grilled meal family style, on platters accompanied by carafes of the local wines. Everyone agreed that there never was a finer feast.

Let's again gather in the Tuscan countryside, but on a golden fall day after the grape or olive harvest. The tables are laden with farm-raised poultry and game, along with olives, tomatoes, zucchini, beans of all kinds, chickpeas, artichokes, and wonderfully rich and earthy mushrooms. The aroma of herbs, including lots of basil, is in the air. There are lemon trees and fruits like apples, cherries, plums, apricots, and pears. With all that in mind, let's pull the party together.

Setting the Scene

Italian country is the scenario for this get-together. The dinner can be in your big country kitchen, on the patio, or at a table outdoors. Celebrate autumn with the colors of falling leaves: salmon, burnt orange, gold, olive green, purplish brown. Throw interesting quilts or colorful cloths in these colors over the tables. Set out big candles or lots of votives on glazed terra cotta plates. Family-style service or buffet is the way to go, with lots of big-platter foods. A two-tiered serving tray is a nice addition, saving space and adding visual interest to the buffet. Serve the grilled bread in a large, rustic basket with room for the bowls of toppings. Arrange two grilled meats together on a large platter. Serve the vegetable side dishes and a big bowl of pasta tossed with olive oil, basil, salt, and pepper at room temperature.

Making Beautiful Music
This dinner party begs for Italian opera (try Puccini or Verdi) or the music of the Three Tenors or Andrea Bocelli.

Perfect Partners
Have a large oval bucket filled with ice on hand to chill the Pinot Grigio and the Vin Santo, a Tuscan dessert wine. For red wine drinkers, serve a nice Rosso di Montalcino or a good Chianti.

Choose from Among These Dishes
Wood-Grilled Country Bread with Four Seasons Toppings (page 45)

Green Bean, Tomato, and Goat Cheese Salad with Lemon-Pesto
 Dressing (page 163)

The BBQ Queens' Knife-and-Fork Grilled Vegetable Salad (page 170)

Bistro Fennel and Baby Bello Mushroom Salad (page 191)

Italian Grilled Veal Chops with Green Olive, Caper, and Fresh
 Tomato Sauce (page 100)

Veal T-Bones with Lemon-Butter Sauce and Gremolata Garnish
 (page 102)

Vineyard Smoked Chicken *Amogio* (page 132)

Smoke-Roasted Root Vegetables with Garlic and Rosemary (page 198)

Stir-Grilled Tomatoes, Red Onion, and Fresh Herbs with Grilled
 Flatbread (page 188)

Wine-Splashed Peaches, Plums, and Berries (page 210)

Almond Bundt Pound Cake (page 224)

Grilled Chocolate Crostini (page 216)

Grilled Pork Tenderloin with Peanut Butter Dipping Sauce and Toasted Sesame Seeds

This is a fun two-step appetizer that can be arranged on platters and passed through a crowd of guests. Arrange the grilled and chilled pork slices on a platter with bowls of the dipping sauce and the sesame seeds. Guests dip a slice of tenderloin in the sauce, then lightly dredge one side in the sesame seeds. This recipe is perfect for entertaining because it needs to be made 1 or 2 days ahead so that the pork can be chilled. So there's one less thing to cook on the day of your party! We have definite thoughts on which peanut butter to use, too, as you might expect. Judith is a Skippy girl and Karen prefers extra-crunchy Jif. Choose your favorite peanut butter, smooth or chunky.

Makes 12 to 15 servings

- **3 pounds pork tenderloins**
- **½ cup hoisin sauce**
- **½ cup soy sauce**
- **3 tablespoons honey**
- **1 tablespoon toasted sesame oil**
- **3 cloves garlic, minced**
- **1 tablespoon minced fresh ginger**
- **1 cup peanut butter**
- **Leafy greens for garnish**
- **1 cup toasted sesame seeds**

1. Rinse the pork tenderloins under cold running water and pat dry. With a paring knife, remove any membrane. Place the tenderloins in a large zipper-top plastic bag and set aside.

2. In a small bowl, combine the hoisin sauce, soy sauce, honey, sesame oil, garlic, and ginger to make the marinade. Place the peanut butter in a separate small bowl. Add 3 to 4 tablespoons of the marinade to the peanut butter and stir to blend into a dipping sauce, adding more if necessary. The dipping sauce should have the consistency of a slightly thickened sauce. Cover and refrigerate the dipping sauce until ready to use. Pour the rest of the marinade over the tenderloins and marinate for 4 to 6 hours or overnight in the refrigerator.

3. Prepare a hot fire in your grill. Remove the pork from the marinade and place on a doubled baking sheet to take outside. Pour the marinade into a small saucepan and boil for 5 minutes prior to using it as a baste.

4. Char the tenderloins for 2 or 3 minutes per side, turning at quarter turns and brushing with the marinade, until all sides are charred and the internal temperature registers 135° to 140°F on an instant-read thermometer. Remove the pork from the grill and let it rest for about 20 minutes. Cover and refrigerate for several hours or overnight.

5. When ready to serve, cut the pork into ¼-inch-thick slices. Arrange the greens on a platter. Place the tenderloin slices atop the greens, with shallow bowls of the peanut butter dipping sauce and the toasted sesame seeds on the side of the platter.

Razzle-Dazzle: Pretty Stems All in a Row

Shop for various stemmed wine and cocktail glasses at garage sales, flea markets, and antique stores. You'll have a unique collection of inexpensive glasses that are festive and fun. Guests can select their favorite glass, and it's also easier to remember whose is whose.

Grilled Mini Lamb Burgers with Cilantro-Mint Butter

Memphis Blues Restaurant in Vancouver, Canada, along with Barbra-Jo's Books to Cooks, hosted a great event for our cookbook *The BBQ Queens' Big Book of Barbecue* (The Harvard Common Press, 2005). The evening began with Cosmopolitans and passed appetizers that included a mini lamb burger. Of course, we had to go home and re-create the great taste, and here it is.

Makes 12 mini burgers

Cilantro-Mint Butter:
- ½ cup (1 stick) unsalted butter, softened
- 1½ tablespoons finely chopped fresh cilantro
- 1½ tablespoons finely chopped fresh mint
- 1 clove garlic, minced

- 1½ pounds ground lamb
- 1⅔ cups crumbled feta cheese
- ⅓ cup minced kalamata olives
- 1 clove garlic, minced
- ¾ teaspoon ground cumin
- ¾ teaspoon ground coriander
- ½ teaspoon kosher salt
- 1 teaspoon freshly ground black pepper
- Olive oil for brushing
- 12 mini pita breads, slit halfway open
- 1 red onion, thinly sliced
- 1 head red-leaf lettuce, shredded

1. To make the cilantro-mint butter, in a small bowl, combine the softened butter, cilantro, mint, and garlic. Set aside.
2. Prepare a hot fire in your grill.
3. Combine the lamb, ⅔ cup of the feta, the olives, and garlic in a large bowl and gently mix together until just blended. Make 12 small patties about ½ inch thick.
4. Combine the cumin, coriander, salt, and pepper in a small bowl. Lightly brush the patties with olive oil on both sides. Sprinkle with the cumin-coriander seasoning on both sides. Wrap the pita breads in a heavy-duty aluminum foil packet. Place the burgers and bread on a doubled baking sheet and carry out to the grill.
5. Put the pita on the indirect side of the grill and close the lid. Let warm for about 5 minutes.
6. Grill the mini burgers over direct heat for about 3 minutes on one side, then turn and place a dollop of the butter on the browned side. Grill an additional 3 minutes for medium-rare to medium. The outside should be browned and the interior just barely pink.
7. Place a burger in each pita and garnish with more of the butter, the remaining feta, sliced red onion, and the lettuce. Serve immediately.

Rioja-Style Grilled Pork Tenderloin Tapas

Rioja, in northern Spain, is a region famous for its wines and the hearty food that goes with them. The seasoning paste on this pork features sassy Spanish paprika; we like to use smoked Spanish paprika for even more flavor. To be really authentic, grill this pork over charcoal and vine clippings (we use wild grapevines, common in the Midwest), or try flavored wood pellets. Of course, you can double, triple, or quadruple this recipe to serve more, more, more.

Makes 4 to 6 servings

Suggested wood: Oak, oak wine-barrel staves, grapevines, or almond

- **1 pound pork tenderloin**
- **3 tablespoons regular or smoked Spanish paprika**
- **¾ teaspoon dried oregano**
- **¾ teaspoon dried thyme**
- **1 bay leaf**
- **1 large clove garlic**
- **1½ teaspoons kosher or sea salt**
- **2 tablespoons olive oil, plus more for brushing**
- **1 large French baguette, cut into 12 to 14 slices**
- **Fresh lemon and orange wedges for garnish**

1. Rinse the pork tenderloin under cold running water and pat dry. With a paring knife, remove any membrane. In a small bowl, combine the paprika, oregano, thyme, and bay leaf. Using a mortar and pestle, mash the garlic clove and salt together to make a smooth paste. Add the paste and the olive oil to the paprika mixture and stir until smooth. Spread the paste over the pork, wrap tightly in plastic wrap, and refrigerate for at least 1 day and up to 3 days before grilling. (The longer you marinate, the stronger the flavor.)

2. Prepare a hot fire in your grill. Remove the pork tenderloin from the refrigerator, unwrap, and slice into 12 to 14 thin medallions. Brush each medallion, on both sides, with olive oil and place on a doubled baking sheet to take outside.

3. In a charcoal grill, spread a handful of vine clippings over the coals. In a gas grill, place dry wood pellets or dry wood chips in the smoker box or in an aluminum foil packet with holes punched in the top. Grill the medallions for about 1 to 2 minutes per side, turning once. Serve each medallion on a round of baguette, accompanied by lemon and orange wedges for squeezing over the pork.

Deck It Out · · · · · · · · · · · · · · · · · ·

For a great rustic touch, arrange a few tendrils of vines and/or leaves on the platter, along with the tapas and citrus wedges.

Raise a Glass · · · · · · · · · · · · · · · · ·

Serve with a hearty red wine from Rioja or a young Cabernet.

Grilled Prosciutto-Wrapped Asparagus with Fig Balsamic Vinegar and Shaved Parmesan

Like a conga line of sarong-wrapped lovelies, this appetizer sizzles and shimmies on even the plainest of white platters. It's easier to grill these ganged onto double skewers, turning once, and then finish the dish with a splash of balsamic vinegar.

Makes 6 to 8 servings

- **2 pounds fresh asparagus, ends trimmed**
- **4 ounces prosciutto, cut lengthwise into 2-inch pieces**
- **Olive oil**
- **Fig balsamic vinegar for drizzling**
- **Shaved Parmesan cheese for garnish**

1. Prepare a medium-hot fire in your grill.
2. Wrap each asparagus spear with a slice of prosciutto. Drizzle the spears with olive oil to lightly coat.
3. Place the spears perpendicular to the grill rack. Grill, turning often, until the asparagus is crisp-tender and the prosciutto has blistered, 8 to 10 minutes. Set the asparagus on a serving platter and splash with the fig balsamic vinegar. Sprinkle with the shaved Parmesan. Serve hot or at room temperature.

More Sparkling Drinks

We love them so much that we decided we needed to include these as well!

Prairie Kir Royale

A brunch barbecue calls for a special cocktail. Instead of mimosas, why not serve something a little different? We love these sparklers, adapted from a recipe in Judith's *Prairie Home Cooking* (The Harvard Common Press, 1999).

Makes 8 servings

- 8 fresh blackberries or raspberries
- 8 teaspoons blackberry or raspberry liqueur
- One 750-milliliter bottle Champagne or sparkling wine, preferably brut and very cold

Place a berry in the bottom of each of eight Champagne glasses, drizzle with a teaspoon of liqueur, and top with Champagne. Serve immediately.

Raspberry Rossini

Instead of the hard-to-find crème de fraises (strawberry liqueur) of the classic Rossini, this version gets its kick from framboise, a raspberry liqueur. Perfect for a spring or early summer outdoor barbecue bash, this festive drink sparkles with bubbly Italian Prosecco.

Makes 8 servings

- 1 quart fresh raspberries
- Sugar to taste
- 2 tablespoons framboise
- One 750-milliliter bottle chilled Prosecco or other sparkling wine

1. In a food processor, puree the berries. Strain out the seeds. Transfer to a large glass pitcher. Taste and stir in a teaspoon or two of sugar to take away any excess tartness, but not so much as to make the berries too sweet.
2. Stir in the framboise, then the Prosecco. Pour into eight Champagne glasses and serve immediately.

Pancetta-Wrapped Radicchio, Fennel, and Potato Bundles

"Bundles" on the grill—several ingredients rolled together and wrapped with something edible (here either pancetta or prosciutto)—are a great way to do appetizers. You can assemble them hours ahead of time, then preside over them at the grill like the important person you are (or get another person who wants to be important to grill these for you, while you socialize).

Makes 6 to 8 servings

- **2 large baking potatoes**
- **2 small heads radicchio, cut into quarters**
- **1 bulb fennel, ends trimmed and cut into 8 wedges**
- **8 thin slices pancetta or prosciutto**
- **Olive oil for brushing**
- **1 recipe Mortar and Pestle Vinaigrette (page 170)**

1. Prick the potatoes all over with a fork. Microwave them on High until done, 7 to 10 minutes. Run the potatoes under cold running water until cool enough to handle, then peel and cut each potato into 4 wedges.
2. Stack one piece of each of the three vegetables together to form 8 bundles, with the largest piece on the bottom and the smallest on the top. This will probably mean the fennel on the bottom, the radicchio in the middle, and the potato on top, but it will depend on the size of your vegetables. Wrap each bundle with a slice of pancetta and secure with a toothpick. (At this point, you may cover and refrigerate the bundles for up to 1 day ahead. Let come to room temperature before grilling.)
3. Prepare a hot fire in your grill. Place the bundles on a baking sheet, brush them with olive oil, and take out to the grill.
4. Grill for 3 to 4 minutes per side, turning once, or until browned and golden. Serve on a platter drizzled with the vinaigrette or on a round plate with the vinaigrette in a small bowl as a dipping sauce.

Mocktails

Sometimes you want to serve a festive drink, but without the alcohol. Be a very good host(ess) and always have a nonalcoholic beverage for those who prefer no alcohol. Water, coffee, iced tea? Yeah, yeah, and fairly boring, too. Remember, this is a barbecue bash, so make something fun and out of the ordinary for the party. These mocktails are so delicious, with lots of citrus and herb flavors, that you may offer them as your only drink. For those who'd like to turn them into an alcoholic cooler, simply add spirits like sparkling wine, vodka, rum, or a fruity liqueur to taste. For a splashy touch, freeze the fruit garnishes that you plan to use. Simply adding sparkling water or club soda to a drink makes it more special, too.

Pomegranate Spritzer

If you're thinking that this sounds sort of like a Shirley Temple (7UP with a splash of grenadine), you're correct. Grenadine is made with pomegranate syrup, although there are some grenadines that are made with other fruit flavors. There is a pomegranate liqueur available, too, called Pama. If you have a mixed crowd of imbibers and abstainers, then serve this one drink with either the syrup or the Pama. Easy enough! We like to serve these grown-up-style, in highball glasses rimmed with lime juice and cinnamon sugar or other store-bought sweet drink rimmers. Feel free to use other fruit flavors, like some of the Monin fruit syrups, to create your own favorite drink.

Makes 4 servings

- **2 tablespoons sugar**
- **1 teaspoon ground cinnamon**
- **1 lime**
- **Ice cubes**
- **3 cups chilled fruit-flavored sparkling water or club soda**
- **1 cup grenadine, or to taste**

1. Combine the sugar and cinnamon in a shallow bowl and mix well.
2. Cut the lime into quarters. Wet the rims of four highball glasses with lime juice, then place each glass, rim edge down, into the cinnamon sugar to coat.
3. Fill each glass with ice cubes. Pour ¾ cup sparkling water into each glass. Top each glass with ¼ cup grenadine, or to taste. Garnish with a wedge of lime.

Freshly Squeezed Citrus Cordial

The syrup in this mocktail can be used as a blueprint to make other citrus syrups by substituting your favorite citrus flavor. The mocktail becomes a cocktail when you add a splash of citrus-flavored liqueur, vodka, or rum. The citrus syrup can be made ahead and refrigerated for several days.

Makes 8 servings

- **6 cups water**
- **1½ cups sugar**
- **1 cup freshly squeezed citrus juice of your choice, strained**
- **Chilled sparkling water or club soda**
- **Citrus fruit wedges of your choice for garnish**

1. To make the citrus syrup, bring the water to a boil in a saucepan. Add the sugar and stir until dissolved. Remove from the heat and cool to room temperature. When cool, add the citrus juice and stir. Refrigerate for several hours or until ice cold.
2. To make each drink, pour ¾ cup of the syrup into a tall glass. Top with sparkling water and garnish with a wedge of citrus.

Virgin Sea Breeze

Tart, tangy, and a little bit sweet is what they say about the BBQ Queens—um, we mean this drink. On a hot and humid day, pour a glass of this, close your eyes, and you're on the beach or at the lake. Ahhhh!

Makes 8 servings

- **4 cups cranberry juice cocktail, chilled**
- **4 cups grapefruit juice, chilled**
- **Ice cubes**
- **Chilled sparkling water or club soda**

1. Pour the cranberry juice and grapefruit juice into a large pitcher. Stir to blend.
2. Pour the juice into eight highball glasses filled with ice cubes. Top with sparkling water.

Pineapple Sunshine

This would be yummy as a slushy, too. Just add the juices to a blender along with ice cubes, and pulse until slushy. Stir in the sparkling water last and pulse again. Then pour into margarita glasses and garnish.

Makes 4 servings

- 1⅓ cups pineapple juice
- 1⅓ cups orange juice
- 1⅓ cups sour mix
- Ice cubes
- Chilled sparkling water or club soda
- 1 orange, quartered
- 4 spears fresh pineapple

1. Combine the pineapple juice, orange juice, and sour mix in a pitcher.
2. Pour the mixture into four highball glasses filled with ice. Top with sparkling water and garnish each drink with an orange quarter and a spear of pineapple.

Sunshine Citrus Mocktail

This is sort of like a Tequila Sunrise, but with only lots of healthy fresh-squeezed juices. Substitute a different flavored syrup for the grenadine if you like, but keep in mind that the tartness of the grapefruit and lemon juices begs for a little something sweet.

Makes about 4 servings

- 2 cups freshly squeezed grapefruit juice
- 1 cup freshly squeezed orange juice
- 1 cup freshly squeezed lemon juice
- ¼ cup grenadine
- Ice cubes
- Chilled sparkling water or club soda
- Orange slices for garnish

1. Combine the grapefruit juice, orange juice, lemon juice, and grenadine in a large pitcher.
2. For each drink, pour 1 cup of the mixture into a tall glass filled with ice cubes. Top with sparkling water and garnish with an orange slice.

Berry-Spice Iced Tea

Fred Thompson has the most delightful drinks books with pretty photos. We like this recipe from *Iced Tea* (The Harvard Common Press, 2002). If you want to change it up a bit, try raspberry- or cherry-flavored tea. Frozen raspberries, black or red, would also make a colorful garnish for this drink.

Makes 6 servings

- **3 cups water**
- **3 black currant–flavored tea bags or 3 teaspoons black currant–flavored tea leaves**
- **Three 3-inch cinnamon sticks**
- **10 whole cloves**
- **⅓ cup sugar**
- **1½ cups cranberry juice cocktail**
- **1 tablespoon freshly squeezed lemon juice**
- **Thinly sliced lemon for garnish**

1. In a small saucepan, bring the water to a gentle boil. Add the tea, cover, and remove from the heat. Let steep for 10 minutes.
2. Remove the tea bags without squeezing, or strain out the leaves using a fine-mesh strainer. Add the cinnamon sticks, cloves, and sugar. Cover and let cool to room temperature.
3. Strain the liquid through a fine-mesh strainer into a pitcher. Add the cranberry juice and lemon juice and stir to combine.
4. Chill, then serve over ice, garnished with lemon slices.

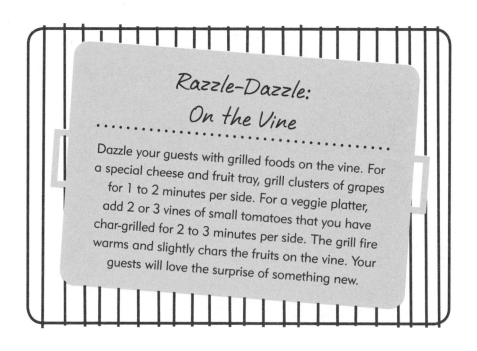

Razzle-Dazzle: On the Vine

Dazzle your guests with grilled foods on the vine. For a special cheese and fruit tray, grill clusters of grapes for 1 to 2 minutes per side. For a veggie platter, add 2 or 3 vines of small tomatoes that you have char-grilled for 2 to 3 minutes per side. The grill fire warms and slightly chars the fruits on the vine. Your guests will love the surprise of something new.

Grilled Siciliano

We like the mix-and-match possibilities in this micro sandwich, which can be assembled a day ahead of time and grilled right before serving. Use whatever filling ingredients sound good and will look good when you cut this long sandwich into miniature slices. We've taken a meat-lover's approach, but go vegetarian if you prefer. You can also double, triple, or quadruple this recipe to serve a bigger crowd.

Makes 8 servings

- **1 long, thin baguette or ficelle**
- **Garlic-flavored olive oil for brushing**
- **8 ounces thinly sliced mortadella, smoked turkey, salami, or pepperoni**
- **8 ounces sliced provolone or fontina cheese**
- **One 8-ounce jar roasted red peppers**
- **½ cup pitted brine-cured kalamata olives**

1. Slice the bread horizontally through the middle, but not all the way through, so the bread loaf is "hinged." Slather the cut sides with olive oil. Arrange slices of the meat on the bottom half, then top with slices of cheese, roasted red peppers, and the olives. Close the "lid" of the sandwich and brush the top with olive oil. Wrap well in aluminum foil. (At this point, you may refrigerate the sandwich for up to 1 day.)

2. Prepare a medium fire in your grill. Heat the sandwich for 15 to 30 minutes, or until thoroughly warmed. To serve, cut on the diagonal into 1-inch-thick slices and arrange on a platter.

Deck It Out

We love long, rectangular platters of little bites arranged in alternate rows: Thai Grilled Flank Steak in Lettuce Cups (page 50), Grilled Siciliano slices, and wedges of Grilled Polenta with Caramelized Onions and Gorgonzola (page 31). It makes for a striking visual presentation.

Take It Easy

Tasty tubes of pureed sun-dried tomato, basil, cilantro, and lemongrass are available in the fresh herb section of many grocery

stores. Anchovy and olive pastes are delicious, too, and are usually found near the canned tuna or in the Italian section. When spread on the bread first, these pastes (or pestos) add a no-work flavor punch to sandwiches like this Grilled Siciliano.

Change It Up

- Try filling this with basil pesto, thinly sliced grilled chicken, and aioli.
- If you want to make a vegetable-based sandwich, substitute grilled slices of zucchini, summer squash, or mushrooms for the meat.

Raise a Glass

Serve this with a Chianti or a young Cabernet if it's meat-filled, or a Soave if vegetable-filled.

Razzle-Dazzle: Beyond Parsley

Just like the Junior League of Kansas City, Missouri, did in its cookbook *Beyond Parsley* (which Karen worked on), think beyond a sprig of parsley when garnishing. For a simple finishing touch on a platter of grilled or smoked food, add small bouquets of mixed fresh herbs. Lovely twining vines of thyme or oregano are a perfect finish. Place thin slices of citrus fruit on a corner of the platter and top with the green bouquet of your choice, but try and match the herbs that you've cooked with for a perfect culinary complement.

Apple-Smoked Salmon

Deeply flavorful, this salmon makes a knockout dish for a brunch or an appetizer for a casual or black-tie barbecue dinner. And the bonus? You can smoke it a day ahead of time, wrap it in plastic, and refrigerate. The salmon can be served hot, cold, or at room temperature. We are indebted to Dennis Horner, an attorney and barbecue contest competitor, for this recipe. He and we like to use Paul Prudhomme's Seafood Magic seasoning for this dish, but feel free to switch to your favorite dry rub.

Makes 10 to 12 servings

Suggested wood: Apple

- **One 2½- to 3-pound boneless, skinless salmon fillet**
- **One 12-ounce bottle zesty Italian dressing**
- **½ cup Seafood Magic or dry rub of your choice**
- **Apple juice for spraying**
- **Thinly sliced lemons and sprigs of fresh dill for garnish**

1. Place the salmon fillet in a plastic container or zipper-top plastic bag. Pour the Italian dressing over the fish. Cover and marinate the fillet for 3 to 4 hours in the refrigerator.
2. Prepare a fire in your smoker. Pour the apple juice into a plastic spray bottle and keep nearby.
3. Remove the salmon from the marinade (do not pat dry) and discard the marinade. Place the marinated salmon on a baking sheet, with the side that had the skin facing down. Sprinkle the dry rub on the top of the fish, then take out to the smoker. Place the fillet on the smoker rack, with the side that has the rub facing up. Close the lid and smoke for 2 to 2¼ hours at 225° to 250°F, spraying every 30 minutes with apple juice. Use two spatulas to carefully transfer the salmon from the smoker to a platter. Garnish with lemon slices and dill sprigs.

Deck It Out

Set out a bowl of Horseradish Crème Fraîche (page 78) to dollop on each serving. This salmon is knife and fork food, so have little plates and forks ready for serving.

Sparkle, Sizzle, Smoke!
A Cozy Dinner à Deux

It's winter, and baby, it's cold outside! But imagine you're indoors listening to the legendary Peggy Lee sing "Fever," Diana Krall doing the classic "I've Got You Under My Skin," or Rita Coolidge subtly suggesting "We're All Alone." Things can sure warm up fast.

Like the velvet voices of these sultry singers, smoky appetizers and a sizzling something hot off the fire make for come-hither fare when paired with glasses of bubbly. Even if you don't have the "I like romantic evenings by the fire"–type setting, you can at least supply the feeling and the flavor. As BBQ Queens, we know that using smoke and sizzle as flavors can lift almost any dish.

There's nothing romantic about a frazzled cook, though, so plan and work ahead so that you can enjoy yourself, too. Go with all appetizers, or one appetizer and the main course, and maybe a dessert. (Nothing too heavy, though!) The great thing about the two sweet endings we suggest is that both can be made ahead—the pears entirely, while the cupcake batter and the frozen truffle mixture can be ready to go in the oven at the last minute. Or just buy a good dessert.

Setting the Scene

We're talking a cozy dinner here, so set a table for just the two of you—in front of the fire would be ideal. Move your furniture around if you have to and place that table—even if it is a card table disguised with a nice cloth—in front of the fire or by a window where you have candles burning. Have an ice bucket or an urn filled with ice nearby to keep that Champagne chilled. This is another time to get out the good stuff: silver, linens, fresh flowers, votive candles. Dim the lights. And enjoy!

Making Beautiful Music

Just about any female torch or soulful jazz singer, such as the abovementioned, sets the proper mood.

Perfect Partners

Creamy textures or rich backgrounds help carry the smoke or grill flavors in each dish, which are well counterpointed by the crisp acidity of sparkling wines. Our absolute favorite Champagne—we like it brut, brut, brut (did we say "dry"?)—is Veuve Clicquot, when the budget allows, of course. But we also bow to Queen Elizabeth's favorite, Bollinger R. D., those great California sparklers Domaine Chandon and Roederer Estate, and Italian Prosecco or Spanish cava. And remember—Champagne or sparkling wine needs to be served very, very cold.

Choose from Among These Dishes

Wood-Roasted Oysters on a Bed of Rock Salt with Two Sauces
(page 76)
Wood-Grilled Shrimp Cocktail with Horseradish Crème Fraîche
(page 78)
Pecan-Smoked Goat Cheese–Stuffed Peppadews (page 36)
Grilled Figs on Rosemary Skewers (page 34)
Grilled Lobster Parcels (page 80)
Wood-Grilled Duck Breast Paillards with Raspberry-Thyme Sauce
(page 143)
Creole Coffee–Rubbed Filet Mignon with Silky Crab Butter (page 94)
Grilled asparagus
Warm Chocolate Truffle Cupcakes (page 216)
Pears Poached in Moscato del Solo (page 212)

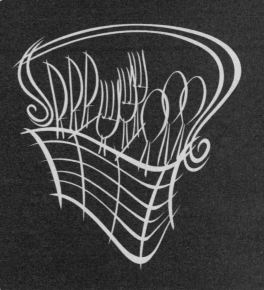

Grilled Mini Tuna Burgers with Rémoulade

A brush stroke of olive oil and tarragon vinegar infuses the tuna with the essence of the Mediterranean coast. The rémoulade is so flavorful that no other garnishes are necessary. Maybe just have extra napkins on hand to catch any of the juicy spills. A version of this recipe was featured in *Bon Appétit* and everyone on staff "loved it!," said food editor Kristine Kidd. Serve the tuna burgers with the mini lamb burgers (page 60) and Sunshine Citrus Mocktails (page 67), spiked with vodka according to guests' tastes, for an upscale-but-not-stuffy cocktail party—or just a new way to do burgers on the weekend.

Makes 8 mini burgers

Rémoulade:
- **1 teaspoon finely chopped fresh Italian parsley leaves**
- **1 teaspoon grated onion**
- **2 large hard-boiled egg yolks**
- **1 teaspoon anchovy paste**
- **1 clove garlic, minced**
- **1 large organic egg or equivalent egg substitute**
- **1 cup extra-virgin olive oil**
- **2 tablespoons capers, rinsed, drained, and patted dry**
- **Juice of ½ lemon, or to your taste**

- **Eight 3-ounce yellowfin tuna steaks, cut 1 inch thick**
- **¼ cup olive oil, plus more for brushing the rolls**
- **2 tablespoons tarragon vinegar**
- **1 bay leaf, slightly crunched**
- **8 small artisanal rolls, sliced in half**

1. To make the rémoulade, place the parsley, onion, hard-boiled egg yolks, anchovy paste, garlic, and whole egg in a food processor or blender and process into a paste. With the machine running, slowly add the olive oil through the feed tube in a thin stream until the mixture forms a mayonnaise-like consistency. Fold in the capers and lemon juice. Cover tightly and chill until ready to serve. (You may make the rémoulade up to 24 hours in advance.)
2. Prepare a hot fire in your grill.
3. Place the tuna on a doubled baking sheet. In a small bowl, mix together the olive oil, tarragon vinegar, and bay leaf and place on the sheet. Brush the cut sides of the rolls with olive oil and set in a basket. Carry everything out to the grill.
4. Grill the tuna steaks for 2½ to 3 minutes per side for medium-rare (3 to 4 minutes for medium). Baste with the oil and tarragon mixture several times while grilling. During the last few minutes of grilling, place the rolls, cut sides down, on the grill rack, and grill until the bread is golden and you have good grill marks.

To serve, place a tuna steak on each bun bottom, top with the rémoulade, and cover with the bun top.

> *Take care when serving dishes with uncooked eggs to the very young, the very old, or anyone with a compromised immune system. Use organic eggs from a source you trust, or use an egg substitute.*

Razzle-Dazzle: Being Green

Who says that floral arrangements have to be made up of flowers? Not us! Leafy green ferns, shade- or sun-loving coleus, lovely vines of ivy, cactus, and pots of fresh herbs all qualify as "floral" arrangements. They're low maintenance and crowd pleasing, and they don't have perfumey smells that might interfere with delectable food aromas. If possible, keep green plants in potted containers or buckets of water. Snip ivy just an hour or two before your party, keep in water until the last minute, and then lay the vines around the table as decoration.

Wood-Roasted Oysters on a Bed of Rock Salt with Two Sauces

When you want to serve an appetizer that is simple yet oh-so-impressive, this is it. Although you no longer have to wait for a month with an "r" in it to serve oysters (as they're now farm-raised in cold waters throughout the year), it can be difficult in inland areas to get oysters during the hot months, so check out their availability before you plan your menu. Serve with both of our smoky sauces or just one—it's your party, after all! Rock salt, a large-grained salt used in old-fashioned ice cream makers, is available in the canning or outdoor cooking section of the grocery store. Have ready a pair of sturdy oven mitts, an oyster knife, and an experienced oyster shucker.

Makes 6 to 8 servings

Suggested wood: 1 cup chips or ⅓ cup pellets (apple, cherry, mesquite, oak, or pecan)

Smoky Cocktail Sauce:
- **1 cup store-bought cocktail sauce**
- **1 tablespoon prepared horseradish, or to your taste**
- **1 teaspoon liquid smoke flavoring, or to your taste**

Chipotle-Garlic Butter:
- **1 cup (2 sticks) unsalted butter, melted**
- **4 cloves garlic, minced**
- **Juice of 1 lemon**
- **1 teaspoon bottled chipotle sauce, or to your taste**

- **Rock salt**
- **24 to 32 oysters in their shells, scrubbed and rinsed**

1. Make the two sauces. Whisk the ingredients of each sauce together in two separate small bowls. Keep the cocktail sauce chilled, and keep the butter sauce warm by the grill.

2. Line two heatproof serving platters with a layer of rock salt and place in a 350°F oven to warm while the grill is heating up.

3. Prepare a hot fire in your grill. If using a charcoal grill, place moistened wood chips (or a foil packet of dry wood pellets with holes poked in the top) directly on the coals right before you want to grill. If using a gas grill, enclose dry wood chips or pellets in a foil packet with holes poked in the top; place the packet on the grill grate over the heat source. You're ready to grill when you see the smoke from the smoldering wood and the fire is hot.

4. Place the oysters, flat shell up, on a large baking sheet (or two), cover with a damp towel, and take out to the grill. (Discard any oysters that have opened.) Using grill tongs, place the oysters, flat shell up, over the hot fire. Close the lid of the grill and grill for 3 minutes, or until the shells have opened. Using oven mitts, remove the cooked oysters to the baking sheet

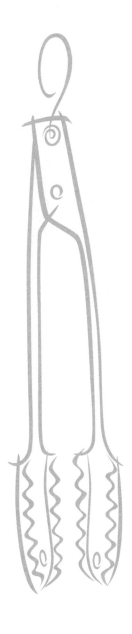

(discard any oysters that have not opened after grilling for 5 minutes). Using an oyster knife, open the oysters completely and remove and discard the top shell. Place the opened oysters on the hot rock salt and top with the sauces of your choice. Serve warm.

Deck It Out

To go all-out, topping-wise, garnish the platter with lemon wedges and small, pretty bowls of vinegar and horseradish, if you like.

Take It Easy

For one quick make-ahead sauce, prepare a Maltaise aioli by thinning a good-quality store-bought mayonnaise with orange juice. Add freshly grated orange zest and smoked paprika to taste. *Voilà!*

Change It Up

We also like kinder, gentler sauces with grilled oysters, more along the lines of a *beurre blanc*.

Raise a Glass

Have ready a chilled bottle of Muscadet or a pale ale to toast your culinary success.

Wood-Grilled Shrimp Cocktail with Horseradish Crème Fraîche

Classic shrimp cocktail—chilled pink steamed shrimp over shreds of iceberg lettuce topped with a pungent tomato-and-horseradish sauce—is not so retro that it's cool again just yet. So we've given shrimp cocktail a BBQ Queen makeover to help it along. Wouldn't shrimp taste better stir-grilled with a kiss of smoke? And served with grilled red onion and tomatoes? Then topped with a horseradish crème fraîche? Yes, yes, yes! Notice the different methods for grilling with a kiss of smoke on charcoal or gas grills. Experiment with moistened versus dry wood chips or packets of dry wood pellets to find out how to get the best smoke flavor from your grill.

Makes 4 to 6 servings

Suggested wood: 1 cup chips or ⅓ cup pellets (apple, cherry, mesquite, oak, or pecan)

Horseradish Crème Fraîche:
- **½ cup heavy cream**
- **½ cup sour cream**
- **1 tablespoon prepared horseradish, or to your taste**

- **1 pound jumbo shrimp, peeled and deveined**
- **1 cup cherry or grape tomatoes**
- **1 medium-size red onion, sliced**
- **½ cup bottled vinaigrette of your choice**
- **Shredded iceberg lettuce**

1. To make the crème fraîche, stir together the cream and sour cream in a small bowl until well blended. Cover and leave at room temperature for several hours or overnight (this helps the crème fraîche to thicken). When ready to serve, stir in the horseradish.

2. Place the shrimp, tomatoes, and onion in a zipper-top plastic bag and pour the vinaigrette over. Seal the bag and let marinate in the refrigerator for up to 2 hours while you start the fire. Oil the interior and exterior of a grill wok and set aside on a baking sheet.

3. Prepare a hot fire in your grill. If using a charcoal grill, place water-soaked wood chips directly on coals or place a foil packet of dry wood pellets with holes poked in the top directly on the coals right before you want to grill. If using a gas grill, enclose dry wood chips or pellets in a foil packet with holes poked in the top; place the packet on the grill grate over the heat source. You're ready to grill when you see the smoke from the smoldering wood and the fire is hot.

4. Set the prepared grill wok over the sink and pour the contents of the bag into it. Let drain. Set the wok on the baking sheet and take out to the grill. Stir-grill, tossing with wooden paddles every 2 minutes or so, for 15 minutes, or until the vegetables have softened and the shrimp are pink and opaque. While you're grilling, close the lid from time to time for increased wood-smoke flavor.

5. To serve, arrange the shredded lettuce, shrimp, and vegetables on small plates, in martini glasses, or in small glass bowls and top with a dollop of the crème fraîche. Serve hot, at room temperature, or cold.

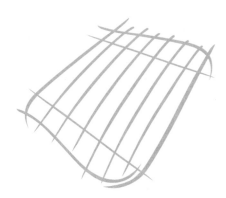

Take It Easy

Cruise through the salad bar of your grocery store and load up on already prepared shredded lettuce, cherry tomatoes, and sliced onion. Then buy ready-made crème fraîche and you're halfway there.

Change It Up

To make it easier to serve a crowd (and to control portions) use small lettuce cups to each hold a dab of the grilled vegetable mixture, 1 grilled shrimp, and a dollop-ette of horseradish crème fraîche. Arrange on a large serving platter.

Grilled Lobster Parcels

The members of our cookbook club are all fans of cookbook author Anne Willan, so we visited her cooking school, La Varenne, at the Château du Feÿ in the Burgundy countryside of France for a week. When we revisited Willan's works at a recent gathering, member Kathy Smith prepared Willan's Lobster in a Parcel (*From My Château Kitchen*, Clarkson Potter, 2000). Our grilled homage follows. Ooh-la-la!

Makes 12 parcels

- **Meat from 2 grilled lobster tails (see page 152)**
- **2 tablespoons unsalted butter**
- **3 tablespoons brandy**
- **2 shallots, finely chopped**
- **2 cloves garlic, minced**
- **1 medium-size carrot, finely chopped**
- **1 cup white wine, preferably Chardonnay**
- **3 tablespoons heavy cream**
- **Kosher salt and freshly ground black pepper to taste**
- **One 1-pound package phyllo pastry dough**
- **Olive oil for brushing**

1. Cut the meat of each tail into six ½-inch pieces and set aside.

2. In a large sauté pan, melt the butter. Add the brandy, light a long match, and carefully ignite the brandy. Let it burn for about 1 minute, being careful to stand back, and removing the pan from the heat to control the flame if it gets too high. Add the shallots, garlic, and carrot and cook for 5 to 6 minutes, until tender. Add the white wine, bring to a boil, and reduce by half. Add the cream and turn off the heat. Season with salt and pepper.

3. Place a layer of phyllo sheets on a clean counter and trim to make 6-inch squares. Cover the sheets with a damp towel until ready to use. Lightly brush a baking sheet with olive oil. Lay one single square of phyllo on the baking sheet and brush lightly with oil. Repeat with 2 more phyllo layers, brushing each with olive oil and setting on top of each other. Place 1 slice of lobster meat in the center of the square. Spoon about 2 teaspoons of the shallot mixture on the lobster. Fold one side of the phyllo over the lobster. Fold the sides of the phyllo inward and cover with the fourth side of the phyllo like an envelope, to form a small rectangular parcel. Repeat with the rest of the phyllo and the lobster and shallot mixtures. Set the parcels on the baking sheet and, using a sharp knife, cut a small air hole

into the top of each parcel. (At this point, you may cover and refrigerate the parcels for several hours.)

4. When ready to bake, preheat the oven to 375°F. Bake the parcels for 20 to 25 minutes, until light golden brown and crispy. Serve warm.

Deck It Out

Throw a French cocktail party, starting the evening with cocktails made from Lillet (visit www.lillet.fr for ideas). Then serve the Grilled Lobster Parcels with glasses of Chardonnay or Champagne. Accompany with foie gras, country pâté, and Smoke-Roasted Fingerlings with Crème Fraîche and Caviar (page 30).

Change It Up

Substitute scallops, shrimp, monkfish, halibut, salmon, or your favorite fish for the lobster.

Raise a Glass

Serve with the same Chardonnay you use in the cooking.

Razzle-Dazzle: Fresh Flowers

Go black tie with fresh flowers, whether you purchase them from a florist or the farmers' market, or they come from your own backyard. The theme of the party helps to dictate the kind of flowers. For an elegant event, monochromatic sprays of flowers add a single main color, and mixed floral bouquets in the same color are dramatic and interesting.

Entrées to Get the Bash in Gear

Long ago, we realized that oven cooking just didn't give our favorite celebration foods the same big flavor that the grill or smoker does. (If we liked indoor cooking and roasting, maybe we'd be the Oven Queens? Not.) In addition to freeing up oven space for side dishes or desserts, using your grill or smoker to cook the entrée is guaranteed to get you more help with the food. There's something about being the tender of the flame that is a lot more appealing than being the peeler of the potatoes.

For any occasion, big or small, we all want food with a "wow" factor. Happily for all of us, the easiest dishes to prepare also look the most festive: regal smoke-kissed prime rib (you'll never do prime rib indoors again, we promise); Latin-style pork roast with garlic-lime barbecue sauce; rosy double-smoked spiral-sliced ham; bronzed turkey, moist with wine-herb butter sauce; golden, juicy rotisseried chicken; a bountiful herb-grilled seafood platter; pink salmon with a bright green aioli; and so many more. Taken right off the grill or smoker, all of these entrées look fabulous served on big platters with little more than a few branches of fresh herbs and seasonal fruits nestled around them. That's what we love about serving food rustic style.

So set your table(s) ahead of time, pour yourself a glass of wine, and get yourself in the barbecue-bash state of mind. Life is a feast, so eat it up!

Smoked Spanish Paprika Sirloin Steak with Rustic Olive Salsa

The BBQ Queens find ideas for new recipes everywhere. Karen's visit to the hair salon yielded this delicious recipe from her stylist Andrea Benjamina and friend Judi Moritz. Andrea raved about the grilled pork chops Judi had recently prepared. Judi applies a heavy dose of regular paprika and a sprinkle of Knorr's Aromat Seasoning to the chops and places them in a zipper-top plastic bag. She mushes it all together with 2 or 3 tablespoons of olive oil and lets it marinate in the refrigerator for several hours. Then she removes the chops from the plastic bag and grills them. They get a nice crust and are absolutely delicious. So a tweak here and a tweak there, and we change the recipe to a Spanish-style steak. Instead of regular paprika, we choose smoked Spanish paprika. There is no need for salt, since the lovely oak smoke of the paprika is strong enough to do the flavor job on its own.

Makes 4 to 6 servings

Rustic Olive Salsa:
- **2 tablespoons honey**
- **⅓ cup sherry vinegar**
- **½ cup olive oil**
- **1 red onion, cut in half and sliced into half-moons**
- **2 cloves garlic, minced**
- **1½ cups picholine or other cured green olives**
- **1 roasted red pepper, cut into chunks (peppers from a jar are fine)**
- **2 oranges, peeled, pith removed, and cut into segments**
- **½ cup coarsely chopped fresh Italian parsley**

- **One 1½ -pound boneless sirloin steak, 1½ inches thick**
- **2 to 3 tablespoons olive oil**
- **2 to 3 tablespoons smoked Spanish paprika**

1. To make the rustic olive salsa, whisk together the honey and vinegar in a small bowl. Continue whisking and slowly add the olive oil in a steady stream, until emulsified. Place the onion, garlic, olives, red pepper, orange segments, and parsley in a larger bowl. Pour the dressing over all and toss to blend. (The salsa will keep for up to 1 day in the refrigerator.)

2. Place the steak in a glass casserole dish. Drizzle with the olive oil and sprinkle with the paprika. Let stand at room temperature for 1 hour.

3. Meanwhile, prepare a hot fire in your grill. Grill the steak for 6 to 7 minutes on each side for medium-rare. Place the steak on a cutting board and let rest for about 10 minutes; cut against the grain into ¼-inch-thick slices. Transfer to a platter and pass the salsa on the side.

Change It Up · · · · · · · · · · · · · · · · · · ·

The Rustic Olive Salsa can change face if you finely chop the onion, garlic, olives, and orange. Its consistency then becomes more like a relish.

Raise a Glass · · · · · · · · · · · · · · · · · · ·

As the saying goes, when in Spain, do as the Spanish do. Serve a good Rioja or a refreshing red sangria (see page 35) with this steak.

Carpetbagger Steak with Four Seasons Stuffings

We fancy up flank steak by stuffing it. Think about colorful seasonal vegetables and change the "stuffing" as you like. Our inspiration came from the pretty pinwheel stuffed flank steaks available ready made at upscale independent grocery stores or chains like Whole Foods Market. However, the cheese can melt like crazy on the grill and make a mess. Tsk, tsk. Our version is mess proof. We place the ingredients on one side of the steak and fold it over rather than roll it. Flank steak is the uptown cut, while round steak is the downtown version. (We like them both!) The secret to these tough but flavorful steaks is tenderizing them twice. Have the butcher run the meat through the tenderizer or cuber once, then turn the steak by 90 degrees and run it through again. This makes it almost fork-tender.

Makes about 4 servings

- **One 1½-pound flank steak or round steak, ¼ inch thick**

Spring Asparagus Stuffing:
- **4 ounces fontina cheese, thinly sliced**
- **12 spears thin asparagus, blanched**

1. Prepare a hot fire in your grill.
2. Lay out the flattened, tenderized steak on a doubled baking sheet. Arrange a layer of cheese, then the layer of vegetables or fruit, on half of the steak. Fold the other half over the filling and secure the edge with several toothpicks.
3. Carefully place the steak over the hot fire and grill for about 4 minutes per side, turning once, for medium-rare. Set the grilled steak on the

Summer Pepper Stuffing:
- **4 ounces soft goat cheese or herbed cream cheese**
- **1 or 2 fire-roasted red bell peppers or piquillo peppers**

Autumn Dried Fruit Stuffing:
- **4 ounces feta cheese, crumbled**
- **1 cup chopped dried fruit, such as apricots and raisins**

Winter Spinach Stuffing:
- **4 or 5 slices provolone cheese**
- **2 to 3 ounces baby spinach leaves**

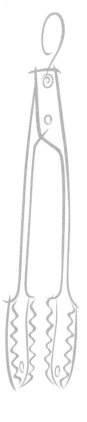

clean baking sheet and let rest for 7 to 10 minutes. Remove toothpicks, slice, and serve hot.

Deck It Out

Make a fancy party around this dish. Begin with cocktails and Wood-Roasted Oysters on a Bed of Rock Salt with Two Sauces (page 76). Blistered Baby Pattypans and Red Onion (page 187) can begin to grill a bit before the stuffed steak goes on the grill. Rustic bread with a flavored butter like Silky Crab Butter (page 94) or Béarnaise Butter (page 152) finishes the side dishes. And make-ahead Almond Bundt Pound Cake (page 224) can be pulled out of the freezer and served with berries and cream.

Change It Up

Think ethnic stuffing: sliced Roma tomatoes with fresh basil leaves and Monterey Jack cheese; cilantro and grated *queso fresco*; Mediterranean cured olives with arugula and Pecorino Romano; or sliced Hass avocado, bacon, and cheddar cheese.

Raise a Glass

Serve any red wine from a Beaujolais to a Merlot to even a Cabernet with this seasonal steak recipe.

Wine and Barbecue

"Drink what you like!" we proclaim. It's the simplest and easiest instruction we can offer you. That being said, here's some helpful advice on general wine and barbecue pairings. To start with, buy your wine from a reputable store with good printed descriptions accompanying the wines. Many stores display the rankings and descriptions alongside each wine. Excellent, knowledgeable clerks can make all the difference in helping you select good wines in your budget range, too.

A couple of our favorite books on wine are *The Sommelier's Guide to Wine* by Brian H. Smith (Black Dog & Leventhal, 2003) and *The Wine Lover's Companion* by Ron Herbst and the late Sharon Tyler Herbst (Barron's, 1995).

We all know that, traditionally, white wine goes with fish and white meats like poultry and pork, and red wine goes with red meat. This rule is becoming more flexible, particularly when it comes to pairing lighter-style red wines with fish and white meats. Also, you probably know that you want to pair the same level of heaviness or heartiness of wine with food, like a heavy Cabernet with a big, rich, full-flavored steak. But contrasting wine and food can also make a great match. Food-wine opposites like salty or smoky ham, turkey, smoked salmon, or blue cheese and a fruity Beaujolais or Pinot Noir are wonderfully complementary.

Brian H. Smith goes a step further and says to choose your wine by echoing the flavors of the fruits and vegetables that are on the plate. For instance, if you are serving grilled chicken with a citrus-herb butter and asparagus, a grassy Sauvignon Blanc might be an excellent choice. Smoked turkey with a cherry conserve might be delightful with a fruity Merlot to echo the cherry. So it is not just the entrée to consider in choosing the wine, but also what the fruit and vegetable accompaniments or sauces are going to be. This might sound confusing, but it actually makes for a broader choice of wines that might go well with your party spread.

Here are some general guidelines for pairing wines with grilled and smoked foods.

Dry, Sparkling White and Rosé Wines

Dry effervescent wines are delicate and light. They are a festive way to start a party, and the tickle to the nose will make your guests smile. Champagne from France, cava from Spain, Prosecco from Italy, and domestic or imported sparkling wine made in the method of Champagne all fit into this category. Pair these wines with fish, shellfish, white meat, berries, fruits, vegetables, and cheeses.

Dry, Light White Wines

These are the lighter white wines that are dry, crisp, and/or tart with varying degrees of fruitiness or grassiness. Choose from Riesling, Pinot Grigio, Chenin Blanc/Vouvray, Orvieto, Sauvignon Blanc/Fumé Blanc/Pouilly-Fumé, and Soave. "Fumé" means smoked, and these wines are often wood-aged and therefore perfect to serve with lightly smoked fare. Pair them with grilled or lightly smoked foods including white, green, and yellow vegetables; citrus, apple, and pears; chicken, turkey, pheasant, and quail; pork and ham; fish and shellfish; and cheeses.

Dry, Medium- to Full-Bodied White Wines

Chardonnay/Pouilly-Fuissé/Chablis, Gewürztraminer, Marsanne, Pinot Blanc, Pinot Gris, Sémillon, Vernaccia, and Viognier are all fuller-bodied white wines. They range from wines aged in wood barrels with resulting buttery, nutty, creamy, and smoky qualities to the flinty and mineral-flavored Chablis. Floral and fruity hints in these wines might include apricot, peach, pear, apple, lemon, melon, or pineapple. Pair them with grilled or smoked fish and shellfish; chicken and turkey; pork; veal; vegetables like sweet potatoes and squash; and most any spicy food.

Dry, Light Red Wines

Gamay, Beaujolais, Pinot Noir, Cabernet Sauvignon Rosé, and Grenache are all light and fruity with red berry flavor. The Pinot Noir also has woodsy and earthy components. Pair with red-colored fruits like plums and berries; red-colored vegetables like tomatoes, peppers, and beets; grilled meats like pork, ham, lamb chops, and hamburgers; fish and shellfish; chicken and turkey.

Dry, Medium- to Full-Bodied Red Wines

Cabernet Franc, Grenache, Merlot, Sangiovese, Tempranillo, and Zinfandel are all the prize-winning middleweights in this category. Tones of cherry, plum, and red berry predominate here, with the Sangiovese having sour cherry notes and the Zinfandel ranging into dark berry flavors. Pair with grilled or smoked meats and stronger-flavored fish like lamb, beef steaks, barbecued pork ribs, duck, veal, venison, tuna, turkey, and sausage; medium- to full-flavored cheeses; pizza; and spicy foods.

Dry, Full-Bodied Red Wines

Brunello, Barolo, Cabernet Sauvignon, and Shiraz are some of the big, full red wines. Their flavors include dark ripe fruits, dark berries, currants, and lots of tannin. Barolo is at the top of the price range. Pair with grilled or smoked dark meats like beef steaks or tenderloins and beef ribs, rack or leg of lamb, venison, duck, goose, and strong cheeses.

Beer and Barbecue

Matching the tastes of different types of beers to grilled and smoked food is an ongoing research project for us. So many beers, so little time! You can hardly have a barbecue without offering your guests a choice of beers, but, you may well ask, "Which beers?" In general, we prefer lighter-tasting beer with appetizers, medium-bodied beer with entrées, and a touch of porter or stout to enhance chocolate in a dessert.

The easiest way to pair beer and grilled and barbecued foods is to think of lager as white wine and ale as red wine. So, for example, contrast a creamy smoked or grilled corn chowder with a light and crispy lager, and complement a smoky beef brisket or coffee-rubbed steak with a full-bodied ale.

Just as wine-and-food-pairing dinners are ever popular, there's a whole new surge of beer aficionados, brewers, and restaurateurs who are promoting dinners in which different beers are paired with different courses. To give you an edge at home, *The Premium Beer Drinker's Guide* by Stephen Beaumont (Firefly Books, 2000) offers great pairing tips. If "easy" is your byword, then we say, "KISS (keep it simple, silly)! Drink what you like and pair what tastes good to you."

Here is our short version of Beer 101.

Lager

This type of beer is made with bottom-fermenting yeast. Lagers are characteristically smooth, elegant, crisp, and clean tasting. Popular examples include American light lager, Vienna-style lagers, and pilsners. Other lagers include bock, steam beer, dopplebock, dunkel, Marzen/Oktoberfest, and Dortmunder, with many of these lagers originating in Germany.

Lager is great with simple, casual grilled foods like hamburgers, chicken, pork tenderloin, or vegetables. Vienna-style lagers like Dos Equis match up well with spicy Mexican food. Oktoberfest (also known as Marzen) and other Vienna-style lagers are great with Thanksgiving smoked turkey and German-style grilled sausages. We love American lager (Budweiser, Miller, or Coors) on hot summer days, poured over ice and served with a big squeeze of lime, sort of like a beer spritzer. Serve this with a delicious grilled appetizer, and it won't fill you up. Pilsners are sometimes a bit sweeter than a regular lager, but still dry and crisp. Serve this refreshing beer (Pilsner Urquell is one of our favorites) with grilled fish, shellfish, or vegetables. We like our lagers well chilled— just like a white wine.

Ale

Ale is made with a top-fermenting yeast. Ales are generally hearty, robust, rich, and fruity. Bitters, a mainstay of English pubs, are golden brown draft ales with hops, on the dry side, and with a lower but delightful carbonation that's bubbly on the nose. Pale ales, wheat beers, and hearty sweet porters are in this category, too. Dark and rich, heavier stouts are made from pale malt and roasted unmalted barley, and have a caramel tone to them.

Golden or blond ales like wheat beers can be fruity and nutty and are great with appetizers and spicy hot foods. They're simply good drinking beers and oftentimes are served with a wedge of lemon, which begs for any kind of grilled or smoked fish as a complement. We're partial to wheat beer from the Boulevard Brewery in our hometown of Kansas City.

Pale ales can have a bigger flavor than lagers, and they match up with grilled lamb, barbecued ribs, smoked prime rib, and smoked poultry. There are more delicate and light aromatic varieties like Belgian blond ales to pour with fish and shellfish. Favorites of ours include brews from the New Belgium Brewing Company, in Fort Collins, Colorado.

Amber ale is tops with barbecued anything. Bitter and India pale ale have lots of hops and can cut right through grease, vinegar, and smoke. So pair them with vinegar-mopped pork butt or ribs, or smoked or grilled fish salads drizzled with vinaigrette.

Brown ale is hopped up, too, so pair it with smoked fish and game, hamburgers, sausages, portobello mushrooms, and our Smoked Rib Roast with Horseradish Crème Fraîche (page 98) or Grilled Venison Chops with Brandy Cream Sauce (page 108).

The hearty, sweet flavor of porter matches well with the more complex flavors of barbecue and grilled or smoked sausages. Try this with Creole Coffee–Rubbed Filet Mignon with Silky Crab Butter (page 94). Burgers with sharp cheddar or blue cheese on top match up nicely, too. We also like to sip porter with chocolate desserts.

Stout's dark, slightly bitter, roasty flavor gives smoked pork, brisket, and prime rib a run for their money. Stout also pairs well with chocolate (try our Grilled Chocolate Crostini on page 216), caramel, and nutty desserts.

Under the Sweet-Scented Pines: A Spanish Tapas Party

Love to take a trip to Spain but just don't have the time or the euros? Then jump on this menu and you'll feel like you're there. Tapas, or "little bites," can be a wonderful way to host a casual cocktail or appetizer party, where your guests can graze from one indoor or outdoor room to the next.

When Karen and husband Dick visited her sister Linda Yeates in Rota, Spain, the food and drink, from the sherry to the very strong coffee, were all memorable. But the most fun was when Linda's neighbors, Roxi McCarthy and Ralph Steinheimer, led an evening of bar hopping. Ralph is a tapas connoisseur and knew which bars had the best offerings. Bar Playa was a cafe specializing in all things seafood. Another bar was known for its Iberico ham, which you soon figured out from the interior décor of dozens of black-hoofed legs of cured ham hanging from the rafters. The *filete* guy at Bar El Rinconcillo had been perfecting his pork fillet for the past 40 years. It was just a thin slice of pork from the tenderloin, marinated in garlic and most likely olive oil and Manzanilla sherry, grilled and served on a lightly toasted slice of baguette.

Setting the Scene

A tapas party means lots of little tables where diners can sit and share their goodies. So either set up a buffet where guests can help themselves, with lots of little tables nearby, or arrange the tapas offerings at different stations around the house, the yard, or your patio. Use lots of wood, rustic ironwork lanterns or candleholders, and terra cotta to set your tables. Set pots of vivid geraniums or bowls of citrus fruit on the tables for color. Choose plain white plates or go for sunny, rich colors like saffron, burnt orange, deep green, or seaside blue and white.

Making Beautiful Music

Any of the many Spanish guitar CD anthologies available would be perfect for this evening, or try anything from the members of the Buena Vista Social Club.

Perfect Partners

Serve Red Wine Sangria and/or White Wine Sangria (page 35), along with chilled dry fino sherry and pilsner or lager beer (Spanish, if you can find it).

Choose from Among These Dishes

Platter of grilled vegetables dressed with Mortar and Pestle Vinaigrette (page 170)

Pancetta-Wrapped Radicchio, Fennel, and Potato Bundles (page 64)

Potato Salad with Aioli (page 195)

Fideo (page 200)

Piquillo Pepper–Stuffed Chicken with Salsa Verde (page 134)

Cilantro Slaw (page 167)

Rioja-Style Grilled Pork Tenderloin Tapas (page 61)

Smoked Spanish Paprika Sirloin Steak with Rustic Olive Salsa (page 85)

Herb-Grilled Seafood Platter (page 150)

Wood-Roasted Oysters on a Bed of Rock Salt with Two Sauces (page 76)

Take It Easy

How easy it is to throw a party with delicious Spanish tapas from your pantry! "Is this authentic?" you ask. Yes, it is. Spanish cafés serve many delectable items from jars and cans.

- Marcona almonds (fried Spanish almonds)
- Assorted olives (anchovy-, cheese-, and almond-stuffed olives, and other cured olives)
- Olive paste spread on toasted or grilled bread
- Pickled or brined anchovies, sardines, cockles, clams, and mussels
- Tuna in olive oil
- Quince paste served with bread or hard cheeses
- Roasted red bell or piquillo peppers
- Marinated garlic cloves, cocktail onions, and peppadews
- Spanish cheeses, such as manchego, mahon, and Cabrales
- Serrano ham, thinly sliced
- Caperberries in brine
- Chickpeas or red kidney beans tossed with olive oil and red wine vinegar
- Marinated octopus or squid

Creole Coffee-Rubbed Filet Mignon with Silky Crab Butter

We love giving classic recipes a newer, fresher interpretation—on the grill, of course! The steakhouse "Oscar" treatment of béarnaise sauce, crabmeat, and steamed asparagus (itself a version of veal Oscar, named after a Swedish king) is our starting point here. What if Oscar took a stroll through the French Quarter of old New Orleans? With that inspiration, we came up with a Creole Coffee Rub for some va-va-voom. Then we finish the steaks with Silky Crab Butter that has béarnaise-like flavor for the aaaaaahhhhh finish. (Or be really true to the Big Easy and use cooked crawfish tails instead of crab.) What better accompaniment than grilled asparagus? Just brush thick spears with olive oil and grill alongside the steaks.

Makes 8 servings

Creole Coffee Rub:
- **2 tablespoons finely ground chicory coffee or espresso**
- **1 tablespoon Spanish paprika**
- **1 tablespoon dark brown sugar**
- **1 teaspoon dry mustard**
- **2 teaspoons fine kosher or sea salt**
- **1 teaspoon freshly ground black pepper**
- **1 teaspoon freshly ground white pepper**
- **1 teaspoon dried tarragon**
- **1 teaspoon dried oregano**
- **2 teaspoons cayenne pepper**

Silky Crab Butter:
- **⅓ cup dry white wine**
- **¼ cup tarragon vinegar**
- **1 tablespoon finely chopped green onion**

1. Prepare a hot fire in your grill.
2. To make the creole coffee rub, combine all the ingredients in a small bowl. Set aside.
3. To make the silky crab butter, bring the wine, tarragon vinegar, green onion, garlic, tarragon, and salt to a boil in a small saucepan over high heat. Continue to boil until the mixture has reduced to 2 tablespoons, about 8 minutes. Reduce the heat to low and whisk in the butter, a cube at a time. When the butter has almost melted, whisk in the mustard, cayenne pepper, and crabmeat. Set aside. (If you wish, make the butter a day ahead of time. Let the butter cool, then form into a log, wrap in plastic wrap, and chill for up to 3 days. To serve, cut the log into 8 rounds and place a round of butter on each hot steak.)
4. Brush the steaks lightly with olive oil and season on both sides with the rub. Grill the steaks, covered, for 3 minutes on each side for medium-rare. Serve each steak with a dollop of the crab butter.

- 1 clove garlic, minced
- 1 teaspoon dried tarragon, plus more to taste
- ¼ teaspoon fine kosher or sea salt
- 11 tablespoons unsalted butter, cut into cubes
- 1 teaspoon Creole or other stone-ground mustard
- ¼ teaspoon cayenne pepper
- 8 ounces backfin lump crabmeat, picked over, or cooked crawfish tails

- Four 8-ounce boneless filet mignon, rib-eye, sirloin, or strip steaks, cut ¾ to 1 inch thick
- Olive oil for brushing

Change It Up

Any good cut of steak would be great with this treatment. The Silky Crab Butter would also be delicious on grilled fish or served on grilled bread as a canapé.

Raise a Glass

With this steak, a deep, rich red Brunello would be fabulous.

Razzle-Dazzle: Salt Rubs

Here are four razzle-dazzle dry rubs that are as easy as 1-2 or 1-2-3.
- *Luscious Lamb Rub:* Add 1 tablespoon dried lavender or rosemary to ½ cup coarse kosher or sea salt.
- *Perfect Pork Rub:* Add 1 tablespoon dried grated orange zest and 1 tablespoon cracked black pepper to ½ cup coarse kosher or sea salt.
- *Chic Chicken Rub:* Add 1 tablespoon granulated garlic and 1 tablespoon lemon pepper to ½ cup coarse kosher or sea salt.
- *Super Steak Rub:* Add 2 tablespoons dark brown sugar and 2 tablespoons cracked black pepper to ½ cup coarse kosher or sea salt.

Grilled Beef Tenderloin

...nd when you want to enjoy life, make this recipe, which is as easy ...o relax! A few days ahead of time (or that day, if you wish), make ...have to do is to grill the tenderloin, mix up the sauce in a bowl, set ...bes, and warm some French bread. If your guests don't gobble up everything in sight that evening, you'll have the makings for wonderful sandwiches the next day.

Makes 8 servings

- **One 6- to 8-pound beef tenderloin**
- **Olive oil for brushing**
- **1 recipe Creole Coffee Rub (page 94), 2 teaspoons reserved for Creole Sauce**

Creole Sauce:
- **1 cup mayonnaise**
- **2 tablespoons prepared horseradish**
- **2 tablespoons Creole or whole-grain mustard**
- **2 teaspoons freshly squeezed lemon juice, or to taste**
- **2 teaspoons Creole Coffee Rub (page 94)**
- **Fine kosher or sea salt and freshly ground black pepper to taste**

- **4 cups baby arugula**
- **8 ounces Parmigiano-Reggiano cheese, shaved with a vegetable peeler**

1. Prepare a hot fire in your grill, using mesquite, if you like.
2. If the tenderloin has a tapered tail, fold it under the meat, then tie the tenderloin at intervals with kitchen twine. Brush the meat with olive oil, then season with the creole coffee rub.
3. To make the Creole sauce, whisk all the ingredients together in a small bowl. Set aside at room temperature. Arrange the baby arugula on a serving platter and set aside.
4. Grill the tenderloin, covered, turning a quarter turn every 5 minutes, for 10 minutes. Turn again, brush again with olive oil, and grill for 10 to 12 more minutes, or until an instant-read thermometer registers 130°F for rare, or when the meat is firm yet a little springy to the touch. Grill longer if desired.
5. Let the tenderloin rest for 5 minutes, then remove the string, slice, and arrange on the platter of arugula. Sprinkle the Parmigiano-Reggiano shavings over the meat and pass the sauce at the table.

Deck It Out

To serve this as part of a holiday dinner, accompany it with Wood-Grilled Country Bread with Four Seasons Toppings (page 45), Grilled Winter Greens with Warm Cranberry-Port Vinaigrette (page 178), and a side of All-Seasons Potato Casserole for a Crowd (page 196).

Raise a Glass

Of course you can serve a big-flavored red wine with this, but we'd suggest beginning the evening with a batch of our Frozen Cosmopolitans (page 49).

Razzle-Dazzle: Edible Flowers

What to do? Should we use edible flowers for bouquets or for garnish? Let's do both! Karen remembers the first time she shopped at an organic farmers' market in the 1980s; it was on the island of Kauai. The fresh mixed salad greens included a colorful array of edible organic nasturtiums, violas, and pansies. It was so memorable that she now plants nasturtiums every year for their bright orange, yellow, and golden colors and for their peppery flavor. Sometimes it's a bumper crop, and sometimes not. But other edible blossoms to adorn your plates or drinks include: chive and other herbs, almond, apple, lavender, orange, plum, peach, squash, daisies, geraniums, jasmine, lilacs, violets, and marigolds.

Smoked Rib Roast with Horseradish Crème Fraîche

A standing rib roast often is the main culinary attraction for a special occasion or holiday dinner, and generally it goes in the oven to roast. But we're here to tell you that there's a better way to go with this expensive holiday classic. Smoke it! A smoked rib roast has all that good charriness on the exterior, but the somewhat bland meat of your mother's standard oven-roasted rib roast is revved up with a new smoky flavor. Even traditionalists who don't like you messing with their holiday dishes will love beef roast this way. Yum!

Makes 8 servings

Suggested wood: Mesquite or hickory

- **One 4- to 6-pound standing rib roast, at room temperature**
- **¼ cup olive oil**
- **2 tablespoons granulated garlic**
- **½ cup cracked black peppercorns**
- **1 recipe Horseradish Crème Fraîche (page 78)**

1. Prepare a medium fire in your smoker.
2. Trim some of the white fat from the roast and discard. Rub the roast with olive oil and press the granulated garlic and cracked pepper into the surface of the meat. Insert a meat thermometer in the center of the roast.
3. Place the roast, fat side up, on a rack in your smoker. Cover and smoke at 225° to 250°F, or until the meat thermometer registers 140°F for rare, 3 to 3½ hours.
4. Remove the roast from the smoker, remove the meat thermometer, and wrap the roast tightly in plastic wrap. Allow to rest for 15 to 20 minutes. Then unwrap, slice, and serve with the horseradish crème fraîche on the side.

Deck It Out

Present the whole roast on a big platter garnished with Stir-Grilled Crispy Shallots (page 185), little bowls of the Horseradish Crème Fraîche, and sprigs of fresh rosemary. Great side dishes include Planked Portobellos with Fresh Herb Grilling Sauce (page 179) and Smoked Gouda Grits (page 201).

Change It Up

Wood-roast your standing rib on the grill with a kiss of smoke. Prepare a dual-heat fire, with a hot fire on one side and a low fire on the other. Use 1 cup wood chips or ⅓ cup wood pellets. If using a charcoal grill, place moistened wood chips (or a foil packet of dry wood pellets with holes poked in the top) directly on the coals right before you want to grill. If using a gas grill, enclose dry wood chips or pellets in a foil packet with holes poked in the top; place the packet on the grill grate over the heat source. You're ready to grill when you see the smoke from the smoldering wood and the fire is hot. Place the roast on the lower-heat side, close the lid, and wood-roast for 2 to 2½ hours, or until the meat thermometer registers 140°F for rare. You will need to replenish the charcoal if using a charcoal grill, and you might need to turn the roast several times to keep one side (the one closer to the hot fire) from getting too browned and done.

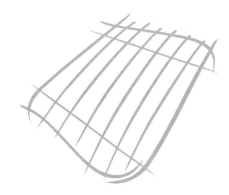

Raise a Glass

Of course, this regal dish deserves a deep, rich red wine, like an Italian Brunello or a Spanish Tempranillo.

Italian Grilled Veal Chops with Green Olive, Caper, and Fresh Tomato Sauce

We like a dual-heat fire for thick chops like these, meaning a hot fire on one side of the grill and a medium or medium-low fire on the other side. You sear the chops on the hot side, then finish grilling them on the other, trattoria style. The sauce is very easy and takes just a few minutes, so if you prefer, you can wait until the chops are resting before making it.

Makes 4 servings

Green Olive, Caper, and Fresh Tomato Sauce:

- ¼ cup olive oil
- 2 cloves garlic, minced
- 1 cup pitted and halved Italian or French green olives
- ¼ cup drained capers
- 1 large tomato, peeled, seeded, and chopped
- ¼ teaspoon red pepper flakes

- **Four 12-ounce veal rib chops, about 1½ inches thick**
- **Olive oil for brushing**
- **Kosher or sea salt and freshly ground black pepper to taste**
- **¼ cup chopped fresh Italian parsley**

1. Prepare a dual-heat fire in your grill, with a hot fire on one side and a medium fire on the other. Oil the grill rack.
2. To make the sauce, heat the olive oil in a large skillet and sauté the garlic until golden, about 2 minutes. Stir in the green olives, capers, tomato, and red pepper flakes and cook, stirring, for 2 minutes. Keep warm until ready to serve.
3. Brush the chops with olive oil and season on both sides with salt and pepper.
4. Grill the chops over the hot fire for 2 to 3 minutes on each side, or until you have good grill marks. Transfer to the medium side and grill for 8 to 10 minutes more, turning once, or until an instant-read thermometer registers an internal temperature of 145°F for medium-rare; if you like your veal more done, aim for 155° to 165°F. Remove the chops from the grill and let rest for 5 minutes. Serve each chop with a spoonful of sauce and a sprinkling of Italian parsley on top.

Take It Easy

Do BBQ Queens ever buy take-out from the store? You betcha! Sometimes you just need to give yourself a break. So to go with this lovely veal chop, offer a duo of Italian cheeses with fresh fruit for an appetizer. Twice-baked potatoes purchased from the store are a great side. Cream puffs from the bakery or freezer section served with Dark Chocolate Ganache (page 237—you do keep this on hand, don't you?) are a perfect ending.

Raise a Glass

Serve Prosecco to start with or throughout the whole meal. For those who prefer a still wine, offer a glass of Sangiovese.

Razzle-Dazzle: Haute Smoke

Smokiness goes to the next level with haute additions to the fire. Instead of wood, add fresh stalks of basil to the fire for basil smoke, rosemary sprigs for rosemary smoke, fennel stalks for fennel smoke, etc. Soak 1 cup dried herbes de Provence in water prior to putting it on the fire for herbes de Provence smoke. Citrus smoke is easy: just throw fresh orange, lime, lemon, or grapefruit peel on the fire. You can try this method with corncobs, corn husks, fresh seaweed, nut shells, and so on, and so on.

Veal T-Bones with Lemon-Butter Sauce and Gremolata Garnish

Company's coming, so let's do something easy but extraordinary. A veal T-bone steak is just the ticket. It's a bit pricey, but your guests will feel so pampered when they take their first bite, especially with a spoonful of the luscious lemon-butter sauce and a sprinkling of the aromatic gremolata that takes it over the top. The orzo pasta makes a pretty bed to set the meat atop. Now all you need is a salad like our Grilled Winter Greens with Warm Cranberry-Port Vinaigrette (page 178).

Makes 4 servings

- **4 veal T-bone steaks, about ¾ inch thick**
- **Olive oil for brushing**
- **Garlic salt and freshly ground black pepper to taste**

Gremolata:
- **Zest of 1 lemon**
- **½ cup chopped fresh Italian parsley**
- **2 cloves garlic**
- **¼ cup grated Pecorino Romano cheese (optional)**

Lemon-Butter Sauce:
- **⅔ cup chicken stock**
- **Juice of 2 large lemons**
- **5 tablespoons unsalted butter**

- **3 cups cooked orzo or small shell pasta**

1. Let the veal steaks come to room temperature. Brush the veal with olive oil and season with garlic salt and pepper. Set on a doubled baking sheet.
2. Prepare a hot fire in your grill.
3. To make the gremolata, finely chop the lemon zest, parsley, and garlic. Place in a bowl, add the Pecorino Romano cheese, if using, and set aside.
4. To make the lemon-butter sauce, bring the chicken stock to a boil in a small saucepan and cook for 3 to 4 minutes to slightly reduce. Add the lemon juice and cook for 1 to 2 minutes. Slowly whisk in the butter, 1 tablespoon at a time, until smooth and slightly thick, 3 to 4 minutes. Keep warm.
5. Grill the steaks over the hot fire for about 5 minutes per side, until they are seared on the surface and just cooked through to 130° to 135°F for medium-rare. Set the steaks aside, keeping them warm.
6. Rewarm the pasta if necessary, and divide it among four dinner plates. Place a steak over the pasta on each plate. Spoon the lemon-butter sauce over the steaks and sprinkle all with the gremolata. Serve immediately.

Deck It Out

Think of this dinner as one that would be perfect under the stars (see page 182). Set a romantic table with candles placed atop mirrors. Choose fresh flowers in your favorite color—whatever is in season. You'll spend extra time on dressing up the table, so choose an appetizer that can be made ahead, like the divine Grilled Lobster Parcels (page 80). For dessert, serve fresh fruit and cheese or one of our fruits in liqueur (see pages 209 to 213).

Change It Up

Any great steak could substitute for the veal steak in this dish. Even a fish steak would be exquisite.

Raise a Glass

Drink choices might include Pinot Grigio or Vernaccia for white wine, Chianti or Rossodi Montalcino for red wine, or an Italian lager-style beer like Moretti or Peroni.

Razzle-Dazzle:
Herb Basting Brushes

Basting brushes made out of fresh herb bouquets are one of the tricks of the barbecue trade. For example, tie together several stalks of fresh rosemary as a fragrant baster that's great for pork, poultry, and lamb. Combine a mixed bouquet of sprigs of dill, lemon balm, and thyme for fish and seafood.

Persian Grilled Leg of Lamb with Tabbouleh Stuffing and Pomegranate Sauce

Beautiful to the eye and heaven to the taste buds, this rolled leg of lamb grills to a turn in minutes. If you can, make the stuffing a day ahead of time, to let the fresh flavors blend. (Of course, the stuffing can also stand alone as the Middle Eastern salad it is!) Begin with the 6- to 7-pound leg of lamb, boned, trimmed, and butterflied (have your butcher do all of that). If you like, use the side of a sturdy saucer or a meat mallet and pound the meat to an even thickness and lay it flat.

Makes 6 to 8 servings

Tabbouleh Stuffing:
- **2 cups water**
- **1 cup bulgur or cracked wheat**
- **⅔ cup finely chopped red onion**
- **2 medium-size tomatoes, peeled, seeded, and diced**
- **½ cup fresh mint leaves, finely chopped**
- **1 teaspoon grated lemon zest**
- **Juice of 1 lemon**
- **¼ cup extra-virgin olive oil**
- **Kosher or sea salt and freshly ground black pepper to taste**

Pomegranate Sauce:
- **2 tablespoons pomegranate syrup or pomegranate molasses (if you can't find either, boil ½ cup pomegranate juice until only 2 tablespoons are left)**
- **7 tablespoons extra-virgin olive oil**
- **2 teaspoons honey**

1. To make the stuffing, bring the water and bulgur to a boil in a saucepan over medium-high heat. Reduce the heat, cover, and simmer until the bulgur is tender, about 15 minutes. Remove from the heat and let it sit, covered, for another 15 minutes. Do not open the lid. Fluff the bulgur with a fork and stir in the remaining ingredients. (At this point, you may cover and refrigerate the stuffing for up to 2 days. Let it come to room temperature before serving as a side dish or using as a stuffing.)
2. Prepare a medium-hot fire in your grill.
3. To make the pomegranate sauce, whisk together the pomegranate syrup, olive oil, and honey. Add the lemon juice, salt, and pepper. Set aside.
4. To fill the lamb, place the boned, butterflied lamb skin side down on a flat surface. Brush with olive oil and season with salt and lemon pepper. Spread the stuffing over the meat. Roll up the meat lengthwise, jellyroll style, and tie with kitchen twine at 1-inch intervals.
5. Grill the lamb for about 10 minutes on each side, turning the roll a quarter turn each time,

- **Fresh squeezed lemon juice to taste**
- **Kosher or sea salt and freshly ground black pepper to taste**

- **One 6- to 7-pound leg of lamb, boned, trimmed, and butterflied**
- **Olive oil for brushing**
- **Kosher or sea salt and lemon pepper to taste**

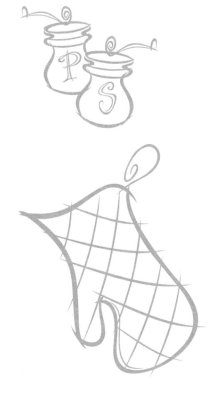

until the internal temperature reads 125° to 130°F for medium-rare to medium, about 40 minutes total. Let the lamb rest for 10 to 15 minutes before slicing and serving with the pomegranate sauce drizzled over it.

Deck It Out

Slice and serve the beautiful spirals of grilled lamb—napped with its easy, vinaigrette-style pomegranate sauce—on a platter over grilled Mediterranean vegetables such as zucchini, yellow summer squash, bell peppers, and eggplant. Along with a bowl of couscous, it's a one-dish company meal the BBQ Queens way!

Take It Easy

For an even easier stuffing, use instant couscous prepared according to the package directions and mixed with the other ingredients, instead of the bulgur.

Raise a Glass

The Middle Eastern flavors of this meal beg for a Pomegranate and Bubbly (page 33) cocktail. Follow those with a delicious red wine such as Barbaresco or Barolo.

Roast-Smoked Lamb Shanks

This is one of those "I never thought of that" recipes. Most anything that is slow-cooked can also be slow-smoked. However, sometimes you want a nicely browned exterior, and that is where the roast-smoke technique comes into play. We think it's a lot easier to pop a roast in a very hot oven (450° to 500°F) to get a nice, crusty, browned exterior. This takes about 10 minutes for smaller pieces of meat like shanks and 20 minutes or so for a larger roast, but the nice part is you can decide how brown you want the roast or shank. The smoker can be set up while the shanks are roasting in the oven. The gas grill version of this is pretty easy, though not as smoky. Place a wood box filled with dry wood chips over the gas fire. Place the shanks on the indirect side of the grill and close the lid. Roast for the 10-plus minutes at 500°F. Open the lid to see if the shanks are nicely browned. Then turn down the heat to 250°F and continue to smoke. No matter what kind of grill you use, this recipe needs time for the lamb to marinate, but the actual prep and cooking is very simple.

Makes 4 servings

Suggested wood: 3 chunks or 1 cup apple or oak chips or the equivalent of vine cuttings, mint stems, or lemon balm stems

- **Four 1-pound lamb shanks**
- **4 cloves garlic, slivered**
- **Juice of 2 lemons**
- **Coarse kosher or sea salt and freshly ground black pepper to taste**
- **¼ cup chopped fresh Italian parsley**
- **1 tablespoon chopped fresh thyme**
- **1 tablespoon chopped fresh oregano**
- **¼ cup olive oil**
- **¼ cup seasoned bread crumbs**
- **2 to 3 tablespoons unsalted butter**
- **2 to 3 tablespoons dry red or white wine**

1. Trim any excess fat from the lamb shanks. Make small slits in each shank and place the garlic slivers in the slits. Set the shanks on a plate. Rub the lemon juice over all and sprinkle with salt and pepper.

2. In a shallow bowl, combine the parsley, thyme, and oregano, and roll the lamb shanks in the herbs to coat. Set in a casserole dish and let stand for about 2 hours at room temperature before roasting. (At this point, you may refrigerate the shanks for up to 24 hours. Let sit at room temperature for a couple of hours before roasting.)

3. Heat the oven (or grill) to 500°F. Lightly brush the herbs off into the pan juices, and pour off and reserve the juices. Then coat the shanks with the olive oil and dredge in the bread crumbs. Place the shanks in a roasting pan (that will also fit in the smoker or grill) and set in the hot oven (or grill). Roast for about 10 minutes or a little bit longer, until the exterior is nicely browned.

4. Prepare a 250°F fire in your smoker.

5. Place the reserved herb marinade in a small saucepan and bring to a boil for 2 minutes. Add the butter and wine and simmer over medium heat for 5 minutes. Set aside.

6. Place a sheet of heavy-duty foil lightly over the roasting pan, but do not crimp closed. Place the pan in the smoker (or on the indirect side of the grill) and slow-cook for about 1 hour. Reheat the marinade to a boil and pour over the shanks. Crimp the foil tightly to the pan and continue to cook for another 1 to 1½ hours. The shanks are done when the meat begins to fall off the bone.

7. Remove the shanks from the pan and keep warm. Skim the fat off the meat juices from the pan. Place the juices in a saucepan and heat, tasting and adjusting the seasonings if desired, and adding a bit more wine if more liquid is needed. Pour the juices over the meat and serve hot.

Deck It Out

Serve the shanks over Oven-Baked Herbed Risotto (page 204) and/or with Smoke-Roasted Root Vegetables with Garlic and Rosemary (page 198). Make a gremolata to sprinkle over the finished plate: finely chop ½ cup fresh Italian parsley leaves, 2 cloves garlic, and the zest from 1 lemon.

Change It Up

Try this recipe with veal shanks or a nice lamb or veal roast.

Raise a Glass

The smoky richness of this dish pairs well with a semi-bold Merlot to a full-bodied Cabernet.

Grilled Venison Chops with Brandy Cream Sauce

Venison—a family of game that includes elk, deer, and even caribou—is a very lean meat and is best when prepared medium-rare. Karen's husband goes elk hunting every year in the Colorado Rockies. We all feast on the elk venison, from the delicious hamburger to the divine steaks, chops, and fillets. When the elk outsmart Dick, we still fare well with tasty grain-fed deer from the Kansas corn and bean fields. You may substitute farm-raised venison, available at some independent butcher shops.

Makes 4 servings

Suggested wood: 1 cup water-soaked grapevines or oak chips

- **Four ½-inch-thick venison chops or steaks**
- **Olive oil for brushing**
- **Kosher or sea salt and freshly ground black pepper to taste**

Brandy Cream Sauce:
- **⅓ cup brandy**
- **⅓ cup heavy cream**
- **2 tablespoons Dijon mustard**

1. Prepare a hot fire in your grill and add the grapevines.
2. Coat the chops with olive oil and sprinkle with salt and pepper.
3. Whisk the sauce ingredients together. Divide the sauce into two small bowls, using one bowl for basting and setting the other bowl aside for serving. Grill the chops directly over the hot fire for about 3 minutes on each side, basting several times with the sauce. Place one venison chop on each of four plates and serve with the reserved bowl of sauce.

Deck It Out
The Grilled Winter Greens with Warm Cranberry-Port Vinaigrette (page 178) and the Stir-Grilled Crispy Shallots (page 185) make good accompaniments.

Change It Up
This recipe is great for beef steaks, too.

Raise a Glass
Accompany this full-flavored lean meat with either a Syrah or Shiraz. To finish the meal, try our brandy-laced Queen Bee (page 234).

Regal Cocktails

There are party drinks and then there are fit-for-royalty party drinks. We've gathered an eclectic collection of regal recipes that happen to go very well with barbecue. To top off many of your drinks in style, try our Razzle-Dazzle tip (page 47) on rimming glasses with edible glitter using gold and silver leaf products from Easy Leaf Products (www.easyleafproducts.com).

Jealous Queen

Someone must have gotten some fairy tale information mixed up. Does this sound like something the mean queen from *Snow White and the Seven Dwarfs* might serve, but with an orange instead of the poison apple? Anyway, we like the name, and the drink is wicked good.

Makes 4 servings

- Ice cubes
- 4 tablespoons (¼ cup) Cointreau, Grand Marnier, or other orange-flavored liqueur
- 8 tablespoons (½ cup) vodka
- 4 dashes of bitters
- 4 dashes of salt

1. Fill a cocktail shaker with ice and add the orange liqueur and vodka. Shake to blend.
2. Fill four wine glasses with ice cubes. Pour one quarter of the mixture into each glass. Add a dash of bitters and a dash of salt to each drink.

Queen Elizabeth

Be careful with this one or your crown might get cockeyed.

Makes 2 servings

- Ice cubes
- ¾ cup gin
- 2 tablespoons dry vermouth
- 2 tablespoons B&B

1. Fill a small pitcher or mixing glass with ice cubes. Add the gin, vermouth, and B&B, and stir to blend.
2. Pour into two highball glasses. Add more ice if you like.

Cinderella's Slipper

If Cinderella had drunk this libation at the ball, she would have lost both slippers. Drink it and have a ball of your own.

Makes 2 servings

- Ice cubes
- 1 cup lemon-flavored vodka
- 3 tablespoons Cointreau
- 3 tablespoons pineapple juice

1. Fill a cocktail shaker with ice cubes. Add the vodka, Cointreau, and pineapple juice and shake.
2. Strain into two large cocktail glasses and serve.

French Kiss

This has a touch of bitter in contrast to some of the sweet drinks offered here. Serve it as an apéritif for those who want something sophisticated and not too sugary. To make it a true French Kiss, pour Dubonnet, Lillet, or Noilly Prat, all from France. If you'd rather have an Italian Kiss, pour Cinzano!

Makes 4 servings

- Ice cubes
- 1⅓ cups white (dry) vermouth
- 1⅓ cups red (sweet) vermouth
- Lemon twists for garnish

Fill four large cocktail glasses with ice cubes. Pour ⅓ cup white vermouth and ⅓ cup red vermouth into each glass. Rub the rim of each glass with a lemon twist and serve.

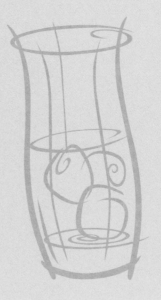

Bourbon Ricky

Any drink with the name "Ricky" brings to our minds *I Love Lucy*, with its great comic pairing of Lucille Ball and Vivian Vance. We've even changed the spelling from the more traditional "Rickey" to suit our comic purposes. This version, made with bourbon, is especially refreshing on a hot summer day.

Makes 4 servings

- Ice cubes
- **12 tablespoons (¾ cup) bourbon**
- **8 tablespoons (½ cup) freshly squeezed lime juice**
- **Chilled club soda**
- **Lime wedges for garnish**

Fill four highball glasses with ice cubes. Add 3 tablespoons bourbon and 2 tablespoons lime juice to each glass. Top with club soda. Stir gently and garnish each glass with a lime wedge.

Cuba Libre

Drinkin' rum and Coca-Cola . . . This tune just makes you want to sway and sip a refreshing grown-up cocktail. Try a cherry-flavored cola, if you like, to add a fresh twist to this classic.

Makes 4 servings

- Ice cubes
- **1 cup dark rum**
- **2 cups or more cola**
- **1 lime, cut into quarters**
- **4 sugarcane swizzle sticks, for garnish**

1. Fill four highball glasses with ice cubes. Pour ¼ cup rum into each glass. Add ½ cup (or more) cola to each glass. Squeeze a lime quarter over each drink, and then drop the lime into the glass.
2. Add a sugarcane swizzle stick and stir.

What's for Brunch?

A casual weekend brunch is a great way to entertain. Both of our families love to have brunch picnics in the spring. When Easter or Passover falls later in the spring, they are also great times to celebrate alfresco.

With a brunch, you can have a lot of freedom with the menu, as it can go more like breakfast or more like lunch. And you can be spontaneous. After all, whose social life is scheduled weeks in advance for a late Sunday morning?

Brunch also gives you permission to think not just outside the box, but outside, period. In Kansas City, any warm spell from November through April can be a great time for a brunch—no bugs, no threatening thunderstorms, no wilting heat, no high winds. One memorable day after Thanksgiving, Judith's family had brunch alfresco when the temperature was in the low 70s. It was a delightful, if unusual, way to start the holiday season.

So just look at the five-day weather forecast, call around to invite friends and family, and plan your menu around the ham, salmon, lamb, or beef suggestions below. If the weather changes, then just cook outdoors and eat inside!

Setting the Scene

Nothing says "fresh morning" like blue and white china and tablecloths paired with yellow flowers. Put pots of butter yellow daffodils, daisies, or mums in a big, rustic basket or fill tall vases with sunflowers for a buffet or serving table. Line baskets with blue and white napkins to hold breads at each seating table. Place a chafing dish on the buffet table to keep the eggs warm, or use a bowl set in a pan of hot water. Make plenty of coffee indoors and bring it outside in thermal carafes.

Making Beautiful Music

Play easy listening, upbeat classical music, or light jazz for this repast. Ella Fitzgerald, Louis Armstrong, Wynton Marsalis, or Yo-Yo Ma are good choices.

Perfect Partners

Serve both alcoholic and nonalcoholic sparklers: Mimosas (see page 33),
Prairie Kir Royales (page 63), Da Das (page 40), or BBQ Queens' Royal Slushes
(page 49), and Cranberry-Orange Sparklers (page 41) or lemonade–club
soda spritzers.

Choose from Among These Dishes

Grilled Pink Grapefruit and Orange Salad with Fresh Avocado (page 174)

An assortment of grilled sausages

Apple-Smoked Salmon (page 71) with Horseradish Crème Fraîche (page 78)

Provençal Grilled Salmon with Rosemary and Mint Aioli (page 145)

Scrambled eggs with chives

Warm breads, muffins, coffeecakes, and/or breakfast pastries

Double-Smoked Ham with Whiskey-Cider Sauce (page 124)

Carpetbagger Steak with Four Seasons Stuffings (page 86)

Persian Grilled Leg of Lamb with Tabbouleh Stuffing and Pomegranate Sauce
     (page 104)

Grilled Cornmeal-Crusted Green Tomatoes with Shrimp Rémoulade
     (page 190)

Grilled asparagus

Blue Cheese Coleslaw (page 173)

Fresh Apple Spice Cake (page 222)

Asian-Style Pork Tenderloins with Grilled Broccoli

Try this pungent Asian-style marinade on just about any kind of meat, fish, or vegetable. We've provided a quick marinade, but if you'd like to add fresh garlic cloves and ginger to it, it would be wonderful. Pork tenderloins are a great company dish to grill because they don't take very long to cook. We like ours with a bit of pink in the middle for medium-rare. Pork does not have to be cooked until well done anymore. Remember that when the meat rests, the internal temperature will climb another 5 or so degrees. So cooking to 140°F means that the meat will climb to at least 145°F while it rests.

Makes 8 servings

- **4 pork tenderloins (3½ to 4 pounds)**
- **6 to 8 large stalks broccoli or broccolini**

Quick Asian Marinade:
- **½ cup soy sauce**
- **½ cup rice vinegar**
- **2 tablespoons toasted sesame oil**
- **2 tablespoons honey**
- **2 teaspoons lemon pepper**

1. Place the tenderloins in a large zipper-top plastic bag.
2. Clean the broccoli, removing the tough outer layer of stem. Slice the peeled stem into thin strips about ¼ inch thick. Separate the florets. Place the broccoli in a separate large zipper-top plastic bag.
3. Combine the marinade ingredients. Pour half of the marinade into each bag. Marinate the pork and the broccoli in the refrigerator for 1 hour.
4. Meanwhile, prepare a hot fire in your grill. Oil a grill wok or basket on both sides and place directly over the fire.
5. Drain the broccoli, reserving the marinade for basting. Place the broccoli in a bowl and set on a doubled baking sheet. Set the marinade on the sheet, too.
6. Remove the tenderloins from their marinade and discard that marinade. Set the pork on the sheet and take everything out to the grill.
7. Place the broccoli in the wok and grill for about 5 minutes, tossing while cooking. Spoon a little marinade over the broccoli while grilling. When the broccoli is tender and slightly charred, move the wok to the indirect-heat side of the grill.

8. Place the meat directly over the hot fire on the grill grates. Grill the tenderloins for 2 to 3 minutes per side, turning a quarter turn at a time, until the internal temperature of the meat registers 140°F. Baste with the remaining vegetable marinade.

9. Let the meat rest for about 5 minutes, then slice diagonally into 1- to 1½-inch-thick slices. Place on a platter and serve with the broccoli on the side.

Deck It Out

Place the pork slices on individual dinner plates accompanied by Asian Noodles (page 199). Top the noodles with the grilled broccoli, and serve with a side of Asian-Style Fruit Slaw (page 172).

Take It Easy

Use your favorite bottled Asian marinade or vinaigrette in place of the Quick Asian Marinade. Buy already cut-up broccoli from the grocery store salad bar.

Change It Up

• Beef tenderloin is a delicious substitute for the pork in this dish. Game meats like venison are good subs, too.

• If you'd rather serve Asian-marinated grilled asparagus than broccoli, be our guest. (And let us be your guest, too!)

Raise a Glass

Pour a cold Asian beer like Kirin or Sapporo, or serve a Sauvignon Blanc.

Latin-Style Barbecued Pork Loin with Aji-li-Mojili

In Puerto Rico and Cuba, this Latin-style recipe known as *lechon asado* would be prepared with a suckling pig and cooked outdoors on a spit over an open charcoal fire. Traditionally, this dish was served for Noche Buena (Christmas Eve) supper, but any time you want a festive party dish that is actually pretty easy, this is it. The pork is first flavored with a sour-orange marinade, then cooked slowly until finger-lickin' good. If you can find sour orange, or *naranja agria*, in Hispanic markets in your area, so much the better, or use our substitute below. The traditional "barbecue sauce" is *aji-li-mojili*, a garlicky sauce sour with lime juice—mmm! We've adapted the traditional asado method to work in the American backyard, either on the grill using an indirect fire or on a rotisserie, with the same succulent results. Check the maximum weight that your rotisserie motor can handle, then buy your pork loin. Rotisserie or grill two at a time and plan for delicious leftovers.

Makes 6 to 8 servings

- **One 5- to 6- pound boneless pork loin roast**

Sour-Orange Marinade:
- **8 cloves garlic, peeled and chopped**
- **2 teaspoons dried oregano**
- **1 tablespoon cracked black peppercorns**
- **1 tablespoon kosher salt**
- **1 cup sour orange juice or ¼ cup orange juice mixed with ¾ cup freshly squeezed lime juice (from 8 to 10 limes)**
- **½ cup olive oil**

1. Place the pork loin in a large zipper-top plastic bag. In a medium-size bowl, whisk together the marinade ingredients, then pour over the pork. Seal the bag and let marinate in the refrigerator, turning several times, for at least 2 hours and up to 24 hours.

2. Set up your grill for rotisserie cooking (see page 23). Prepare a medium fire, about 350°F. Remove the roast from the marinade, but do not pat dry, and place the marinade in a saucepan. Bring the marinade to a boil and cook for 3 minutes; keep warm by the grill.

3. Push the rotisserie rod through the center of the roast so that it is balanced, then place on the spit. Cover and cook, basting with the cooked marinade every 30 minutes, until an instant-read thermometer registers an internal temperature of 145°F for medium, 3 to 4 hours total; if you like your pork more done, aim for 155° to 165°F. Let the pork loin rest for 10 minutes before slicing.

Aji-li-Mojili:

- **4 cloves garlic, minced**
- **1 cup olive oil**
- **2 tablespoons white wine vinegar**
- **¼ cup freshly squeezed lime juice (from 3 to 4 limes)**
- **½ teaspoon salt**
- **¼ teaspoon red pepper flakes**

4. To make the *aji* sauce, whisk all the ingredients together in a small bowl. To serve, slice the pork loin and drizzle with the sauce.

Deck It Out

Serve the pork loin on a platter garnished with fresh orange and lime slices and sprigs of oregano. Serve Cilantro Slaw (page 167) and Sweet Potato Salad with Ginger-Lime Vinaigrette (page 197) on the side.

Change It Up

If you don't have a rotisserie, prepare an indirect fire in your grill (a hot fire on one side, no fire on the other). Place the pork loin on the no-fire side. Cover and grill, basting every 30 minutes, until an instant-read thermometer registers an internal temperature of 145°F for medium, 3 to 4 hours total; if you like your pork more done, aim for 155° to 165°F. Let the pork loin rest for 10 minutes before slicing. You may need to turn the pork roast during grilling if one side gets too browned. You can also smoke the pork loin at 225° to 250°F, using apple wood or other fruit wood, for 3 to 4 hours (see page 18 for how to smoke).

Raise a Glass

While the pork loin is on the spit, offer your guests their choice of drinks, Cuba Libres (page 111) or mojitos.

Smoky Marinated or Rubbed Pork Butt with Sautéed Spinach

Here is a smoked pork butt recipe with an option for marinating and basting with the succulent flavors of smoke and either honey, mustard, and orange zest, or an Italian-style rosemary-garlic paste. Either dish is homey and rustic, perfect to serve family and friends. The butt is laced with fat and smokes for several hours without drying out. Our mantra is "Grill or smoke for another meal." So why not prepare two butts and use one of the toppings on each? There'll be plenty for company and maybe even some leftovers for delicious sandwiches the next day.

Makes 8 servings

Suggested wood: 3 to 5 chunks water-soaked apple or oak, or 3 or 4 branches fresh rosemary

• **One 4- to 5-pound pork butt roast**

Orange-Mustard-Honey Marinade/Baste:
• **½ cup wildflower honey**
• **½ cup zesty barbecue sauce**
• **2 tablespoons grated orange zest**
• **¼ cup freshly squeezed orange juice**
• **¼ cup country-style German mustard**
• **1 tablespoon Worcestershire sauce**
• **1 teaspoon grated fresh ginger**
• **½ teaspoon kosher or sea salt**
• **¼ teaspoon red pepper flakes**

1. If making the orange-marinated pork, combine all the marinade ingredients in a small bowl. Place the pork butt in a large zipper-top plastic bag. Pour half of the marinade into the bag and refrigerate for several hours or overnight. Refrigerate the rest of the marinade for basting.

2. If making the pork with rosemary paste, place the rosemary, garlic, salt, and pepper in a food processor and puree. With the machine running, slowly add the oil to form a paste. Apply the paste to the pork and coat well. This pork may be smoked right away.

3. Prepare a 225°F fire in your smoker. When ready to smoke, place the water-soaked wood over the fire.

4. Place the pork butt, fat side up, in a disposable aluminum pan, place in the smoker, and smoke for 30 to 40 minutes per pound. (Pork butt should be fork-tender when it is done. It has enough fat throughout that it can withstand longer cooking times without drying out.) If making the orange-marinated pork, let the pork smoke for 1 hour before basting. Then use the refrigerated marinade and apply liberally every 20 to 30 minutes. The rosemary-pasted pork does not need to be basted. Add

Smoked Spanish Paprika Sirloin Steak with Rustic Olive Salsa (page 85)
and Wood-Grilled Shrimp Cocktail with Horseradish Crème Fraîche (page 78)

Grilled Farmers' Market Antipasto Platter (page 29)

Grilled Corn with a Butter for Every Occasion (page 164)

Persian Grilled Leg of Lamb with Tabbouleh Stuffing and Pomegranate Sauce (page 104)

Stir-Grilled Tomatoes, Red Onion, and Fresh Herbs with Grilled Flatbread (page 188)

Cilantro Slaw (page 167)

Latin-Style Barbecued Pork Loin with Aji-li-Mojili (page 116)

Clockwise from top left: Pomegranate and Bubbly, Sangria, and Cinderella's Slipper (pages 33, 35, and 110)

Grilled Figs on Rosemary Skewers (page 34)

Guava-Glazed Spatchcocked Chicken (page 130)

Provençal Grilled Salmon with Rosemary and Mint Aioli (page 145)

Pecan-Smoked Goat Cheese–Stuffed Peppadews (page 36)

Blistered Baby Pattypans and Red Onion (page 187)

Chocolate Ice Cream Cake (page 228)

Fresh Rosemary and Garlic Paste:
- ¼ cup fresh rosemary leaves
- 10 large cloves garlic
- 1 tablespoon kosher or sea salt
- 1 tablespoon coarsely ground black pepper
- 2 tablespoons olive oil

Sautéed Spinach:
- ¼ cup olive oil
- 1½ pounds baby spinach leaves
- ¼ cup toasted pine nuts
- Kosher or sea salt and freshly ground black pepper to taste

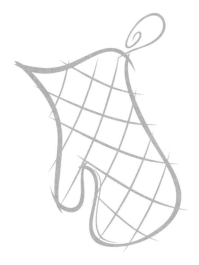

additional wood after about 2 hours if needed. Keep smoking until the pork butt is fork-tender and an instant-read thermometer inserted in the thickest part of the roast registers 170° to 180°F. Remove the roast from the smoker, cover with plastic wrap, and let stand for 10 minutes.

5. To make the spinach, heat the olive oil in a large pan over medium-high heat. Add the spinach and toss to coat with oil. Cook for 2 or 3 minutes for just slightly wilted spinach (some of the leaves will still hold their shape), or cook for 5 to 6 minutes for a more wilted dish. Add the toasted pine nuts and season with salt and pepper.

6. When cutting the pork, let the pieces of meat fall into chunks rather than slicing them. Place the spinach on a platter and place the pork chunks on the platter, partially over the spinach, for a nice presentation.

Deck It Out ·

Decorate your table with linens in fall colors, miniature pumpkins, and vases of sage branches. Along with the spinach, serve either Smoke-Roasted Root Vegetables with Garlic and Rosemary (page 198) or All-Seasons Potato Casserole for a Crowd (page 196). Since this makes such a nice autumn menu, finish it off with Fresh Apple Spice Cake (page 222).

Change It Up · · · · · · · · · · · · · · · · · · ·

Pork is so versatile that you may substitute any of your favorite rubs or marinades, homemade or store bought. Simple single-ingredient applications include coarse salt, onion or garlic salt, cracked pepper, hoisin sauce, smoked Spanish paprika, or mustard, to name just a few.

Raise a Glass ·

Appropriate red wines to serve with this run the gamut: try a fruity Beaujolais, an earthy Pinot Noir, a smoky Merlot, or a zesty Zinfandel.

Cherry-Smoked Rack of Pork with Cider-Mustard-Bourbon Sauce

As the centerpiece of an autumn meal or even a worthy replacement for the Thanksgiving turkey, a smoked rack of pork looks and tastes festive. Whether you mail-order yours from premium purveyors like Niman Ranch (www.nimanranch.com) or Pipestone Family Farms (www.pipestonefamilyfarms.com), find a good deal at Costco, or select one at your hometown butcher shop, you can take it easy by slow-smoking the rack in a bullet smoker outside. At a slow and steady 225° to 250°F, your rack of pork will take on a burnished appearance over 4 to 5 hours.

Makes 8 to 10 servings

Suggested wood: Cherry; apple, hickory, or oak also work

Mustard-Garlic-Herb Slather:
- **12 cloves garlic**
- **2 tablespoons kosher or sea salt**
- **2 tablespoons finely chopped fresh sage or 1 tablespoon crumbled dried sage**
- **2 tablespoons finely chopped fresh rosemary or 1 tablespoon dried rosemary**
- **1 tablespoon lemon pepper**
- **2 tablespoons olive oil**

1. To make the slather, place all of the ingredients in a food processor and pulse until you have a paste.
2. Rinse the rack of pork under cold running water and pat dry. Using a rubber spatula, spread the slather over the meaty top and sides of the rack of pork. Loosely cover with aluminum foil and let rest in the refrigerator for at least 2 hours and up to overnight.
3. Prepare a fire in your smoker. Place the meat, fat side up, in a disposable aluminum pan and let come to room temperature for 1 hour.
4. Place the pan in the smoker and close the lid. Smoke at 225° to 250°F for 4 to 5 hours, or until an instant-read thermometer inserted in the center registers 140° to 150°F.

- **2 tablespoons Dijon mustard**
- **One 8- to 10-pound rack of pork**

Cider-Mustard-Bourbon Sauce:
- **2 cups apple cider**
- **1 teaspoon chicken flavor base or 1 chicken bouillon cube**
- **1 cup heavy cream**
- **1 tablespoon Dijon mustard**
- **1 tablespoon whole-grain mustard**
- **1 tablespoon Worcestershire sauce**
- **2 tablespoons bourbon, Calvados, brandy, or Cognac**
- **Sea salt and freshly ground white pepper to taste**

5. While the pork is smoking, make the sauce. Bring the cider and chicken flavor base to a boil in a saucepan over high heat and cook until the mixture has reduced to ½ cup, about 20 minutes. Whisk in the cream, Dijon and whole-grain mustards, Worcestershire sauce, and bourbon, and bring to a boil. Remove from the heat and season with salt and pepper. Keep warm.

6. Remove the meat to a cutting board, tent loosely with aluminum foil, and let rest for 15 to 30 minutes before carving. To serve, carve the pork and nap each slice with the sauce.

Deck It Out ·······················

If you feel like showing off, place the whole smoked rack on a pretty serving platter, surrounded by lady apples, tiny Seckel pears, branches of fresh sage and rosemary, and bay leaves. Wow! It gets even better when you carve the rack and nap each slice with the pale caramel-colored sauce. Serve this with Oven-Baked Herbed Risotto (page 204) or Smoked Gouda Grits (page 201) and some simple green vegetables.

Change It Up ·····················

This recipe also works with boneless pork loin or a crown roast of pork, which is a larger rack of pork with the rib ends "frenched" (to make the points of the crown) and the rack tied to form a circle. Slow-smoke a loin or crown roast for about 30 minutes per pound.

Raise a Glass ·····················

Settle back with a fruity, lighter-style ale or the wine of your choice, like a dark berry-flavored Zinfandel.

Zinfandel-Glazed Baby Back Ribs with a Kiss of Smoke

We love our slow-smoked ribs in *The BBQ Queens' Big Book of Barbecue* (The Harvard Common Press, 2005). But we know that many grill guys and gals don't slow-smoke over wood. So what to do? Figure out how to do really good indirectly grilled ribs with a kiss of smoke—and here they are. We begin with a sultry, smoky rub and finish with a sauce that has a depth of smokiness from the Zinfandel wine and a bit of liquid smoke. Words of wisdom first: grilling is usually hot and fast, but for this recipe we lower the heat. Most items that are grilled are tender cuts of meat, so we suggest baby backs instead of spare ribs because they are smaller and more tender. We also give you an indoor-outdoor version that calls for slow-baking the ribs first. What about boiling ribs? We think this boils away lots of the flavor and say, won't the baking do almost as well? However, we are not the Barbecued Ribs Police, merely the BBQ Queens. We won't give you a ticket.

Makes 6 to 8 servings

- **3 whole slabs (about 1½ pounds each) baby back ribs**

Smoky Hickory Rub:
- **⅓ cup hickory-smoked salt**
- **⅓ cup celery salt**
- **⅓ cup granulated garlic or garlic powder**
- **¼ cup smoked Spanish paprika**
- **¼ cup dry mustard**
- **¼ cup lemon pepper**
- **¼ cup packed dark brown sugar**

Zinfandel Barbecue Sauce:
- **One 24-ounce bottle ketchup**
- **One 12-ounce bottle chili sauce**
- **1 cup Zinfandel**
- **¾ cup dark honey**

1. Prepare an indirect fire in your grill or smoker to 225° to 250°F. Remove the membrane from the back of the ribs.

2. Combine the rub ingredients in a large glass jar with a tight-fitting lid. Secure the lid and shake to blend. Sprinkle the rub on both sides of the ribs. (There will be leftover rub, and it's delicious on poultry as well as pork. Store the rub in the pantry, for up to 3 months, for best results.) Set the ribs, slightly overlapping, on the indirect-heat side of the grill. Close the lid and cook.

3. While the ribs begin to cook, prepare the barbecue sauce. In a large saucepan, combine all of the sauce ingredients. Whisk to blend and bring to a boil. Lower the heat to medium and cook for 30 minutes to 1 hour. If the sauce is too thin, continue to cook until it thickens. If the sauce is too thick, add a little water to thin it. Keep warm.

- ½ cup red wine vinegar
- ½ cup firmly packed dark brown sugar
- ¼ cup Dijon mustard
- 2 tablespoons Worcestershire sauce
- 1 tablespoon liquid smoke
- 1 tablespoon hickory-smoked salt
- 1 tablespoon ground chipotle chile pepper
- 1 tablespoon ground ancho chile pepper

- One 12-ounce squeeze bottle margarine
- ½ cup honey, in a squeeze bottle

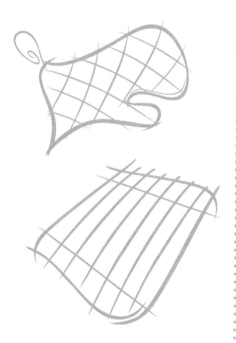

4. After the ribs have cooked for 1½ hours, turn the ribs over and drizzle with margarine, brushing it evenly over the meat. Cover and cook for another 30 minutes. Turn the ribs again and drizzle with the margarine and honey, brushing them evenly over the meat. Cover and cook for another 30 minutes. Repeat with the margarine and honey, and cover and cook for 30 minutes more. When the ribs are tender and the meat is beginning to pull off the bone, brush the ribs on both sides with some of the barbecue sauce. Cook the ribs for a final 15 to 20 minutes. Serve the remaining barbecue sauce on the side.

Deck It Out

For a spectacular presentation, serve the whole slabs on a large platter. These delicious ribs call for an all-out barbecue bash. Serve a panoply of sides, including Heirloom Tomato Bowl with Lemon and Feta (page 186), Quick Coleslaw (see page 173), Potato Salad with Aioli (page 195), and Grilled Corn with a Butter for Every Occasion (page 164).

Change It Up

You may bake the ribs in a 325°F oven for 2 hours, basting with the margarine and honey. When the meat is tender and beginning to pull off the bone, finish cooking the ribs on the grill, about 10 minutes over a medium-hot fire. As soon as you remove the ribs from the grill, brush them with the barbecue sauce.

Raise a Glass

Drink Zin!

Double-Smoked Ham with Whiskey-Cider Sauce

A double-smoked ham is so fragrant, it can be served naked (without any baste or sauce) if you like. However, the accompanying glaze and sauce recipes are so simple and appealing that you really should give them a try. Select either a whole ham or a spiral-cut ham. Serve this for brunch with a casserole of eggs and Brandied Fruit Compote (page 193). Or go the dinner route and serve with All-Seasons Potato Casserole for a Crowd (page 196) and a mixed green salad.

Makes 8 to 10 servings

Suggested wood: Apple, hickory, pecan, or oak, or a combination

Whiskey-Cider Sauce:
- **2 cups apple cider**
- **¼ cup whiskey**
- **¼ cup unsalted butter**
- **2 tablespoons dark brown sugar**

- **1 cup apricot preserves**
- **2 teaspoons dry mustard**
- **1 tablespoon cider vinegar**
- **One 5- to 7-pound bone-in precooked or smoked ham (shank or butt)**
- **20 whole cloves**

1. To make the sauce, place the cider and whiskey in a small saucepan over high heat and cook until reduced by half. Whisk in the butter and brown sugar. Set aside until ready to baste.
2. Combine the apricot preserves, mustard, and vinegar in a small bowl. Coat the ham with the mixture, then stud the ham with the cloves and let stand for 1 hour at room temperature to marinate.
3. Meanwhile, prepare an indirect fire in your smoker.
4. Put the ham in a disposable aluminum pan and place in the smoker. Cover and smoke at 225° to 250°F until it turns bronze and reaches the desired level of smokiness (1 to 2 hours). Baste with whiskey-cider sauce and pan juices after the first 45 minutes of smoking. Remove from the smoker, slice, and serve hot, warm, or at room temperature.

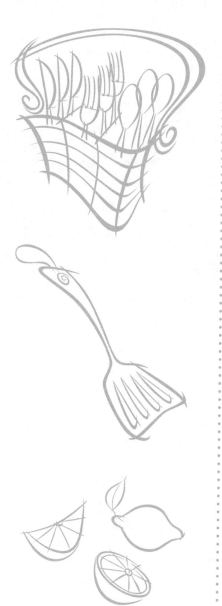

Take It Easy

Plan ahead to do less work before the next round of company arrives. If you have leftover ham, cut off any rind and place chunks of ham in the bowl of a food processor. Process until finely minced. Add 2 to 3 tablespoons mayonnaise and 1 to 2 tablespoons Dijon mustard and pulse to combine. You may also add a bit of apricot preserves, if you like. The amounts will depend upon how much leftover ham you have. Serve in a crock, accompanied by crackers.

Change It Up

Stovetop smoke the ham by following steps 1 and 2. Set up the stovetop smoker with 1 to 2 tablespoons finely shredded dry corncobs or the wood of your choice. Place the tray and rack in the smoker. Set the ham on the rack. Cover the ham with a large piece of heavy-duty aluminum foil and crimp around the pan to cover tightly. Smoke for 45 minutes to 1 hour over medium heat. Baste with the whiskey-cider sauce a couple of times during cooking, being careful to avoid the hot smoke and steam when you open the foil.

Raise a Glass

Serve the ham for brunch, and begin with a mimosa-style drink like Da Das (page 40) or Limoncello Spritzers (page 40). If you make the ham spread above, serve it with Beaujolais or a chilled Riesling.

Mamma Mia! An Italian Antipasto Party

We love the antipasto offerings at Lidia's in Kansas City, which include a mélange of fresh and raw, grilled, preserved, and sautéed goodies prepared under the guidance of chef/owner and cookbook author Lidia Bastianich. These appetizer offerings—*antipasto* means "before the meal"—would make a great appetizer party. Your guests simply take their plates up to the antipasto tables—or to the hot grill—and start taking spoonfuls of this, a slice of that, a forkful of something else, and so on.

There are two ways to serve antipasti at a party: Give each separate dish its own serving platter or mix all the dishes on several platters. It's your party, and your choice.

Setting the Scene
Italian families like to bring tables and chairs in all shapes and sizes out into the courtyard for a family feast. You can do the same. Simply drape the tables with sheets or tablecloths in the same colors or patterns. Go with the retro-trattoria look of red-checked tablecloths or sheets, white plates, and maybe a dripping candle in a straw-wrapped Chianti bottle. Or go more earthy and Tuscan or Umbrian with olives, golds, and russets, with an herb or olive topiary as the centerpiece of each table. String white lights among the trees and you'll feel positively moonstruck.

Making Beautiful Music
Dino: The Essential Dean Martin is finger-snapping upbeat, or try Italian pop stars Zucchero or Pino Danieli.

Perfect Partners
Serve chilled pomegranate spritzers (pomegranate juice and sparkling wine or water), chilled Italian white wines like Pinot Grigio and Vernaccia, cool (but not chilled) Italian reds like young Chianti and Rosso di Montalcino, and Italian beers, such as Moretti and Peroni.

Choose From Among These Dishes

Real Grilled Cheese (see below)

Grilled Polenta with Caramelized Onions and Gorgonzola (page 31)

Grilled Farmers' Market Antipasto Platter (page 29)

Grilled Prosciutto-Wrapped Asparagus with Fig Balsamic Vinegar and
Shaved Parmesan (page 62)

Pancetta-Wrapped Radicchio, Fennel, and Potato Bundles (page 64)

Wood-Grilled Pizza with Two Toppings (page 42), cut into small wedges

Grilled Veal Bundles with Fontina, Sage, and Prosciutto (page 52)

Grilled Pepper Roll-Ups with Feta-Olive-Lemon Filling (page 180)

Real Grilled Cheese

For an antipasto treat, try grilling a firm cheese like fontina or a young, sliceable Pecorino or a cheese in a casing like Brie or Camembert. If you aren't sure if the cheese will hold up on the grill, test a small portion. Apply a bit of olive oil to the slice of fontina or the whole wheel of cheese in a casing (the casing will hold the cheese inside, so do not cut until it is off the grill). Grill over medium to medium-high heat for 2 to 4 minutes per side. The cheese should be crisp and golden on the outside and melting on the inside. Another way to "grill" the cheese is to wrap small portions in 1 or 2 pieces of prosciutto to totally enclose it. Then grill the prosciutto-cheese parcels. The exterior will be crisp, with a meltingly seductive cheese inside.

Umbrian-Style Grilled Whole Chicken

Green and hilly Umbria in central Italy has long been overshadowed by its more famous cousin to the west—Tuscany. Still relatively undiscovered, this region is home to Assisi; the hill town of Deruta, known for its painted ceramics; and great grilling almost everywhere, mostly over charcoal and fruit woods such as apple, cherry, or pear. Umbrian style means using simple ingredients. In this recipe, garlic and fresh herbs blend with green olives and grilled lemons to exquisitely flavor the best free-range chickens you can find. It's the weekend, after all, and time to savor the good life.

Makes 6 to 8 servings

Suggested wood: 1 cup chips or ⅓ cup pellets (apple, cherry, peach, or pear)

Stuffing:
- ¼ cup extra-virgin olive oil
- 18 green olives, pitted
- 2 cloves garlic, chopped
- 2 tablespoons freshly squeezed lemon juice
- 2 tablespoons chopped fresh rosemary leaves
- 2 tablespoons chopped fresh sage leaves
- 1 tablespoon freshly ground black pepper
- Kosher or sea salt to taste

1. To make the stuffing, combine all the ingredients together in a medium-size bowl. To make the paste, combine all the ingredients together in a small bowl.
2. Rinse the chickens under cold running water, remove the giblets and neck from the cavities, and pat dry. Stuff each chicken with half of the stuffing. Rub each chicken with half of the paste. Cover and refrigerate for at least 2 hours and up to 12 hours.
3. Prepare an indirect fire in your grill, with high heat on one side. If using a charcoal grill, place moistened wood chips (or a foil packet of dry wood pellets with holes poked in the top) directly on the coals right before you want to grill. If using a gas grill, enclose dry wood chips or pellets in a foil packet with holes poked in the top; place the packet on the grill grate over the heat source. You're ready to grill when you see smoke from the smoldering wood and the fire is hot.
4. Place the chickens, breast side up, on the no-heat side, close the lid, and grill for 30 to 40 minutes. Open the lid and turn the chickens over. Close the lid and grill for 30 to 40 minutes more, or until an instant-read thermometer

Herb and Garlic Paste:
- **2 tablespoons extra-virgin olive oil**
- **2 cloves garlic, minced**
- **2 tablespoons freshly squeezed lemon juice**
- **1 tablespoon chopped fresh rosemary leaves**
- **1 tablespoon chopped fresh sage leaves**
- **½ teaspoon fine kosher or sea salt**

- **Two 3- to 4-pound chickens**
- **4 large lemons, cut into quarters**

inserted in the thickest part of a thigh registers 160°F. (You might need to turn the chickens several times to keep one side from getting too browned and done.) During the last minutes of grilling, grill the lemon wedges on both sides until they have good grill marks.

5. To serve, place the chickens on a large platter surrounded with the grilled lemon wedges. Let rest for 10 minutes, then carve and serve, drizzled with juice from the grilled lemons.

Deck It Out

Add bunches of fresh rosemary and sage to the platter. Serve with Bistro Fennel and Baby Bello Mushroom Salad (page 191) and/or Oven-Baked Herbed Risotto (page 204).

Change It Up

Grill the chickens on a rotisserie (see page 23 for information on rotisserie cooking).

Raise a Glass

Pair this fragrant meal with a white wine that has notes of citrus, like a Gavi, or a peppery red Syrah.

Guava-Glazed Spatchcocked Chicken

Brined first, then glazed with guava and rum, these flattened whole chickens stay juicy and delicious. Brining is the process of soaking meat, poultry, or seafood in a salty tenderizing solution. Thanks to salt's natural ability to draw out flavors and juices in foods, brining causes the chickens to retain tenderness during cooking. When brining is done properly, your meats will not taste salty, but, rather, even juicier than usual.

Makes 4 to 6 servings

- **2 whole chickens (3 to 4 pounds each)**

Rum and Bay Brine:
- **3 tablespoons kosher or sea salt**
- **1 quart water**
- **1 bay leaf**
- **8 whole black peppercorns**
- **½ cup light or dark rum**

Guava Glaze:
- **¾ cup guava jelly**
- **1 tablespoon grated fresh ginger**
- **2 tablespoons rum**
- **Freshly squeezed lemon or lime juice to taste**

- **Olive oil for brushing**

1. To spatchcock the chickens, turn each chicken breast side down. With a pair of kitchen shears, cut along each side of the backbones, from neck to tail. Snip out the backbones completely. Also remove the wishbones. Turn the chickens breast side up, press down to flatten, and thread 2 or 3 metal skewers through each chicken to help them keep their flattened shape.

2. In a large pot, bring all of the brine ingredients to a boil until the salt dissolves. Let cool to room temperature, then pour the brine into a large zipper-top plastic bag or a roasting pan. Add the chickens, making sure they are totally immersed in the brine. Seal or cover and refrigerate for at least 2 hours and up to 24 hours.

3. Prepare a dual-heat fire in your grill, with a hot fire on one side and a medium fire on the other. Oil a grill rack.

4. To make the glaze, combine the guava jelly, ginger, and rum in a small saucepan over medium heat until the jelly melts. Whisk together, then add the lemon juice. Reserve about half of the glaze for serving, and keep the rest warm by the grill.

5. Remove the chickens from the brine, discard the brine, and rinse the chickens under cold running water. Pat dry and brush with olive oil on both sides. Place on a doubled baking sheet to take out to the grill.

6. Sear the chickens on the hot side of the grill for 4 to 5 minutes per side, or until you get good grill marks. Transfer the chickens, meat side up, to the medium-fire side and brush with the glaze. Close the lid of the grill and cook for 10 minutes. Turn the chickens, brush with glaze again, close the lid, and cook for another 10 minutes, or until an instant-read thermometer registers an internal temperature of 155°F in the thigh meat. Remove the skewers. Cut the chickens into serving portions and serve with the reserved glaze.

Deck It Out ·

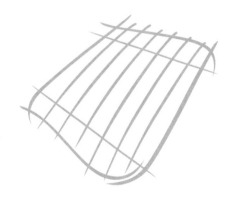

Serve each portion drizzled with more glaze and garnished with an unsprayed edible flower, such as a nasturtium or a lemon blossom. Side dish options include Sweet Potato Salad with Ginger-Lime Vinaigrette (page 197), Grilled Pink Grapefruit and Orange Salad with Fresh Avocado (page 174), and Grilled Corn with a Butter for Every Occasion (page 164).

Change It Up · · · · · · · · · · · · · · · · · ·

You may also use this brine and glaze on pork chops, pork loin, pork tenderloin, leg of lamb, or rack of lamb.

Raise a Glass · · · · · · · · · · · · · · · · · ·

Serve a slightly sweet wine, such as a fruity American Riesling, to counter the brine and match the fruitiness of the glaze.

Vineyard Smoked Chicken Amogio

This is a great crowd pleaser, and it's our version of beer-can chicken—a whole chicken seated on an open can of beer and slowly cooked on the grill. *Amogio* is the Sicilian marinade composed of lemon juice and/or white wine, olive oil, garlic, and herbs. It is used as both a soak and a drizzle, so if you want to have extra, make a double batch. *Amogio* is especially good on grilled poultry, veal, wild game, fish, and seafood. The vertical chicken roasters with a cylinder are handy for this recipe, because wine or other liquid can be poured into the cylinder. Any of our salads would be good accompaniments for the chicken, so choose one that is in season. Smashed Red Potatoes with Green Onions and Cream Cheese (page 194) or Italian Sausage, Pine Nut, and Wild Mushroom Stuffing (page 205) are perfect side dishes. Any grilled corn or mushroom dish would add additional flavors for a feast.

Makes 10 to 12 servings

• **Three 3½- to 4-pound chickens**

Amogio:
• **¼ cup minced fresh garlic, or more to your taste**
• **¾ cup olive oil**
• **¾ cup dry white wine**
• **¾ cup freshly squeezed lemon juice (from 4 to 5 large lemons)**
• **½ cup chopped fresh Italian parsley**
• **2 tablespoons chopped fresh mint**
• **½ teaspoon red pepper flakes**

• **Several bunches grapevines or herb stalks for smoking**
• **3 vertical chicken roasters**
• **One 750-milliliter bottle dry white wine**

1. Rinse the chickens under cold running water, remove the giblets and neck from the cavities, and pat dry. Place each chicken in a zipper-top plastic bag.

2. Combine the *amogio* ingredients in a medium-size bowl and whisk together. Add ½ to ⅔ cup of the marinade to each bag of chicken and seal. Reserve and refrigerate the remaining marinade. Marinate the chicken for at least 1 hour, and preferably overnight, in the refrigerator.

3. Prepare a medium-hot indirect fire in your grill. When ready to cook, add the grapevines to the charcoal, or place on top of a piece of foil directly over a gas flame. (Replenish vines 2 or 3 times during cooking, as needed. Replenish charcoal during cooking as needed.)

4. Fill each roaster cylinder with the wine. Remove the chicken from the marinade, discarding the marinade. Position a chicken on top of each roaster, following the manufacturer's instructions. Set the chickens on the indirect-heat side of the grill. Cover the grill and cook the chickens over medium heat for about 1½ hours, basting with half of the reserved refrigerated

marinade. (Save the remaining marinade to pour over the cooked chickens.) When done, the internal temperature will register 175°F when an instant-read thermometer is inserted into the thickest part of the thigh, not touching the bone. The chicken should be a beautiful mahogany color. (If the chicken begins to get too brown, tent a piece of foil over it.)

5. Using tongs, remove the chickens from the roasters carefully, so that the hot liquid does not spill and burn you. Let rest for 5 minutes. While they are resting, heat the remaining reserved *amogio* until warm.

6. When ready to serve, place 1 whole chicken centered on a large platter, but pushed toward the back. Carve the meat off the remaining 2 chickens and place the pieces in a semi-circle around the whole chicken. Stuff sprigs of herbs around the platter for garnish. Drizzle the heated *amogio* over the chicken pieces and serve.

Deck It Out

Serve the chicken on a platter garnished with bunches of grapes and unsprayed ivy leaves.

Change It Up

For cooking on a can instead of a roaster, lower the chicken's cavity onto the liquid-filled can. Pull the chicken legs forward to balance the bird so that it stands upright. Removing the chicken from the can is a bit trickier than from the roaster. Wear a heat-resistant mitt and hold on to the can while lifting the chicken off with tongs.

Raise a Glass

A nice wheat beer or a dry Pinot Grigio will work very well with this dish.

Piquillo Pepper–Stuffed Chicken with Salsa Verde

Mark Bittman put us on to piquillo peppers, those small red peppers that are descendants of Peru's *chile de arbol*. Piquillos are not edible raw; instead, they're smoke-roasted, then packed in jars. They're deeper in color, smokier, and zippier in flavor than red bell peppers, but feel free to substitute if you can't get piquillos. We ordered ours from Zingerman's (www.zingermans.com). You can also just arrange piquillo peppers on a platter with olives, peppadews, and other goodies for an almost effortless appetizer, or stuff the piquillos the same way as Grilled Pepper Roll-Ups with Feta-Olive-Lemon Filling (page 180). The salsa verde, an herby green sauce, is great on anything grilled. (We use lemon zest, as lemon juice turns the sauce an unappetizing gray-green.) And, of course, any leftovers taste mighty fine the next day. Serve this with Grilled Corn with a Butter for Every Occasion (page 164).

Makes 8 servings

Salsa Verde:
- **1 cup fresh Italian parsley leaves**
- **3 cloves garlic, minced**
- **2 tablespoons capers, drained**
- **1 teaspoon grated fresh lemon zest**
- **1 cup olive oil**
- **Fine kosher or sea salt to taste**

- **8 small boneless, skinless chicken breasts (4 to 5 ounces each)**
- **8 ounces fresh goat cheese, Boursin, or cream cheese, softened**
- **16 preserved piquillo peppers**
- **Fine kosher or sea salt and freshly ground black pepper to taste**
- **Olive oil for brushing**

1. Prepare a medium-hot fire in your grill.
2. To make the salsa verde, place the parsley, garlic, capers, lemon zest, and olive oil in a food processor and puree until smooth. Season with salt and set aside.
3. Place each chicken breast between waxed or parchment paper and flatten with a meat mallet until an even ½-inch thick. With a knife or rubber spatula, spread 1 ounce of cheese down the center of each chicken breast, then top with 2 piquillo peppers, opened and spread out. Season with salt and pepper. Fold the short ends of each chicken breast in, then start from a long end and roll up. If you wish, fasten with toothpicks. Brush with olive oil and place on a doubled baking sheet to take outside.
4. Grill the chicken for 8 to 10 minute per side, turning once. Serve the chicken with the salsa verde on the side.

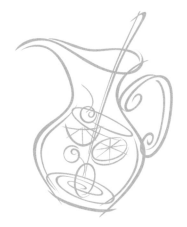

Deck It Out

For a pretty platter of "pick up" food, after the grilled chicken has cooled, refrigerate it for several hours or overnight. Carefully slice it into ½-inch-thick slices, and arrange them in a slightly overlapping pattern on a platter with a bowl of the salsa verde on the side for dipping.

Change It Up

The sky's the limit on all the different stuffings you can think of. Keep it simple and choose just two ingredients: feta cheese and chopped olives, peppery cheese and green chiles, cheddar cheese and bacon, Brie or Camembert cheese and prosciutto, fontina cheese and basil, and so on.

Raise a Glass

Make up a batch of The World's Best Frozen Margaritas (page 48) a day ahead.

Razzle-Dazzle: Smoke in a Bottle

Can you get razzle-dazzle smoke flavor from a bottle? You bet! Try sprinkling on smoked salt like Danish smoked salt or hickory-smoked salt, Tabasco Chipotle Pepper Sauce, smoked Spanish paprika, liquid smoke, ancho chile powder, chipotle chile powder, and chili powder. Though they're not from a bottle, add smoked cheeses to your dishes, like Spanish Idiazabal cheese or Dutch smoked Gouda.

Stuffed Prosciutto-Wrapped Turkey Breast

If turkey isn't something you usually throw on the grill, then we have a surprise for you. This is sensational. It looks *très chic* stuffed with green parsley, golden raisins, and pungent blue cheese. It's wrapped like a present, with the prosciutto adding another layer of flavor while keeping this very lean piece of meat nice and juicy. The Saga blue cheese is creamy, pungent, and perfect for this recipe, but any good blue cheese will do, like Stilton from England, Roquefort from France, Gorgonzola from Italy, or Maytag from Iowa.

Makes 4 to 6 servings

Suggested wood: 1½ cups dry chips, in a combination of apple, cherry, and oak

- **Two 1½- to 2-pound turkey breast halves**
- **½ cup crumbled Saga blue cheese, plus more for garnish**
- **2 tablespoons golden raisins, plus more for garnish**
- **2 tablespoons chopped fresh Italian parsley, plus more for garnish**
- **2 tablespoons olive oil**
- **2 tablespoons Dijon mustard**
- **2 tablespoons freshly squeezed lemon juice**
- **6 thin slices prosciutto**

1. Slice a pocket in each turkey breast and stuff with the blue cheese, raisins, and parsley. Set the meat in a shallow dish.

2. In a small bowl, whisk together the olive oil, mustard, and lemon juice. Pour over the turkey breasts. Cover with plastic wrap and marinate in the refrigerator for 2 to 4 hours, turning 2 or 3 times.

3. When ready to grill, prepare an indirect hot fire in your grill. Place the dry wood chips in a smoker box and place over the hot fire.

4. Remove the turkey from the marinade and wrap each breast with 3 slices of prosciutto. Sear over the hot fire for about 5 minutes on each side. Move the turkey to the indirect side of the grill and close the lid. Continue to cook for another 20 minutes, or until an instant-read thermometer registers 160° to 165°F when inserted in the thickest part of the breast meat. (The meat will continue to cook for another 5 degrees or more while resting.)

5. Let rest for about 5 minutes, then slice on the diagonal. Present on a platter with a garnish of crumbled blue cheese, golden raisins, and parsley.

Deck It Out

Serve the turkey on a platter, garnished with bunches of fresh herbs and mild black olives. Serve this turkey in the summer with Grilled Corn with a Butter for Every Occasion (page 164) and Blistered Baby Pattypans and Red Onion (page 187). Wine-Splashed Peaches, Plums, and Berries (page 210) makes for a luscious sweet ending to this terrific repast. In colder weather, serve Grill-Roasted Red Pepper, Arugula, and Niçoise Olive Salad (page 184) and Pears Poached in Moscato del Solo (page 212).

Change It Up

Substitute different stuffings, such as slices of Brie or Camembert with fresh basil leaves; Monterey Jack cheese, crumbled cooked bacon, and whole roasted green chiles; cooked wild rice, toasted pecans, and sweet dried cranberries; and so on.

Raise a Glass

Match a sweeter, fruity wine to contrast with the saltiness of the blue cheese and prosciutto. An Italian spumante or a California sparkler would be our choice to serve along with everything.

¡Viva la Vida!
A Summer Fiesta

Viva la vida means "long live life" in Spanish. A fiesta is a celebration that reminds us to seize the day, be in the moment, enjoy ourselves. Colorful, vibrant, and casual, a fiesta should also be fun and carefree. The food should do the same without being ordinary. Leave the tacos and fajitas for a weekday, and turn your hand to something more celebratory. Many of the dishes we suggest can be made ahead of time so that you can enjoy a little salsa dancing, too.

Setting the Scene
Set out pots of zinnias from your garden or a farmers' market for instant color. Use bright, hot colors like red, orange, yellow, and lime green in linens, tablecloths, or fabrics to drape the tables. Acrylic serving bowls are great, because they go with everything. You can also buy them in fun, colorful patterns. Shop for inexpensive large tiles in food-safe glazed terra cotta or with folk patterns to use as "platters" or to protect the table from hot dishes. And don't forget sparkling colored lights and a piñata. A fiesta wouldn't be a fiesta without them!

Making Beautiful Music
Salsa music, Jennifer Lopez, Ricky Martin, or your favorite Latin dance-music artist is a must for this party.

Perfect Partners
Have your own house-blend margaritas (try The World's Best Frozen Margarita, page 48) and homemade lemonade or limeade on tap in a large glass container with a spigot so that guests can help themselves. Have other drinks like Mexican beer icing away in metal beverage tubs, and serve pitchers of Red Wine Sangria and White Wine Sangria (page 35) filled with sliced citrus fruits and fresh sugarcane. If you dare, whip up batches of caipirinhas, that lethal South American cocktail based on cachaça.

Choose from Among These Dishes

Wood-Roasted Oysters on a Bed of Rock Salt with Chipotle-Garlic Butter
   (page 76)

Latin-Style Barbecued Pork Loin with *Aji-li-Mojili* (page 116)

Piquillo Pepper–Stuffed Chicken with Salsa Verde (page 134)

Smoked Spanish Paprika Sirloin Steak with Rustic Olive Salsa (page 85)

Corn Husk–Wrapped Shrimp with Grilled Corn (page 156)

Fideo (page 200)

Potato Salad with Aioli (page 195)

Cilantro Slaw (page 167)

Grilled Corn with Ancho Butter (page 164)

Wine-Splashed Peaches, Plums, and Berries (page 210; use Red Wine
   or White Wine Sangria, page 35)

Choco-licious Sheet Cake (page 223)

Planked Stone Fruit with Butter-Rum Glaze (page 213) or grilled
   pineapple with Dulce de Leche Sauce (page 236)

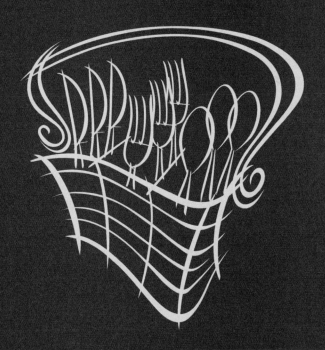

Herb-Smoked Turkey with Pinot-Tarragon Butter Baste

A Thanksgiving groaning board, aptly named for the vast amount of food offered, doesn't have to be made up of the traditional starchy mashed potatoes, stuffing, and such. Lighten it up! We show you how in Deck It Out (below right). During the holidays, cooking the turkey outdoors frees up valuable oven space, too. Once you try this aromatic herb-smoked turkey, you'll want to cook it all year round because it tastes so good.

Here are some tips that will help you indirect grill or smoke your turkey to perfection: Turkey is a lean bird that tends to dry out rather quickly. Our method of larding with an herbed compound butter between the skin and meat, draping with oiled cheesecloth, and basting with a butter sauce is a triple precaution that produces a moist, juicy bird. Remember that the temperature and wind conditions outdoors will affect your cooking time, so allow plenty of time to smoke. (A 12-pound turkey usually smokes in about 4 hours. However, every time the lid is opened for peeking or basting, it will add to the cooking time. So allow another hour, at least. The legs should wiggle easily out of the socket when it is done.) Our smoking flavor of choice for this recipe is herbs. If you want to throw some wood on the fire, go for it.

Makes 8 to 10 servings

Thyme Butter:
- ½ cup (1 stick) unsalted butter, softened
- 2 tablespoons chopped fresh thyme
- 1 clove garlic, minced
- Grated zest of 1 lemon
- Kosher or sea salt and freshly ground black pepper to taste

- One 12-pound turkey, rinsed and patted dry
- 8 thin bacon strips or 4 slices prosciutto
- Cheesecloth
- ¼ cup olive oil

1. Prepare an indirect fire in a grill or a smoker and maintain a temperature of about 250°F.
2. To make the thyme butter, combine the butter, thyme, garlic, lemon zest, salt, and pepper. Carefully spread the butter mixture between the skin and meat of the turkey, trying not to tear the skin. Sprinkle the cavity with salt and pepper. Cut the zested lemon in half and place in the cavity. Truss the legs and place the turkey in a roasting pan that will fit in your grill or smoker. Lay the bacon strips over the turkey. Soak a 15-inch length of cheesecloth in olive oil and place on top of the turkey.
3. When ready to smoke, add a bunch of fresh herbs to a charcoal fire. In a gas grill or electric smoker, lay the herbs on a piece of foil and set directly over the heat source.
4. Place the turkey on the indirect side of the

- **Herbs of your choice for the grill or smoker: thyme, tarragon, lemon balm, and/or rosemary, plus more for garnish**

Pinot-Tarragon Butter Baste:
- **2 cups Pinot Noir or other dry, fruity red wine**
- **1 cup (2 sticks) unsalted butter**
- **4 sprigs fresh tarragon**
- **Kosher or sea salt and freshly ground black pepper to taste**

grill or smoker and slow-smoke for 15 to 20 minutes per pound. Keep the lid closed the first hour of smoking.

5. While the turkey is smoking the first hour, make the baste. In a medium-size saucepan, bring the wine just to a boil, lower the heat to medium, and cook for 10 to 15 minutes, until the wine is reduced by a third. Return the heat to high and add the butter and tarragon. Cook for 2 to 3 minutes, until smooth and just a little thick. Lightly season with salt and pepper.

6. After the first hour of smoking, begin basting the turkey with the butter baste every 20 to 30 minutes. Baste with pan juices, too. Remove the cheesecloth and bacon for the last 30 minutes of cooking to allow the bird to brown. Cook until the internal temperature is about 165°F when an instant-read thermometer is inserted into the meaty part of the thigh. Remove from the grill or smoker and let rest for 15 minutes before carving.

7. Combine the pan juices and any remaining baste. Skim the top for excess fat and strain. Reheat until boiling, and serve spooned over the carved meat or on the side. Garnish the platter with extra herbs.

Deck It Out

For something a little different and on the light side, serve one of our Bistro Salads (pages 189 to 192) on the side or Sweet Potato Salad with Ginger-Lime Vinaigrette (page 197). For a wonderful Thanksgiving with a smoky twist, serve this turkey with Grilled Winter Greens with Warm Cranberry-Port Vinaigrette (page 178). While you're smoking the turkey (if there is room) put Smoke-Roasted Root Vegetables with Garlic

and Rosemary (page 198) on the smoker. And make dessert ahead of time! Our choice is Panettone Bread Pudding with Eggnog Custard (page 226).

Take It Easy

Both of our families pitch in and bring sides and desserts for holiday dinners. It's a great way to let the host relax a bit and concentrate on preparing the main entrée, like this smoked turkey. And, oops, on cleaning the house.

Change It Up

• If sage is your favorite flavor with turkey, make sage butter instead.
• If you prefer white wine to red, use Chardonnay in the sauce instead of the Pinot Noir.

Raise a Glass

Since we're cooking with Pinot Noir, we're drinking it, too.

Wood-Grilled Duck Breast Paillards with Raspberry-Thyme Sauce

Duck breasts, whether wild or farm raised, are best when cooked to a perfect medium-rare. The temperature should be about 135°F when an instant-read thermometer is inserted in the thickest part of the meat. When the breast meat rests for 5 minutes, the temperature will rise another 5 degrees, to 140°F. Avoid overcooking, or the duck will get tough. The game flavor pairs well with fruit relishes, so along with the raspberry sauce, serve a fresh fruit relish or salsa like chopped fresh pear, apple, cranberry, or orange mixed with minced garlic, fresh chopped herbs, and finely chopped red onion.

Makes 4 servings

Suggested wood: 1 cup water-soaked pecan, apple, oak, or cherry chips

- **4 boneless, skinless duck breasts**
- **1 tablespoon olive oil**
- **Coarse kosher salt and freshly ground black pepper to taste**

Raspberry-Thyme Sauce:
- **2 tablespoons unsalted butter**
- **2 tablespoons red wine vinegar**
- **1 tablespoon sugar**
- **2 tablespoons chopped fresh thyme**
- **1 cup seedless raspberry jam**
- **¼ cup chicken broth or stock**

1. Prepare a medium-hot fire in your grill. When the fire is hot, add the water-soaked wood chips directly to the charcoal fire, or place in a smoker box to set in a gas grill.
2. Using the rim of a sturdy saucer or a meat mallet, flatten the duck breasts. Pound the breasts, starting in the middle and working your way out to the sides, until the meat is an even ¾-inch thickness. Lightly score the top of the breasts with 2 or 3 slashes (which keeps the meat from curling). Then lightly coat with the olive oil and season with salt and pepper.
3. To make the sauce, melt the butter in a small saucepan. Add the vinegar and sugar and reduce by half over high heat. Add the thyme, jam, and broth, and simmer until thick.
4. Place the duck breasts on the grill directly over the fire. Grill for 3 to 3½ minutes on each side for medium-rare, 140° to 145°F.
5. Place a duck breast on each of four dinner plates and serve with the sauce spooned over the top.

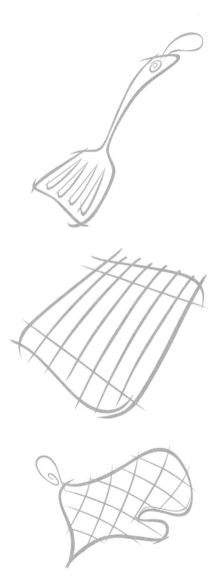

Deck It Out

For a pretty garnish, place a tangle of fresh thyme atop each duck breast and place a few red raspberries on top. Serve Grilled Winter Greens with Warm Cranberry-Port Vinaigrette (page 178) with this dish. You could also make extra vinaigrette and use it as the finishing sauce on the grilled duck breast instead of the raspberry-thyme mixture.

Change It Up

Duck sandwiches are an excellent reason to grill extra. Cold or hot grilled duck sandwiches make a perfect lunch or supper the following day. Buy some good-quality crusty rolls and butter both sides. Place a duck breast, thinly sliced red onion, 1 or 2 slices of crisp bacon, and crumbles of either feta or blue cheese on top. Top with the other piece of the roll. Serve as is, or wrap securely in aluminum foil and warm in a 350°F oven for 10 to 15 minutes. Enjoy!

Raise a Glass

Our choices for libations include our Raspberry Rossini (page 63), Beaujolais, Pinot Noir, or Merlot.

Provençal Grilled Salmon with Rosemary and Mint Aioli

Grilled wild salmon is reason enough to celebrate spring and the beginning of summer. Whether the salmon is from the Pacific Northwest or from Alaska's famous Copper River, it will be a natural deep orange-red color and delectable.

Makes 6 to 8 servings

Rosemary and Mint Aioli:
- **2 large organic egg yolks or equivalent egg substitute**
- **2 anchovy fillets, minced, or 1 tablespoon anchovy paste**
- **2 cloves garlic, minced**
- **1 teaspoon chopped fresh rosemary**
- **1 tablespoon chopped fresh mint**
- **½ teaspoon Worcestershire sauce**
- **½ teaspoon red wine vinegar**
- **1 cup olive oil**
- **1 tablespoon freshly squeezed lemon juice, if needed**
- **Fine kosher or sea salt to taste**
- **Hot pepper sauce of your choice to taste**

- **One 3- to 3½-pound salmon fillet**
- **Olive oil for brushing**
- **1 to 2 tablespoons herbes de Provence**
- **Kosher or sea salt and freshly ground black pepper to taste**

1. Prepare a hot fire in your grill.
2. To make the aioli, whisk the egg yolks together and add the anchovies, garlic, rosemary, mint, Worcestershire sauce, and vinegar. Slowly drizzle in the olive oil while whisking. If the mixture gets too thick, add lemon juice. Season with salt and hot pepper sauce. Mix thoroughly, cover, and chill until ready to serve. (At this point, you may cover and refrigerate for up to 1 day.)
3. Brush the salmon with olive oil, then sprinkle with the herbes de Provence, salt, and pepper. Place on a doubled baking sheet and take out to the grill.
4. Grill the salmon, flesh side down, for 7 to 8 minutes. Using 2 spatulas, loosen the salmon from the grill and carefully roll it over, so the skin side is down. Grill for another 7 to 8 minutes, until it just begins to flake when prodded with a fork. Serve the salmon on a platter, passing the aioli separately.

> *Take care when serving dishes with uncooked eggs to the very young, the very old, or anyone with a compromised immune system. Use organic eggs from a source you trust, or use an egg substitute.*

Deck It Out

Place the salmon on a platter garnished with thin overlapping slices of lemons and limes, and sprigs of fresh rosemary and mint. Serve Smashed Red Potatoes with Green Onions and Cream Cheese (page 194) and Bistro Beet Salad (page 192) alongside.

Change It Up

Smoke the salmon. Brush it with olive oil and season with fresh rosemary, salt, and pepper. Prepare a fire in your smoker using a fruit wood like apple or cherry. Also add fresh sprigs of rosemary to your smoker. Smoke the salmon at 225° to 250°F for 1 to 1½ hours, or until the salmon just begins to flake when prodded with a fork.

Raise a Glass

If you're in the mood for an apéritif, begin this dinner with a bittersweet French Kiss (page 110), followed by a chilled Sauvignon Blanc as the dinner wine.

Razzle-Dazzle: Drizzles

Keep your favorite flavored oils, flavored butters, vinaigrettes, and marinades on hand in the refrigerator for drizzling over finished dishes at a moment's notice. High-quality aged balsamic vinegar makes an elegant drizzle all on its own.

Grilled Halibut with Grilled Red Pepper and Garlic Rouille

A whole grilled fish fillet makes a grand statement when served on a platter with an accompanying sauce, so if you can get a 4-pound fillet, go for it. But you can also make this dish using smaller fillets or steaks. The grilled red pepper and garlic rouille uses two types of red peppers—bell and chile. Grill these and finish the sauce before you put the fish on to grill. Any leftover rouille tastes great on anything grilled (chicken or vegetables or sandwiches), but especially on fish and shellfish.

Makes 8 to 10 servings

Grilled Red Pepper and Garlic Rouille:
- **1 medium-size red bell pepper**
- **3 hot cherry or small red chile peppers**
- **5 large cloves garlic**
- **Olive oil for brushing**
- **2 large organic egg yolks or equivalent egg substitute**
- **1 cup olive oil**
- **1 teaspoon grated lemon zest**
- **Freshly squeezed lemon juice to taste**
- **Kosher or sea salt and freshly ground black pepper to taste**

- **4 pounds halibut fillet, skin removed**
- **Olive oil for brushing**
- **Fine kosher or sea salt and freshly ground black pepper to taste**

1. Prepare a hot fire in your grill. Lightly oil a large grill wok on both sides and set on the hot grill. Oil a grill grate or a perforated grill rack and set on the hot grill.
2. To make the rouille, brush or spray the bell pepper, chile peppers, and garlic cloves with the olive oil, and place in the grill wok. Grill for 10 to 15 minutes, turning occasionally with wooden paddles or grill spatulas, until the peppers have blistered all over and the garlic has softened. When the peppers have cooled slightly, remove the skin, seeds, and stems, using a paring knife. Remove the skin from the garlic. Place the prepared peppers and garlic in a food processor and puree. Add the egg yolks and puree again. With the machine running, drizzle in the olive oil until the rouille has the consistency of a loose mayonnaise. Stir in the lemon zest and add the lemon juice, salt, and pepper. (At this point, you may cover and refrigerate the rouille for up to 2 days. Let it come to room temperature before serving.)
3. To grill the fish, brush on both sides with the olive oil. Place the fish on the prepared grill rack. Grill for 10 minutes per inch of thickness, turning once halfway through. The fillet is

done when it begins to flake when tested with a fork in the thickest part.

4. Remove from the grill, season with salt and pepper, and serve hot with the rouille on the side.

Take care when serving dishes with uncooked eggs to the very young, the very old, or anyone with a compromised immune system. Use organic eggs from a source you trust, or use an egg substitute.

Deck It Out

Serve the fish on a colorful platter, surrounded by grilled lemon slices and marinated red cherry peppers. You may also place the rouille in a squeeze bottle and squeeze dots or a pattern of rouille around the fish, along with green dots of extra-virgin olive oil. Serve a bowl of Cilantro Slaw (page 167) alongside.

Change It Up

Use salmon, blackfish, monkfish, or arctic char in place of the halibut.

Raise a Glass

Serve a crisp Chenin Blanc or Chablis if white wine is your preference, or a light-bodied red like Pinot Noir.

Grilled Swordfish with Papaya Relish and Lemongrass Essence

Lemongrass, traditionally used in Thai cuisine, has a vibrant lemon flavor, and here it lends a lovely Eastern flair to grilled swordfish. If it is not available, try substituting lemon zest, lemon balm, or lemon verbena for similar results. Swordfish is a sturdy, meaty fish, steak-like in texture. It tends to dry out quickly, so grill it for only 6 to 7 minutes per inch of thickness. If swordfish isn't available, substitute dorado, mahi-mahi, or halibut in this recipe.

Makes 8 servings

Suggested wood: ½ cup apple chips, water-soaked, or ½ cup dry apple chips or pellets

Papaya Relish:
- **2 ripe papayas, diced**
- **⅔ cup finely chopped fresh cilantro**
- **6 tablespoons finely diced red onion**
- **1 teaspoon grated fresh ginger**
- **Grated zest and juice of 2 limes**

Lemongrass Essence:
- **¼ cup dry white wine**
- **1 shallot, chopped**
- **2 teaspoons finely chopped lemongrass**
- **1 cup (2 sticks) unsalted butter, cut into cubes**
- **Kosher or sea salt and freshly ground black pepper to taste**

- **Eight 6- to 7-ounce center-cut swordfish steaks**
- **Whole pink peppercorns for garnish**

1. To make the papaya relish, combine all the ingredients in a small bowl. Store tightly covered in the refrigerator until ready to use.

2. To make the lemongrass essence, combine the wine, shallot, and lemongrass in a small saucepan over medium-low heat. Cook until the liquid reduces by two thirds. Whisk in the butter, a cube at a time, and mix well. Strain through a fine-mesh strainer and season with salt and pepper. Set aside.

3. Prepare a hot fire in your grill. Add the soaked wood chips to the hot charcoal fire or the dry chips or pellets to the gas fire. Grill the swordfish over direct heat for 3½ to 4 minutes per side until medium-rare to medium.

4. Spoon the papaya relish onto each dinner plate. Place a swordfish steak in the center of each plate, pour the lemongrass essence over the fish and around the rest of the plate, and garnish each plate with pink peppercorns.

Deck It Out

For a summer lemon feast, serve this swordfish with Green Bean, Tomato, and Goat Cheese Salad with Lemon-Pesto Dressing (page 163) and Queen of Tarts (page 235) with store-bought lemon curd.

Herb-Grilled Seafood Platter

Grilled baby squid (*calamari a la plancha*) is a mainstay in tapas bars, along with grilled
octopus. In our book *Fish & Shellfish, Grilled & Smoked* (The Harvard Common Press,
2002), we prepared baby octopus in a peppered sherry marinade that is oh-so-delicious
that we had to offer a variation here. The great thing about small seafood is how quickly
it grills. So get all of your other dishes ready to serve, grill the fish, and enjoy your party!

Makes about 8 servings

- **Eight 3-ounce salmon fillets**
- **1½ pounds baby squid, cleaned
  (or octopus or cuttlefish pieces)**
- **1½ pounds small fresh sardines,
  smelts, or anchovies, cleaned**

Sherry Marinade:
- **½ cup dry sherry**
- **½ cup extra-virgin olive oil**
- **12 cloves garlic, minced**
- **½ cup finely chopped fresh
  Italian parsley**
- **1 tablespoon smoked Spanish
  paprika**

- **Stalks of your favorite herbs for
  smoking, such as rosemary, mint,
  parsley, or basil**

1. Place the salmon, squid, and sardines in
   separate glass bowls. Combine the marinade
   ingredients and drizzle one third of the
   marinade over each bowl of seafood. Cover
   and marinate in the refrigerator for at least
   1 hour.
2. Meanwhile, prepare a hot fire in your grill. (If
   using charcoal, throw an assortment of fresh
   herbs on the fire right before grilling, if you
   like.) Oil a perforated grill rack on both sides.
3. Grill the salmon fillets first, about 10 minutes
   per inch of thickness, turning once halfway
   through cooking.
4. Grill the squid until lightly charred and opaque,
   1 to 2 minutes per side.
5. Grill the sardines on a perforated grill rack for
   about 3 minutes per side.
6. Place all the seafood on a platter and serve
   tapas style.

Deck It Out ·

This is a pretty dressed-up dish as it is. To
turn it into a tapas party, serve this seafood
platter with an assortment of finger foods

and salads for your own tapas party. We suggest Potato Salad with Aioli (page 195), Grilled Prosciutto-Wrapped Asparagus with Fig Balsamic Vinegar and Shaved Parmesan (page 62), and Planked Portobellos with Fresh Herb Grilling Sauce (page 179). To serve the platter as part of a holiday dinner, we suggest Mediterranean Orange Salad with Pecan-Crusted Goat Cheese (page 176), Oven-Baked Herbed Risotto (page 204), and Golden Raspberry Meringues with Pistachios (page 233).

Change It Up

Sometimes it is difficult to find squid, sardines, and the like. If that's the case, substitute your favorite fish or shellfish, like halibut or catfish for the sardines and shrimp or scallops for the squid.

Raise a Glass

To accompany this party platter, offer red or white sangria (see page 35), sherry, or a Spanish beer.

Razzle-Dazzle: Simple Sprays

Fruit juices like cranberry, orange, limeade, lemonade, and apple add a bit of flavor to meat and poultry on the grill or in the smoker. The secret weapon is a clean empty plastic spray bottle. Fill it up and spray it on!

Grilled Lobster Tails with Béarnaise Butter

When you want a luxurious, intimate dinner, treat you and yours to this grilled feast. Yes, lobster is expensive, but you're worth it. If you're making dinner for two, go ahead and cook the four tails. Save the leftovers to make Grilled Lobster Parcels (page 80).

Makes 4 servings

- **Four 6- to 8-ounce lobster tails, in their shells**

Béarnaise Butter:
- **1 cup (2 sticks) unsalted butter, softened**
- **¼ cup chopped fresh shallots**
- **2 tablespoons white wine vinegar**
- **¼ cup chopped fresh tarragon leaves**
- **½ teaspoon kosher or sea salt**
- **1 teaspoon hot pepper sauce, or to taste**

- **1 loaf artisanal bread, cut in half**

1. Prepare a hot fire in your grill.
2. Carefully cut the lobster tails in half lengthwise and set them on a doubled baking sheet.
3. To make the béarnaise butter, combine all of the ingredients in a medium-size bowl. Spoon 2 to 3 tablespoons into each of four small ramekins to serve with the grilled lobster. (If not using immediately, shape into a roll, wrap in waxed paper or plastic wrap, and refrigerate or freeze.)
4. Butter the bread with the remaining butter.
5. Place the lobster tails on the grill, cut side down, and grill for 2 minutes. Turn the tails and grill shell side down for another 4 to 5 minutes. Move to the indirect side when just done. The shell may char, but the meat should be an opaque white. Grill the bread for 1 to 1½ minutes, cut and buttered side down, until lightly browned.
6. Serve the lobster immediately, with chunks of the crusty grilled bread and a ramekin of béarnaise butter alongside.

Deck It Out

Place the lobster, grilled bread, and ramekins of butter on a beautiful serving platter for an impressive presentation. If you like, sprinkle each plate with gremolata (a mixture of freshly chopped parsley, lemon zest, and

garlic.) A second platter with a bountiful amount of sliced fresh tomatoes is all the accompaniment you need.

Change It Up

• The béarnaise butter is delicious with other shellfish and fish. For a more everyday version of this dish, use monkfish, scallops, or shrimp instead of lobster tails.

• Instead of direct grilling, you can also place the fish or shellfish of your choice on a presoaked plank with a shallow carved center. Place several tablespoons of the butter atop the fish, and cook on the indirect side of a hot grill with the lid closed for 20 to 30 minutes, or until the fish is opaque.

Raise a Glass

Oooh, what drink choices you have. Serve something sparkling, or a Chardonnay, Semillon, or even a Muscadet with this meal.

Razzle-Dazzle: Juice Glasses

Want to start another collection of glasses? Try finding old-fashioned juice glasses and use them for serving inexpensive wine. It's very Italian or South of France, where many villagers traditionally use their own local glassware, usually unstemmed, when drinking the local wine. And this is a great way to serve wine to perambulating guests, who might be putting their glasses down who-knows-where.

Red, White, and Blue:
An All-American Barbecue

Whether your favorite holiday for a big barbecue bash is Memorial Day, the Fourth of July, or Labor Day, this menu is for you. It will change a bit with choosing the veggies that are at their peak, so feel free to mix and match. This is (like all of our menus) a blueprint to help you get started. The biggest decision you'll have is whether this will take place at your home by the lake, or your condo in the mountains, or oh, we almost forgot, your cottage by the sea. Or maybe this is simply in your own backyard! After you decide, think about how much grill and smoker space you have and in what order you will precook or grill most of the dishes.

Setting the Scene
Decorate with American flags, red, white, and blue banners, bouquets of red and white flowers tied with blue ribbons, themed paper goods, and plastic tumblers in red and blue. Don't forget the sparklers (as in fireworks) . . . you get the picture?

Making Beautiful Music
Aaron Copland is a perfect music choice for Fourth of July festivities. Other good music choices include the Boston Pops, John Philip Sousa, Willie Nelson, John Mellencamp, and Bruce Springsteen.

Perfect Partners
To make it easier on you as the host (BBQ Queens want to have fun, too), fill great big tubs with plenty of ice to make a help-yourself bar. Have one tub filled with bottled water, lemonade, and soft drinks. The other tub will keep the beer and wine chilled.

Choose from Among These Dishes

Your favorite deviled eggs

Vineyard Smoked Chicken *Amogio* (page 132)

Zinfandel-Glazed Baby Back Ribs with a Kiss of Smoke (page 122)

Corn Husk–Wrapped Shrimp with Grilled Corn (page 156)

Potato Salad with Aioli (page 195)

Your favorite baked beans

Grilled Cornmeal-Crusted Green Tomatoes with Shrimp Rémoulade (page 190)

Heirloom Tomato Bowl with Lemon and Feta (page 186)

Grilled Corn with a Butter for Every Occasion (page 164)

Blue Cheese Coleslaw (page 173)

Cilantro Slaw (page 167)

Vanilla Cupcakes with White Chocolate–Cream Cheese Frosting (page 218)

Choco-licious Sheet Cake (page 223)

Fresh strawberries and blueberries over premium vanilla ice cream

Corn Husk-Wrapped Shrimp with Grilled Corn

Serve this recipe in the summer, when the corn is sweet and the husks are tender and supple. The husks infuse the shrimp with a fragrant aroma. For a minimalist approach, just drizzle a bit of olive oil and salt and pepper over the shrimp. The beautiful pink shrimp contrasts nicely against the green husk wrapper. It's a fun and novel company dish because it's like opening a present. The shrimp can be assembled in the corn husks and refrigerated for several hours so that when it's time to grill, the prep work has already been done. That leaves you plenty of time to enjoy a cool drink before grilling and dining alfresco.

Makes 6 servings

- **6 ears of corn, with the husks on**
- **½ cup (1 stick) unsalted butter**
- **⅔ cup chopped fresh chives or fresh Italian parsley**
- **2 pounds large shrimp, peeled and deveined**
- **Kosher or sea salt and freshly ground black pepper to taste**
- **Olive oil for brushing**

1. Prepare a hot indirect fire in your grill.
2. Peel back the corn husks and remove the silk on all 6 ears of corn. Break off the corn cob at the base, leaving the husk attached to the stem. Set the cleaned ears of corn aside.
3. Melt the butter in a small saucepan and add the chives. Place the shrimp in a large bowl. Pour the chive butter over the shrimp and toss to coat.
4. Fold back a few of the leaves of each corn husk and place ⅓ pound shrimp in each husk. Season with salt and pepper. Close the husks and tie together with strips of the corn husk or kitchen twine. (You may do this earlier in the day and refrigerate the packets until ready to grill.)
5. Brush the ears of corn with olive oil and season with salt and pepper. Place everything on a doubled baking sheet and carry out to the grill.
6. Place the shrimp in corn husks on the grill directly over the fire, and grill for 5 minutes. Then move to the indirect side of the grill. Place the ears of corn directly over the fire to lightly char them, turning several times, for

2 to 3 minutes. Move the corn to the indirect side of grill, also, and continue to cook for another 5 minutes with the grill lid closed.

7. Serve the shrimp packets by folding back the top of the corn husks to display the shrimp inside, with an ear of grilled corn on the side.

Deck It Out ·····················

Add a duo of dipping sauces for the shrimp, like your favorite store-bought or homemade cocktail sauce along with Garlic and Horseradish Mayonnaise: mix together 1 cup mayonnaise, 1 minced garlic clove, 1 tablespoon or more prepared horseradish, and a spritz of lemon juice. Offer a platter of fresh sliced heirloom tomatoes or Grilled Cornmeal-Crusted Green Tomatoes with Shrimp Rémoulade (page 190) on the side to complete the meal.

Take It Easy ·····················

Make a cool meal for a hot day and entertain while hardly cooking a thing the day of the party. Smoke or grill the shrimp packets and the corn a day ahead. Refrigerate the packets on a baking sheet covered with plastic wrap. Make a relish from the grilled corn: Cut the kernels off the cobs and place in a bowl. Add 1 chopped red onion, 1 chopped red bell pepper, and the juice from 1 lemon. When ready to serve, slice 4 or 5 beefsteak tomatoes and arrange on a platter. Spoon the relish down the center and drizzle with extra-virgin olive oil. Serve with the shrimp packets, crusty bread, and a bottle of chilled Sauvignon Blanc.

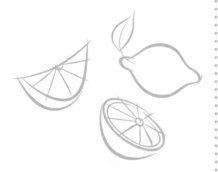

Change It Up

- Substitute scallops, catfish, cod, haddock, salmon, or halibut for the shrimp.
- The seafood-stuffed corn husks are easy to smoke, too. Simply prepare a smoker with an aromatic wood like mesquite, oak, or fruit wood, and smoke the packets at 225°F for 35 to 45 minutes.

Raise a Glass

Choose a lager-style beer on ice with a wedge of lime, or a dry to semisweet white wine, like a Sauvignon Blanc or Riesling.

Grilled Shrimp and Baby Bok Choy with Ginger-Soy Butter Sauce

In this simple yet sophisticated entrée, the flavors and colors blend together so well that you'll break out another bottle of Chardonnay to celebrate! The sauce is really a version of the French *beurre blanc*, so divine. Use the biggest shrimp you can find here, and if you can find Asian prawns, which are more similar to lobster, use those. Scallops would also be delicious with this.

Makes 4 servings

Ginger-Soy Butter Sauce:
- **1½ cups dry white wine, such as Chardonnay**
- **2 tablespoons rice wine vinegar**
- **2 tablespoons grated fresh ginger**
- **2 large shallots, minced**
- **1 cup (2 sticks) unsalted butter, chilled and cut into cubes**
- **1 tablespoon soy sauce**
- **½ teaspoon toasted sesame oil**

1. To make the sauce, bring the wine, rice wine vinegar, ginger, and shallots to a boil in a saucepan over high heat and reduce until only 2 tablespoons of liquid remain, 7 to 10 minutes. Remove from the heat and whisk in the butter, a cube at a time, until the sauce has emulsified. (If it starts to separate, whisk in an ice cube and keep whisking until the sauce comes back together.) Whisk in the soy sauce and sesame oil and set aside.
2. Prepare a hot fire in your grill.
3. Place the shrimp and baby bok choy on a doubled baking sheet to take out to the grill.

- **16 jumbo shrimp, rinsed and patted dry**
- **4 to 6 heads baby bok choy, rinsed, patted dry, ends trimmed, and sliced in half lengthwise**
- **Olive oil for brushing**
- **Kosher or sea salt and freshly ground black pepper to taste**

Brush the shrimp and bok choy with olive oil on both sides, and season with salt and pepper.

4. Grill the shrimp for about 3 minutes before turning. If the shrimp stick, cook them a little longer, until they turn easily. After turning, grill long enough to heat through, about 2 minutes. Grill the baby bok choy on the cut side for 1 to 2 minutes or until the exterior has browned and the interior is still crisp. To serve, arrange a quarter of the bok choy on each of 4 plates, top with 4 shrimp, and spoon the sauce over all.

Deck It Out

Garnish, if you like, with finely minced red and yellow bell pepper and chive stems. Serve with Asian-Style Fruit Slaw (page 172) or Asian Noodles (page 199).

Change It Up

Plank the shrimp, drizzled with half the sauce, on a wooden oven plank (because it has a deeper well to hold the butter). To do this, soak the oven plank in water for at least 30 minutes. Prepare a hot, indirect fire in your grill (heat on one side, no heat on the other). Arrange the shrimp on the plank and drizzle with the butter. Place the plank on the unheated side of the grill, close the lid, and cook for 30 to 45 minutes, or until the shrimp are opaque and firm to the touch. During the last 15 minutes, steam the baby bok choy. To serve, arrange the shrimp and the remaining butter on the bok choy and garnish with diced bell pepper.

Raise a Glass

Since we're cooking with Chardonnay, that's what we're drinking.

Sides that Go Great with Those Entrées

We found our inspiration for the recipes in this chapter from Greek tavernas, French bistros, Asian noodle shops, and good old American kitchens. From a variety of simple slaws and fresh vegetable salads to casseroles and gratins and, of course, grilled vegetables, our barbecue-bash sides offer something for everyone. Some are grilled and some are not (some don't even have to be cooked), giving you plenty of flexibility.

The side dishes we've created for this chapter are all versatile enough to complement several different entrées. By all means, mix and match sides and entrées according to your and your guests' tastes, and make as few or as many sides as you like, depending on how many guests you're feeding and how fancy a spread you want to lay out.

Many of these side dishes have a certain magical phrase in their description: "Can be made ahead of time." This is always music to our ears, and we're betting that you will feel the same way. Making side dishes ahead of time allows us all precious extra minutes to make ourselves look stylish before show time.

Green Bean, Tomato, and Goat Cheese Salad with Lemon-Pesto Dressing

One of our secret "frozen assets" is packages of frozen French green beans or *haricots verts*. "Frozen vegetables?" you might sniff. "In the case of these tiny green beans, yes," we reply. They cook quickly to a beautiful and uniform green, and taste nearly as good as fresh. This recipe can easily be increased to serve more people.

Makes 4 servings

Lemon-Pesto Dressing:
- ½ cup prepared basil pesto
- 2 tablespoons freshly squeezed lemon juice
- ¼ cup olive oil
- Kosher or sea salt and freshly ground black pepper to taste

- 12 ounces fresh or frozen tiny French green beans or *haricots verts*
- 8 ounces ripe Roma tomatoes, sliced on the diagonal
- 4 ounces fresh goat cheese

1. To make the dressing, whisk all the ingredients together in a bowl and set aside.
2. Bring a large pot of water to a boil. Plunge the beans in and cook for 2 minutes. Drain the beans in a colander, then transfer the hot beans to a bowl of ice water. (This will keep their color bright.) Drain again and pat dry.
3. In a large mixing bowl, toss the beans with half the dressing. Add the tomatoes and gently toss with the remainder of the dressing. Spoon the salad onto a serving platter and crumble the goat cheese on top. Serve at room temperature.

Deck It Out

For a slightly more formal presentation, arrange the beans in a line down the platter, shingle the tomatoes on top of the beans, then drizzle with dressing and crumble the goat cheese over the tomatoes.

Take It Easy

Make like a BBQ Queen and keep bags of frozen *haricots verts* or baby green beans on hand for simple yet sophisticated side dishes anytime.

Change It Up ·

- Use Mortar and Pestle Vinaigrette (page 170) instead of the Lemon-Pesto Dressing.
- Use small yellow teardrop or other heirloom tomatoes in place of the Romas.

Grilled Corn with a Butter for Every Occasion

When corn is sweet and fresh it simply must be eaten. Sometimes it is so wonderful that it barely needs to be cooked. When there is an abundance of corn, it begs to be prepared with just a bit of a twist. Instead of dropping the ears in a pot of boiling water (never for more than 6 minutes), try grilling or smoking them in their husks with a flavored butter. What could be better for a simple meal with family and friends than grilled shrimp with grilled or smoked corn, rustic bread, and a flavored butter (or two or three. . .)?

Makes 12 servings, or maybe just 6

- **12 ears of fresh, tender, sweet corn in season, in the husk**
- **½ cup flavored butter of your choice (see page 166)**

1. Pull back the husks from each ear and remove the corn silk. Pull the husks back over the corn and place in a large bowl or bucket of cold water. Soak for 30 minutes while you prepare your fire and one or more of the butters.
2. Prepare a hot fire in your grill.
3. Remove the corn from the water and drain. Slightly open the husks and brush some of the softened flavored butter on the corn kernels. Close the husks and tie the ends with strips of the corn husk or kitchen twine.
4. Place the ears of corn directly over the fire and grill for 6 to 8 minutes, turning with tongs as the husks begin to brown. If the husks get too charred, move the ears to the indirect side of the grill and finish grilling with the lid closed for a few minutes more. The corn is tender and fresh to begin with, so you only need to char the husks a bit, warm the corn kernels, and

melt the butter. Let diners pull back their own husks so that the corn stays nice and warm. Serve with additional flavored butter.

Change It Up

To smoke the corn, prepare a fire in your smoker. Place water-soaked wood chips (oak, maple, pecan, or fruit) or grapevines in the smoker according to the manufacturer's directions. Follow steps 1 and 3 above to prepare the ears of corn. Place the corn in the smoker and smoke at 225° to 250°F for about 1 hour.

Razzle-Dazzle: Grill the Whole Thing

Sometimes veggies on the grill just seem too time-consuming, with all that slicing and dicing. So think big! Grill the whole vegetable with the skin on for a dramatic presentation. Whole tomatoes, whole onions in their skins, whole potatoes, whole summer squash, whole peppers, and so on. The larger and denser, the more time it will take (so you might want to microwave a big baking potato or yam for a couple of minutes first). A whole tomato will get done quickly if you're mainly warming it. Vegetables like zucchini are wonderful with lots of char. Grill them like we do for Blistered Baby Pattypans and Red Onion (page 187). Once you try it a couple of times, it will be very easy to eyeball when the vegetables are done.

A Butter for Every Occasion

Flavored butters can add that touch of panache to a dish like nothing else. They're so easy to make and, what's even better, can be *made ahead*—words that thrill any dinner preparer or party giver. Make up the butter, then spoon it into ramekins or roll it into a log on waxed paper or plastic wrap. Keep it in the refrigerator for up to 1 week or in the freezer for several months. Just be sure to label and date the packages so you know what you're pulling out of the freezer. Make one of these festive butters, or come up with your own signature blend.

Begin with ½ cup (1 stick) softened unsalted butter. Then mix in the following for different flavored butters.

Chipotle Butter: Add 1 tablespoon chipotle chile powder.

Ancho Butter: Add 1 tablespoon ancho chile powder.

BBQ Rub Butter: Add 1 tablespoon of your favorite dry barbecue rub or seasoning.

Lemon-Garlic Butter: Add 2 minced cloves garlic and the grated zest of 1 lemon.

Fresh Herb Butter: Add 1, 2, or 3 tablespoons of the finely chopped fresh herb of your choice, or a medley of fresh herbs, such as thyme, Italian parsley, tarragon, and rosemary, and 1 teaspoon fresh lemon juice.

Caper Butter: Add 1 tablespoon or more caper paste or capers smashed with a fork.

Olive Butter: Add 1 tablespoon or more olive paste.

Anchovy Butter: Add 1 tablespoon or more anchovy paste.

Sun-Dried Tomato Butter: Add 1 tablespoon or more sun-dried tomato paste.

Maggi Butter: Add 1 tablespoon Maggi Liquid Seasoning, 1 tablespoon chopped fresh Italian parsley, and ¼ teaspoon dry mustard.

Onion Butter: Add 6 finely chopped green onions, 1 teaspoon Worcestershire sauce, and ¼ teaspoon dry mustard.

Red Pepper Butter: Add 2 tablespoons or more finely chopped red bell pepper (fire-roasted, smoked, grilled, or raw).

Blue Cheese Butter: Add 3 tablespoons crumbled blue cheese.

Feta Butter: Add 3 tablespoons crumbled feta cheese.

Goat Cheese Butter: Add 3 tablespoons softened goat cheese.

Cilantro Slaw

Adapt this slaw by simply changing the fresh herb and/or chile that you use. We also like Italian parsley, chives, and basil. Choose jalapeño or banana peppers if you like a mildly hot flavor. Go for a habanero only if you dare!

Makes about 8 servings

- **1 small red onion, thinly sliced**
- **1 small chile, minced**
- **Grated zest of 1 lime**
- **Juice of 2 limes**
- **One 10-ounce package finely shredded cabbage or coleslaw mix**
- **½ cup chopped fresh cilantro leaves**
- **Extra-virgin olive oil for drizzling**
- **Kosher or sea salt and freshly ground black pepper to taste**

1. Combine the onion, chile, lime zest, and lime juice in a small bowl and toss to coat. Refrigerate until ready to use.
2. When ready to serve, place the shredded cabbage and cilantro in a large serving bowl. Add the onion mixture. Drizzle with olive oil to just moisten, season with salt and pepper, and stir to combine all. Serve immediately.

Razzle-Dazzle: Chop! Chop! Chop!

Sprinkle a savory finishing touch on a plate or platter of food with chopped fresh herbs. For something even more colorful, sprinkle finely diced bell peppers in a trio of colors like red, yellow, and purple. An oh-so-French way to finish off the plate is with a persillade, a flavorful mixture of chopped parsley and garlic. The Italian version, called gremolata, combines chopped parsley, garlic, and lemon zest.

Lemongrass and Sugarcane:
A Barefoot Summer
Poolside Bash

Fun in the sun doesn't have to translate into hot dogs, burgers, and potato salad. When you want to entertain around the water, there are other, more creative ways to be carefree. Start with our Asian-inspired menu. Try to keep to foods that your guests can eat with their fingers or just a fork. If you like, you can simply skewer chunks of swordfish or salmon on spikes of lemongrass, then grill and serve with papaya relish.

Setting the Scene
Take a tropical print as your cue for table toppers, and serve foods on real or ceramic banana leaves, woven rattan or sea grass trays, and bamboo bowls and cutting boards. Set out pots of tropical or leafy green plants to suggest the tropics, and maybe some battery-operated fans to create a gentle "tropical" breeze. . . .

Making Beautiful Music
Go retro with the soundtrack to *South Pacific*, nouveau with something from Enya, or classic with gamelan music.

Perfect Partners
Ice down bottles of Tsingtao beer, Sauvignon Blanc, or Gewürztraminer. Serve big pitchers of lemonade or limeade with fresh sugarcane stalks or stems of lemongrass as swizzle sticks. And remember: On a really hot day, you can never have too much ice.

Choose from Among These Dishes

Grilled Pork Tenderloin with Peanut Butter Dipping Sauce and Toasted
  Sesame Seeds (page 58)

Grilled Lamb Chops with Thai Chili-Peanut Dipping Sauce (page 53)

Thai Grilled Flank Steak (page 50), thinly sliced (omit the lettuce cups)

Grilled Swordfish with Papaya Relish and Lemongrass Essence (page 149)

Asian Noodles (page 199)

Sweet Potato Salad with Ginger-Lime Vinaigrette (page 197)

Cilantro Slaw (page 167)

Asian-Style Fruit Slaw (page 172)

Planked Stone Fruit with Butter-Rum Glaze (page 213)

Iced Pineapple Rum 'n' Cream (see Change It Up, page 230)

The BBQ Queens' Knife-and-Fork Grilled Vegetable Salad

With a variety of grilled vegetables arranged colorfully on a plate, this salad seems more like an entrée since you eat it with a knife and fork. It's a version of a salad we developed for *Food & Wine* magazine. You'll be amazed at how much flavor just a tablespoon of the vinaigrette provides when you drizzle it over the salad. If you don't have a mortar and pestle, press the garlic clove into a bowl, then mash it to a paste with the salt using a fork. Stir in the remaining ingredients. Accompany this big-flavor dish with a slice of artisanal bread, lightly brushed with olive oil and grilled—and a glass of Pinot Noir. As a side dish, this goes well with a grilled steak or fish fillet. Leftovers make delicious sandwich fillings the next day.

Makes 4 servings

- **1 large red or Spanish onion, cut into ½-inch-thick slices**
- **2 small eggplant, trimmed and cut lengthwise into ½-inch-thick slices**
- **2 small zucchini, trimmed and cut lengthwise into ½-inch-thick slices**
- **2 small yellow squash, trimmed and cut lengthwise into ½-inch-thick slices**
- **1 medium-size red bell pepper**
- **1 medium-size yellow bell pepper**
- **2 large heads romaine lettuce, cut into quarters**
- **Olive oil for brushing**
- **Fine kosher or sea salt and freshly ground black pepper to taste**

Mortar and Pestle Vinaigrette:
- **1 large clove garlic**
- **1 teaspoon coarse kosher or sea salt**

1. Prepare a hot fire in your grill. Soak 3 or 4 wooden skewers in water for 30 minutes.
2. Thread the skewers with the onion slices so that they look like large lollipops. Brush the skewered onion slices, the eggplant, zucchini, and yellow squash slices, the bell peppers, and the romaine quarters with olive oil and season with salt and pepper. Place on a large tray or baking sheet to take out to the grill.
3. Grill the vegetables in succession. Grill the eggplant, zucchini, and yellow squash slices for 3 to 4 minutes per side, turning with grill tongs to get good grill marks. Grill the bell peppers for 3 to 4 minutes per side, turning several times, until blackened all over. Grill the onion slices for 4 to 5 minutes per side, turning once. Grill the romaine quarters for 1 to 2 minutes per side, turning as soon as the greens begin to char. When each vegetable is done, transfer it to the tray. Bring everything indoors.
4. To make the vinaigrette, crush the garlic with the salt in a mortar and pestle and turn the pestle to mash the garlic and salt into a paste.

- **1 tablespoon freshly squeezed lemon juice**
- **3 tablespoons extra-virgin olive oil**

- **¼ cup toasted pine nuts**
- **4 ounces goat cheese**

Using the pestle, stir in the lemon juice, then the olive oil, until well blended. Set aside.

5. With a paring knife, cut off the stem of each grilled pepper, then slice in half lengthwise and remove the seeds. Using a scraping motion with your knife, remove the charred skin from each pepper, then cut into wide strips. Arrange the grilled vegetables on four plates, removing the onions from the skewers. Drizzle each plate with 1 tablespoon of the vinaigrette, then sprinkle with the toasted pine nuts. Crumble some goat cheese on each salad and serve.

Change It Up ···················

To make an awesome pasta salad out of this, chop the vegetables after you have grilled them. Cook 12 ounces of fusilli, penne, or orecchiette until *al dente*. Drain, then toss with the grilled vegetables and the vinaigrette in a large serving bowl. Top with the toasted pine nuts and crumbled goat cheese. Or instead of the vinaigrette, toss the pasta and vegetables with aioli from Potato Salad with Aioli (page 195), topping the salad with pine nuts (and skipping the goat cheese).

Asian-Style Fruit Slaw

If nectarines are not top quality, substitute canned mandarin oranges that you have drained, then refreshed in ice-cold water to get rid of the canned taste. Shredded radishes would be a nice addition to this slaw, too.

Makes 14 to 16 servings

- ¼ cup vegetable oil
- ¼ cup rice vinegar
- 1 tablespoon finely minced fresh ginger
- 1 tablespoon soy sauce
- One 10-ounce package green cabbage coleslaw mix
- One 10-ounce package red cabbage coleslaw mix
- 2 fresh nectarines, sliced into thin wedges
- ½ cup green onions sliced on the diagonal
- ½ cup coarsely chopped cashews
- ⅓ cup chopped fresh cilantro leaves
- ¼ cup finely slivered candied ginger

1. To make the dressing, combine the vegetable oil, vinegar, fresh ginger, and soy sauce in a glass jar with a tight-fitting lid. Shake to blend and refrigerate until ready to use.
2. In a large serving bowl, combine the green and red cabbages, nectarines, green onions, cashews, cilantro, and candied ginger. Refrigerate until ready to serve.
3. Toss the slaw with the dressing and serve immediately.

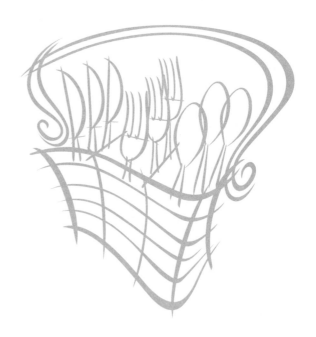

Blue Cheese Coleslaw

We're Midwest girls, and we prefer Maytag blue cheese from Newton, Iowa, for its mellow, creamy blue cheese bite. But try whatever kind you like best. Shredded apple or radish is also nice in this, and crumbled crisp bacon is a welcome addition.

Makes 10 to 12 servings

- **6 tablespoons vegetable oil**
- **3 tablespoons cider vinegar**
- **2 teaspoons sugar**
- **½ teaspoon garlic salt**
- **One 16-ounce package coleslaw mix**
- **8 green onions, chopped**
- **4 ounces blue cheese, crumbled**
- **⅓ cup toasted walnuts or pecans**

1. To make the dressing, combine the vegetable oil, vinegar, sugar, and garlic salt in a glass jar with a tight-fitting lid. Shake to blend and refrigerate until ready to use.
2. In a large serving bowl, combine the coleslaw mix, green onions, blue cheese, and walnuts. Refrigerate until ready to serve.
3. Toss the slaw with the dressing and serve immediately.

Quick Coleslaws

We love the convenience of packaged slaw. Even though the best-case scenario for slaw involves slicing or shredding fresh napa cabbage and carrots, sometimes that extra prep time just isn't there. As BBQ Queens, we embrace convenience foods that are good and fresh and make sense. In *Weeknight Grilling with the BBQ Queens* (The Harvard Common Press, 2006), one of our mantras is "Let the salad bar be your sous chef." In the same vein, make good-quality convenience foods your sous chef, too. There are many different varieties of packaged slaw, from classic slaw with the green (looks more like white to us) cabbage, a tiny bit of red, and shredded carrots, to all–red cabbage slaw, all–green cabbage slaw, and even the thinnest sliced angel-hair slaw. Also, there is no rule that says slaw has to be made with cabbage (or is there?). Try broccoli slaw, carrot slaw, finely sliced or shredded radish slaw, and on and on. . . . If you find any of these packaged, by all means use them to make your own signature slaw.

How much slaw makes a serving? About 1 cup per person, or 1½ to 2 ounces, should suffice.

If you are entertaining in warm weather, when regular salad greens won't hold up on a buffet, think slaw. Have the slaw and other goodies in a serving bowl, covered with plastic wrap, in the refrigerator. Keep the dressing ready, so all you have to do is dress the slaw at the last minute and set it out for everyone to enjoy.

Grilled Pink Grapefruit and Orange Salad with Fresh Avocado

For a brunch gathering or a casual meal of grilled fish or shellfish, this easy, refreshing, and colorful salad looks and tastes great. Grilling the citrus fruit adds just a touch of caramelization and makes the fruit even juicier. And the aroma? Fabulous!

Makes 8 servings

Lemon-Pepper Dressing:
- **3 tablespoons freshly squeezed lemon juice**
- **1 tablespoon clover honey**
- **½ cup olive oil**
- **Kosher or sea salt and freshly ground black pepper to taste**

- **3 pink grapefruit**
- **3 large oranges**
- **Olive oil for brushing**
- **One ripe but firm avocado, pitted, peeled, and thinly sliced**

1. Prepare a hot fire in your grill.
2. To make the dressing, whisk all the ingredients together in a small bowl; set aside.
3. Trim the ends off the fruit (but do not peel), then slice into ½-inch-thick slices. Brush the slices with olive oil and grill for 1 minute on each side, or until slightly browned. Arrange the slices on a platter and top with the avocado. Pour the dressing over all and serve immediately.

Deck It Out ·····················
Arrange the grapefruit slices around the rim of the platter, then fill in the center area with the orange slices. Fan the avocado slices down the center.

Change It Up ·····················
This is also lovely made with ungrilled fruit. Simply peel, seed, and slice the grapefruit and oranges and proceed.

Grilled Greek Taverna Salad

As a side dish to serve with grilled chicken, fish, or steak or as a summery meal on its own, we love this version of the traditional Greek salad. The romaine lettuce and red onion sizzle on the grill for extra flavor. Make this when summer tomatoes are at their peak.

Makes 6 to 8 servings

Greek Vinaigrette:
- ¼ cup extra-virgin olive oil
- 1 tablespoon red wine vinegar
- 1 tablespoon freshly squeezed lemon juice
- 2 cloves garlic, minced
- 1 teaspoon dried oregano
- Kosher or sea salt and freshly ground black pepper to taste

- 2 wooden skewers, soaked in water for 30 minutes
- 1 large red onion, cut into 1-inch-thick slices
- 2 hearts of romaine lettuce
- Olive oil for brushing
- 3 small cucumbers, diced
- 3 medium-size tomatoes, diced
- 4 ounces feta cheese, crumbled
- ½ cup oil- or brine-cured kalamata olives, pitted

1. To make the vinaigrette, whisk all the ingredients together in a small bowl. Set aside.
2. Prepare a hot fire in your grill.
3. Thread the skewers with the onion slices so that they look like large lollipops. Cut the hearts of romaine in half lengthwise. Brush the onion slices and the romaine halves with olive oil. Grill the onion slices for about 5 minutes per side, or until blistered. Grill the romaine, cut side down, for 1 to 2 minutes, or until the lettuce has browned.
4. Chop the romaine and onion and arrange on a serving platter. Top with the cucumbers, tomatoes, feta, and olives. Drizzle the dressing over the top and serve.

Deck It Out

Strew sprigs of fresh oregano around the platter for garnish.

Take It Easy

Okay! Okay! We know this is a grill book, but this recipe is a winner even if you just want to toss all the ingredients together raw. Then it would be an Ungrilled Greek Taverna Salad.

Mediterranean Orange Salad with Pecan-Crusted Goat Cheese

Fresh oranges and smoky goat cheese marry well in this salad. Use blood oranges or tangerines and their zest when they are in season. Serve this salad with the entrée of your choice; it pairs especially well with poultry, pork, and game.

Makes 4 servings

Orange Zest Dressing:
- **Grated zest of 1 orange (about 1½ tablespoons)**
- **⅓ cup white wine vinegar**
- **⅔ cup vegetable oil**
- **2 cloves garlic**
- **1 teaspoon kosher or sea salt**
- **4 teaspoons sugar**

- **Four 1½-ounce slices soft goat cheese**
- **Olive oil for drizzling**
- **¼ cup chopped toasted pecans or hazelnuts**
- **1 head red-leaf lettuce, torn into bite-size pieces**
- **2 oranges, peeled, pith removed, and segmented**
- **16 kalamata olives, pitted**

1. To make the dressing, combine all of the ingredients in a glass jar with a tight-fitting lid. Shake to blend and refrigerate until ready to use (up to several days).
2. Place the goat cheese slices on a small baking sheet. Drizzle with olive oil, lightly brushing to coat evenly. Sprinkle the pecans on top of the cheese. Bake, grill over an indirect fire, or smoke at about 250°F to gently warm the cheese. Avoid too high heat or the rounds will melt. (To stovetop-smoke: place 1 tablespoon Cameron pecan smoking chips in the bottom of the smoker. Place the heat deflector and the rack in the smoker. Set an aluminum pan filled with ice in the smoker. Set the cheese on another aluminum pan and place on top of the ice. This will keep the cheese from melting. Heat the smoker over medium-high heat until wisps of smoke appear. Lower the heat to medium and smoke for 5 to 7 minutes. Let rest for 2 or 3 minutes.)
3. Arrange the lettuce on four salad plates. Place one quarter of the orange segments and four of the olives on each plate. Place the warm goat cheese on top of each salad. Drizzle with the dressing and serve immediately.

Deck It Out

In the winter, sprinkle pomegranate seeds over the dish for a final jewel-like garnish. In the summer, sprinkle grilled corn kernels and chopped fresh chives and/or fresh basil leaves over all for a grand and flavorful finish.

Change It Up

Try lemon or lime zest in the salad dressing and use grapefruit segments for a totally different salad. You may also use canned mandarin orange segments. Refresh them in ice-cold water to get rid of the canned flavor.

Razzle-Dazzle: Whole Onions

Whole grilled onions are impressive, attractive, easy, inexpensive, and oh-so-good-for-you. Leave the outer skin of the onion intact and char the onion to a deep, burnished black color. When ready to serve, the outer skin slides off and the inner onion is sweet and caramelized. Or try another variation: Cook unpeeled whole onions for 40 to 50 minutes, rolling them around on a hot grill until well charred. Check to see that they are tender when pierced with a knife. Sit them upright on a serving platter. When they're cool enough to handle, cut a 2-inch-deep X in the top of the onion. Peel back the leaves and some of the onion layers. Sprinkle a little bit of brown sugar, salt, and pepper over the onion. Top with a pat of butter and serve hot.

Grilled Winter Greens with Warm Cranberry-Port Vinaigrette

When fresh tomatoes are out of season and bitter greens like frisée are in, turn to this salad. We love greens on the grill, a technique that can turn an "Isn't this nice?" salad into an "I want seconds!" one. A whole head of frisée looks like the yarn end of a mop when it is spread out, while a head of romaine is cylindrical, but either type of green works in this recipe. Both grill to perfection and taste great with the tangy, rose-colored vinaigrette.

Makes 8 servings

- **8 small heads frisée or 4 large heads romaine lettuce**
- **Olive oil for brushing**
- **Kosher or sea salt and freshly ground black pepper to taste**

Warm Cranberry-Port Vinaigrette:
- **1 cup fresh cranberries**
- **½ cup sugar**
- **¼ cup cider vinegar**
- **¼ cup orange juice**
- **¼ cup vegetable oil**
- **½ teaspoon red pepper flakes**
- **½ teaspoon ground cinnamon**
- **½ teaspoon garlic salt**
- **2 tablespoons port, brandy, Cognac, or bourbon**

1. Prepare a medium-hot fire in your grill.
2. Trim the stem end of the frisée or cut the romaine in quarters. Brush the open end of the heads of frisée or the cut sides of romaine with olive oil, then sprinkle with salt and pepper. Place the greens on a baking sheet to take out to the grill.
3. To make the vinaigrette, bring the cranberries, sugar, and vinegar to a boil in a medium-size saucepan over medium-high heat and cook until the cranberries pop, 5 to 7 minutes. Stir in all of the remaining ingredients and set aside.
4. Grill the greens on the oiled sides for about 2 minutes, or until browned. Serve the warm greens on salad plates, grilled side up and drizzled with the vinaigrette.

Deck It Out

A little smoked goat cheese crumbled over the top would be perfection.

Take It Easy

For a time-saving vinaigrette, use a good-quality cranberry compote—about 2 cups—heated in a saucepan with the port. Thin with a little cider vinegar if necessary.

Planked Portobellos with Fresh Herb Grilling Sauce

A tip for getting maximum wood flavor when cooking on a plank is to have as much of the food touching the plank as possible. If you are using a sauce or prepared butter on planked foods, we prefer the thicker baking planks that are slightly hollowed out. The food sits in the hollow and sauce can be applied without its running off the sides of a flat plank. Whether you buy whole portobellos and slice them, or buy presliced, make sure the flesh is firm and whitish. If the mushroom looks shriveled, buy a different variety of mushroom that is nice and fresh, and brush this lovely herb sauce on it.

Makes 4 servings

Suggested wood: 1 cedar or oak grilling plank, soaked in water for at least 30 minutes

Fresh Herb Grilling Sauce:
- **2 cups mixed finely chopped fresh herbs (Italian parsley, mint, basil, rosemary, thyme, oregano, etc.)**
- **2 cloves garlic, minced**
- **Grated zest and juice of 1 lemon**
- **¾ cup extra-virgin olive oil**
- **Hot pepper sauce to taste**
- **Kosher or sea salt and freshly ground black pepper to taste**

- **2 large, firm portobello mushrooms, stems trimmed, thickly sliced**
- **1 loaf of rustic bread, sliced, for sopping the sauce**

1. Combine all of the sauce ingredients in a large glass jar with a tight-fitting lid. Shake to combine. The sauce will keep in the refrigerator for up to 3 days.
2. Prepare a medium-hot fire on one side of the grill. (The heat may need to be increased while planking if the outdoor elements are on the cool and windy side.)
3. Place the slices of portobello closely together or slightly overlapping so that each piece touches the plank. Drizzle 2 to 3 tablespoons of the sauce over the slices. Place the plank on the indirect heat side of the grill. Close the lid and let cook for 30 to 40 minutes. Baste with additional sauce every 10 to 15 minutes.
4. Serve with additional sauce and the bread on the side.

Change It Up

Plank Prep à la Judith: Place the plank over direct heat for 3 to 4 minutes, until it begins to smoke and pop. With oven mitts, carefully turn the plank over so the charred side is up. Arrange the mushrooms on the plank and proceed with the recipe.

Grilled Pepper Roll-Ups with Feta-Olive-Lemon Filling

Let's give a royal wave to Nigella Lawson, our favorite grill gal, and Paula Wolfert, our favorite expert on the cuisine of the Mediterranean. This is our BBQ Queen salute to their recipes. These colorful peppers look and taste great and are perfect to take to someone's house when you have to bring a dish to a party, as a vegetarian entrée, or as a side dish with just about any grilled or smoked entrée in this book.

Makes 8 servings

Feta-Olive-Lemon Filling:
- **8 ounces crumbled feta cheese**
- **1 tablespoon olive oil**
- **½ cup finely chopped pitted kalamata or niçoise olives**
- **2 tablespoons finely chopped green onions (white and some of the green parts)**
- **1 teaspoon grated lemon zest**
- **2 tablespoons toasted pine nuts**

- **1 large red bell pepper**
- **1 large yellow bell pepper**
- **Olive oil for brushing**
- **Kosher or sea salt and freshly ground black pepper to taste**

1. To make the filling, mix together the feta cheese, olive oil, olives, green onions, lemon zest, and pine nuts in a medium-size bowl. Set aside.

2. Prepare a hot fire in your grill. Brush the peppers with olive oil, season with salt and pepper, and place on a baking sheet to take out to the grill.

3. Grill the peppers, turning several times, for 5 to 10 minutes, or until blistered and softened all over. Let them cool slightly. With a paring knife, cut each pepper into quarters lengthwise. Trim off the stems, seeds, membranes, and blistered skin. Place about ¼ cup of the feta filling on the end of a grilled pepper quarter and roll up. (If you're nervous, secure each roll with a toothpick.) Arrange the roll-ups on a platter. Serve warm or at room temperature.

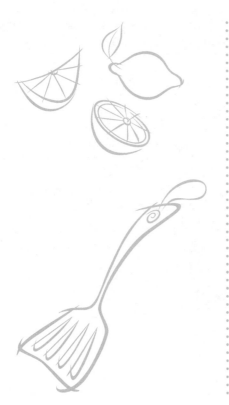

Deck It Out

Arrange the yellow and red peppers on a cobalt blue platter for a visual pop.

Take It Easy

Whole fire-roasted red bell peppers are available in jars at the grocery store. They are delicious and let you skip the step of grilling the peppers in this recipe. We like saving time!

Change It Up

Use strips of grilled eggplant, zucchini, yellow summer squash, or preserved piquillo peppers instead of the bell peppers. Or instead of making roll-ups, spread the cheese evenly over the inside of the pepper strips and arrange pinwheel-style on a plate as an appetizer, or arrange on top of a salad.

Razzle-Dazzle: A Tisket, A Basket

Yes! Baskets are a wonderful way to organize things for a party. Splay a colorful array of napkins, or silverware rolled in napkins, in a basket. Display flowers and decorative greens in a basket or baskets. Sturdy, boxy baskets are great for stacking on a buffet table to give height to a centerpiece. What about a bread basket or a crudités basket? A cookie basket? Get creative!

An Evening Under the Stars:
A Black-Tie Barbecue

On a summer evening, Karen and Dick were married by the water at her parents' home. The moon and stars reflecting off the lake created a special glow. After the ceremony for the budding BBQ Queen and her king, the dinner was, of course, a barbecue! A black-tie barbecue, to be exact.

What's a black-tie barbecue? It's a long-summer-dress-with-bare-feet sort of occasion for which you emphasize the special beauty of the evening without any fussiness or formality. It's like a very stylish picnic for which you've packed silver candlesticks and a bottle of Champagne.

We like to describe the food for this type of occasion as "haute smoke," or using smoke and the sizzle of the grill to lend flavor to high-style recipes that can be served in a more casual way. Forget a plate stacked high with artfully arranged food that took four chefs to create. A black-tie barbecue means rustic food on high-style platters and maybe even eating with your fingers—a little bit.

Setting the Scene

A summer night is a magical time to have a special event, whether it's a wedding reception, a fundraising gala, a special birthday, a welcome home, or even a business dinner. Our inspiration here is a white garden on a summer night, the pale flowers reflecting the light of the moon and stars. Sort of like *A Midsummer Night's Dream* without the misunderstandings.

Whether you're by a lake or pool or simply in your own backyard, reflect the lovely glow of the moon and stars with mirrors. Set up two or three serving tables with framed mirrors, placed at the back of the tables, leaning against a wall or other support. Place mirrors in the center of each seating table. Choose clear, lustrous, and white as your pared-down color scheme for the evening. Set out an assortment of white candles in votives, hurricane lamps, or lanterns, on or near the mirrors. Also use miniature outdoor lights and torchieres. Use large clear or white acrylic serving bowls, clear or white platters and serving dishes, and stainless-steel or other metal buckets to hold beverages outdoors. Drape tables in white, using tablecloths, white bed linens, or lengths of fabric. Flowers can be simple. Stay with the white theme and choose spicy-scented carnations (they hold up well) with a bit of greenery—or white roses, if your budget allows. Set out pots of tall white cosmos, from a garden nursery, around the serving tables.

Making Beautiful Music

If you possibly can, book live music for this event like a string quartet or a nice trio. If it's not in your budget, then go for the retro songbooks of Rod Stewart and Tony Bennett, and maybe rotate with some female vocalists like Alison Krauss or Karrin Allyson.

Perfect Partners

Serve the appetizers with a sparkling wine, the entrées with a chilled, full-bodied white wine such as Chardonnay or Soave or a light red such as Beaujolais or a young Pinot Noir, and the desserts with espresso or a thermal carafe of regular coffee, with brandy and grappa set out for adding to it.

Choose One or Two Appetizers

Grilled Prosciutto-Wrapped Asparagus with Fig Balsamic Vinegar and
    Shaved Parmesan (page 62)
Smoke-Roasted Fingerlings with Crème Fraîche and Caviar (page 30)
Grilled Figs on Rosemary Skewers (page 34)

Choose One Entrée

Grilled Venison Chops with Brandy Cream Sauce (page 108)
Grilled Lobster Tails with Béarnaise Butter (page 152)
Veal T-Bones with Lemon-Butter Sauce and Gremolata Garnish (page 102)

Choose One or Two Sides

Bistro Fennel and Baby Bello Mushroom Salad (page 191)
The BBQ Queens' Knife-and-Fork Grilled Vegetable Salad (page 170)
Green Bean, Tomato, and Goat Cheese Salad with Lemon-Pesto Dressing
    (page 163)

Choose One Dessert

Queen of Tarts (page 235)
Wine-Splashed Peaches, Plums, and Berries (page 210)
Angel food cake with vanilla ice cream or frosted with
    whipped cream and dusted with shredded coconut

Grill-Roasted Red Pepper, Arugula, and Niçoise Olive Salad

As you can see throughout this book, we love Mortar and Pestle Vinaigrette on just about anything, including this yummy salad. This salad goes especially well with lamb, fish and shellfish, or chicken. For an extra-special finish, scatter a few of those roasted and salted whole Marcona almonds on the top.

Makes 4 servings

- **2 medium-size red bell peppers**
- **4 cups arugula or other leafy greens**
- **½ cup pitted oil-cured niçoise olives**
- **1 recipe Mortar and Pestle Vinaigrette (page 170)**
- **Roasted, salted Marcona almonds for garnish**

1. Prepare a hot fire in your grill.
2. Grill the peppers, turning several times, for 5 to 10 minutes, or until blistered and softened all over. Let them cool slightly, then, with a paring knife, cut each pepper into quarters lengthwise. Trim off the stems, seeds, membranes, and blistered skin.
3. In a large bowl, combine the peppers, arugula, and olives. Toss with the vinaigrette and top with the almonds.

Take It Easy
Cruise the salad bar for ingredients, and use good-quality jarred roasted red peppers.

Stir-Grilled Crispy Shallots

We love onions with beef—fried, crispy onions with a grilled filet mignon or a slice of grilled onion with a juicy burger. More of an accompaniment than a true side dish, these smoky, slightly sweet, and crispy shallots taste wonderful with a grilled sirloin, filet mignon, or whole beef tenderloin. Put these on the grill 10 to 15 minutes before you start to grill the beef.

Makes about 2½ cups, for 8 to 10 servings

- **24 shallots, quartered**
- **1 tablespoon fresh rosemary leaves or 2 teaspoons dried rosemary**
- **½ cup olive oil**
- **Kosher or sea salt and freshly ground black pepper to taste**

1. Prepare a hot fire in your grill. Lightly oil a large grill wok on both sides and set on the hot grill.
2. Place the shallots and rosemary in a large bowl. Drizzle the olive oil over them and lightly toss to coat. Season with salt and pepper.
3. At the grill, place the shallot mixture in the grill wok and close the grill lid. Cook for 3 to 5 minutes, open the grill and toss with wooden paddles or grill spatulas, and close the lid again. Repeat until the shallots are tender and crispy, about 10 more minutes. Serve warm or at room temperature.

Razzle-Dazzle: Flatware

Mix-and-match flatware doesn't really have to match at all. If you need to stretch your knives, forks, and spoons for a fete, then get thee to a flea market or an antiques store. Even a kitchen factory outlet store may have bins of assorted flatware on sale for a song. Don't be a slave to matchy-matchy!

Heirloom Tomato Bowl with Lemon and Feta

Fellow 'Que Queen barbecue competitor Jean Tamburello brought a bowl of fresh garden tomatoes swimming in a bowl of luscious amber liquid to a barbecue contest a couple of years ago. It was divine, and we tried to figure out what kind of vinaigrette Jean had made to dress the tomatoes. We finally asked. To our amazement, she told us it was just a hearty pour of extra-virgin olive oil. It mingled with the freshly picked, acidic garden tomatoes to make its own vinaigrette. So why improve on something that good, you ask? Just because. Any farmers' market or home-grown tomatoes will do, but heirlooms are especially nice. Jean usually makes this with Romas and beefsteaks. The different tomatoes cut into wedges, chunks, or slices add eye-appealing shapes to this dish. It is so colorful that it begs to be served in a large glass bowl. And when the tomatoes are this good, plan on about ¾ pound per person. Any leftovers can be whirled in a blender to make a tasty gazpacho.

Makes 8 servings

- **6 to 7 pounds assorted heirloom tomatoes**
- **½ to 1 cup extra-virgin olive oil**
- **Grated zest and juice of 1 lemon**
- **Kosher or sea salt and freshly ground black pepper to taste**
- **8 ounces crumbled feta cheese**

1. Cut some of the tomatoes into wedges. Cut the smaller tomatoes in half. Slice or chunk the rest. Place all the tomatoes in a large glass serving bowl. Pour the olive oil over all. Add the lemon zest and juice. Season with salt and pepper, remembering that the feta cheese is salty, and gently toss to combine.
2. Just before serving, sprinkle the feta cheese over the top. Serve immediately, or allow to sit at room temperature for several hours, which will yield a juicier result.

Deck It Out

Another tasty topping for the tomatoes is simple to make and looks elegant. Heat 3 to 4 tablespoons olive oil in a small sauté pan. Add 1 cup fresh bread crumbs and toss to coat. Cook until golden brown, and sprinkle on top of the tomatoes just before serving.

Change It Up · · · · · · · · · · · · · · · · · ·

Add chopped oil-cured olives, sprinkle with fresh herbs, and/or add chopped or slivered red onions.

Blistered Baby Pattypans and Red Onion

The great thing about firing up the grill is that you have the option of cooking both the side dish and the entrée on it. And we all know that vegetables taste great on the grill. We see these baby pattypan squash at the market a lot these days—even in January, when we did a photo shoot for a "Love Your Grill" feature. Just stir-grill these until they're crisp-tender, then drizzle with a dressing and toss with some sheep's milk cheese, goat cheese, or *queso fresco*.

Makes 4 servings

- **2 pounds assorted green and yellow baby pattypan or other miniature squash**
- **1 large red onion, cut into 8 wedges**
- **2 tablespoons olive oil**
- **Kosher or sea salt and freshly ground black pepper to taste**
- **1 recipe Lemon-Pesto Dressing (page 163) or Mortar and Pestle Vinaigrette (page 170)**
- **4 ounces sheep's milk cheese, goat cheese, or *queso fresco*, crumbled**

1. Prepare a hot fire in your grill. Oil the interior and exterior of a grill wok and place on a baking sheet to take out to the grill. In a zipper-top plastic bag, combine the squash and onion. Drizzle with the olive oil, season with salt and pepper, and toss to coat. Place on the baking sheet and take out to the grill.

2. Place the grill wok on the grill grate over the heat. Dump the contents of the bag into the wok and stir-grill, tossing with wooden paddles every 2 minutes or so, for 15 minutes, or until the vegetables are charred slightly. Transfer the vegetables to a serving bowl and toss with the dressing. Top with the crumbled cheese and serve hot, warm, or at room temperature.

Stir-Grilled Tomatoes, Red Onion, and Fresh Herbs with Grilled Flatbread

You'll need a grill basket or large grill wok for this recipe. Most grill woks are about 12 inches in diameter, but we prefer the larger 15-inch ones. They have more grill surface and make it easier to toss a larger amount of veggies without spilling out onto the grill (where the smaller pieces of food can fall through the grill grates). When stir-grilling a medley of vegetables, think about the color and eye appeal of the dish. If you have pretty heirloom tomatoes, substitute them for the Romas. This is a wonderful side dish for just about any kind of grilled or smoked meat. It's also a great meatless meal when served with extra grilled flatbread to sop up the delicious marinade.

Makes 6 servings

- **8 Roma tomatoes, quartered**
- **1 cup grape tomatoes, halved**
- **1 cup yellow teardrop tomatoes**
- **1 large red onion, cut into thick slivers**
- **$^2/_3$ cup extra-virgin olive oil**
- **$^1/_3$ cup red wine vinegar**
- **2 cloves garlic, minced**
- **Kosher or sea salt and freshly ground black pepper to taste**
- **1 large loaf flatbread**
- **Olive oil for brushing the bread**
- **Balsamic vinegar for drizzling**
- **$^1/_2$ cup loosely packed fresh basil leaves**
- **$^1/_4$ cup finely chopped fresh mint or lemon balm**

1. Set the tomatoes and onion in a large plastic or stainless-steel mixing bowl. Combine the extra-virgin olive oil, red wine vinegar, garlic, salt, and pepper in a cup and pour over the vegetables. Place the vegetables on a baking sheet and marinate at room temperature for 30 minutes. Brush the flatbread on both sides with olive oil and place on another baking sheet.

2. Prepare a hot fire in your grill. Oil both sides of a grill basket or grill wok and set on the baking sheet with the flatbread.

3. Carry both baking sheets out to the grill. Place the wok directly over the hot fire. Using a large slotted spoon, drain the vegetables and place in the wok, reserving the marinade. Toss the vegetables with long-handled wooden spoons and grill for 6 to 8 minutes. Grill the flatbread for a couple of minutes on each side to lightly brown and warm the bread.

4. Serve the vegetables in a shallow bowl or plate that can hold a drizzling of the reserved marinade and the balsamic vinegar. Gently tear the basil leaves and sprinkle over the vegetables,

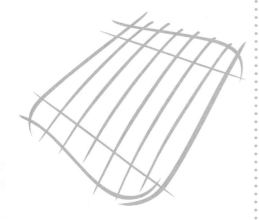

along with the mint. Cut or tear the flatbread into small pieces and serve alongside.

Deck It Out

This is beautiful served on a big platter for a buffet or alfresco dinner. Top with fresh shavings of a wonderful hard cheese like an aged goat cheese, Asiago, or Pecorino Romano, or crumbled blue or feta cheese. Garnish with pretty whole sprigs of fresh basil and mint.

Change It Up

Oh my—make this dish with sliced mushrooms, summer squash, or whatever else is tender and fresh.

Bistro Carrot Salad with Raspberry Vinaigrette

We love shredded raw vegetable salads, especially in colder weather when fresh tomatoes are less than desirable. You can make the three bistro salads—with carrots, fennel (page 191), or beets (page 192)—a day or so ahead of time. They are great with grilled entrées, and they make great leftovers. Because they are simple and flavorful, delicious and healthy, your family and friends will love them, too. In this recipe, the crunchy sweetness of the shredded carrots is beautifully offset by the tart raspberry-mustard vinaigrette.

Makes 8 to 12 servings

- **1 pound carrots, peeled and shredded**
- **2 tablespoons raspberry vinegar**
- **1 teaspoon Dijon mustard**
- **¼ cup olive oil**
- **Kosher or sea salt and freshly ground black pepper to taste**

Place the shredded carrots in a medium-size serving bowl. In a small bowl, whisk together the vinegar, mustard, and olive oil to make a smooth dressing. Toss the carrots with the dressing, then season with salt and pepper. Serve cold or at room temperature.

Grilled Cornmeal-Crusted Green Tomatoes with Shrimp Rémoulade

When you're longing for tomatoes and can't resist picking green ones, or if you've got lots to use up at the end of the tomato season, make this dish. The tartness of the green tomatoes and the creaminess of the rich shrimp rémoulade contrast nicely to make this an interesting side dish, appetizer, or even entrée. Both firm green and just barely ripe tomatoes work in this recipe.

Makes 6 servings

- 1½ cups Rémoulade (page 74)
- 8 to 12 ounces cooked salad (small) shrimp
- 1 cup all-purpose flour
- 1 teaspoon kosher or sea salt
- 1 teaspoon seasoned pepper
- 2 large eggs, beaten
- 1½ cups cornmeal
- 3 to 4 large green tomatoes, sliced into twelve ¾-inch-thick slices
- Olive oil for drizzling

1. Combine the rémoulade and cooked shrimp in a small bowl. Refrigerate until ready to serve.
2. Mix the flour with the salt and seasoned pepper in a shallow bowl. Place the beaten eggs in another shallow bowl and the cornmeal in a third shallow bowl. Dredge the tomato slices in the seasoned flour, then in the egg, then in the cornmeal. Set the tomato slices on a baking sheet lined with parchment paper and refrigerate for about 30 minutes, to set the coating.
3. Lightly oil the grates on your grill and prepare a hot fire in your grill.
4. Remove the tomatoes from the refrigerator and lightly drizzle the top side with olive oil. Grill over the hot fire for 2 to 3 minutes per side, until golden brown and tender.
5. Overlap the grilled tomatoes in two rows on a rectangular platter and spoon the shrimp rémoulade down the center. Serve immediately.

Deck It Out

Make a tomato stack as pretty as any restaurant would serve. After you slice the tomatoes, spread a ½-inch-thick layer of goat cheese or Boursin cheese between two slices of tomato. Refrigerate until the cheese is firm. Then continue with steps 2 through 4. Arrange the tomatoes on a platter and spoon some of the rémoulade over the top of each tomato stack.

Change It Up ·················

Instead of the shrimp rémoulade, place a thin slice of goat cheese or ½ tablespoon Boursin cheese on each tomato.

Bistro Fennel and Baby Bello Mushroom Salad

No-cook vegetable salads prepared with fresh lemon juice and extra-virgin olive oil get nods of approval from us every time. Here, the slight licorice flavor of the fennel shines through and complements the earthy mushrooms. Cremini mushrooms are the baby versions of portobellos—they are the same size as white mushrooms but are the earthy brown of portobellos. You may substitute a good Parmesan cheese for the Romano if you like.

Makes 6 servings

- **4 small fennel bulbs**
- **8 ounces cremini mushrooms, stems trimmed and sliced**
- **4 ounces Pecorino Romano cheese**
- **Grated zest and juice of 1 lemon**
- **6 tablespoons extra-virgin olive oil**
- **Kosher or sea salt and freshly ground black pepper to taste**

Clean the fennel by discarding the tough outer layer, rinsing the stalks under cold water, and patting dry. Holding aside the fronds, slice the tender stalks into slices (similar to cutting celery). Line a large serving bowl with the fronds. Place the sliced fennel and mushrooms in the bowl. Shave the cheese over all. Sprinkle the lemon zest and drizzle the lemon juice over the salad. Drizzle the oil over the salad and season with salt and pepper. Toss to coat. Place the reserved fronds around the rim of the bowl as a garnish. Serve at room temperature.

Bistro Beet Salad

Yes, this is a raw beet salad! There is no need to cook the beets, which are nutritious and delicious just as they are. Be sure to wear gloves when you grate the beets to avoid staining your hands red.

Makes 4 servings

- **4 medium-size beets, peeled and finely grated**
- **1 bunch green onions, thinly sliced (white and some of the green parts)**
- **1 teaspoon red wine vinegar**
- **1 teaspoon freshly squeezed lemon juice**
- **¼ teaspoon ground cumin**
- **⅛ teaspoon ground coriander**
- **3 to 4 tablespoons extra-virgin olive oil**
- **Coarse kosher or sea salt and freshly ground black pepper to taste**

Place the grated beets and green onions in a glass serving bowl. Combine the vinegar, lemon juice, cumin, and coriander in a cup or small bowl. Slowly drizzle in the olive oil and whisk to incorporate. Pour over the beets and toss to combine. Season with salt and pepper and serve at room temperature.

Deck It Out

Prepare this and the two other bistro salads (pages 189 and 191) and serve them together, in three mounds on a large oval or rectangular white platter.

Take It Easy

Let the grocery store salad bar be your sous chef. Load up on one or more shredded vegetables, then toss with a bottled or homemade dressing for an easy bistro-style salad.

Change It Up

To turn this into an entrée salad, double the dressing and toss half with 4 to 5 cups of assorted greens. Place the greens on a platter and spoon the beet salad over the top. Garnish with wedges of hard-boiled eggs, cooked new potatoes, oil-cured olives, and a sprinkling of caperberries.

Brandied Fruit Compote

This is sweet and tart, and we dare you to eat just one spoonful. It is also very adaptable and can be made with the dried fruits of your choice. We like to buy a 12- or 16-ounce bag of assorted chopped dried fruits so that the only chopping left to do is the onion, apricot, and apple. It is divine served with any kind of poultry or pork.

Makes 5 to 6 cups

- **1 cup brandy**
- **1 cup cider vinegar**
- **2 cups assorted chopped dried fruit (apples, figs, tart red cherries, etc.)**
- **½ cup dried apricots, chopped**
- **½ cup golden or dark raisins**
- **½ cup dried cranberries**
- **⅓ cup honey**
- **½ cup (1 stick) unsalted butter**
- **1 medium-size onion, chopped**
- **2 tart apples, cored, peeled, and chopped**

1. In a large saucepan, boil the brandy and cider vinegar together until reduced by one third, about 8 minutes. Add the dried fruit mixture, apricots, raisins, cranberries, and honey to the brandy. Stir and set aside.
2. In a large skillet, melt the butter over medium heat and sauté the onion until translucent, about 4 minutes. Add the onion and apples to the dried fruit mixture and let sit for about 30 minutes or so, to let the fruit begin to plump. Serve hot, warm, or at room temperature.

Deck It Out · · · · · · · · · · · · · · · · · · ·

Serve this as Jack O' Lantern Compote: Cut off the top of a medium-size sugar pumpkin to make a lid. Hollow out the pumpkin (but don't remove too much from the bottom). Pack the cavity of the pumpkin with the compote. Put the lid back on the pumpkin and place the pumpkin on a baking sheet. Bake in a 350°F oven for 45 minutes to 1 hour, or until the compote is bubbling and the pumpkin is tender. To serve, spoon out both the pumpkin flesh and compote into glass compote dishes.

Change It Up · · · · · · · · · · · · · · · · · ·

Use this compote as a stuffing for a pork loin or pork chops, or to fill the center of a crown roast of pork.

Smashed Red Potatoes with Green Onions and Cream Cheese

This is so easy, yet so good! This is one of those recipes that you can make for 4 or 44, and it pleases everyone from the tiniest tot to Great-Aunt Edna (or whoever the queen bee is in your family).

Makes 4 servings

- **1 pound red potatoes**
- **8 ounces cream cheese, softened**
- **6 green onions, chopped (white and some of the green parts)**
- **Kosher or sea salt and freshly ground white pepper to taste**

1. Place the potatoes in a medium-size heavy saucepan and add just enough water to cover. Bring to a boil and let boil until the potatoes are tender, 12 to 15 minutes.
2. Drain the potatoes and transfer to a serving bowl. With a potato masher or a fork, smash the potatoes together with the cream cheese and onions. Season with salt and pepper and serve hot.

Deck It Out ·····················

Serve the potatoes generously garnished with chopped fresh chives or finely minced green onion.

Potato Salad with Aioli

Of all the potato salads in the world, this one is our favorite, a version of the Tapas-Style Potato Salad in our book *Fish & Shellfish, Grilled & Smoked* (The Harvard Common Press, 2002). Although the classic Spanish method of preparation is to let the potatoes cool, then blend them with the garlic-flavored mayonnaise, we have come to like the tender and melting effect of dressing the hot potatoes with the aioli. The potatoes seem to absorb the dressing better. For us, this potato salad goes with almost anything—if it even makes it out of the kitchen! So make sure to double, triple, even quadruple this recipe to have enough for great leftovers.

Makes 4 servings

- **4 large baking potatoes**

Aioli:
- **½ cup good-quality mayonnaise**
- **3 cloves garlic, minced**
- **½ teaspoon smoked paprika (optional)**

- **2 tablespoons chopped fresh Italian parsley leaves**

1. Either bake or boil the potatoes. To bake, preheat the oven to 375°F, pierce each potato, and bake for 45 to 55 minutes, until tender. To boil, place potatoes with water to cover in a large pot. Bring to a boil over high heat, and boil for 20 to 25 minutes, until fork tender.
2. In a large serving bowl, blend together the mayonnaise, garlic, and smoked paprika, if using. Cut the warm potatoes into small pieces and blend with the garlic mayonnaise using a rubber spatula. Blend in the parsley and serve.

Deck It Out

Serve the potato salad mounded on a colorful platter, and dust more paprika around the edge of the salad. Garnish the center with more chopped Italian parsley.

All-Seasons Potato Casserole for a Crowd

Everybody needs a great potato casserole that can please any guest, and this dish fills the bill. You can put everything together a day or two ahead of time and keep it covered in the fridge until it's time to bake it.

Makes 12 servings

- **5 pounds baking potatoes, peeled and cut into chunks**
- **1 pound cream cheese, softened**
- **1 cup half-and-half**
- **½ cup (1 stick) unsalted butter**
- **2 teaspoons onion powder**
- **Kosher or sea salt and freshly ground white pepper to taste**

Topping:
- **1 small zucchini, shredded**
- **1 small yellow squash, shredded**
- **1 large carrot, peeled and shredded**
- **2 tablespoons chopped fresh Italian parsley**
- **4 tablespoons (½ stick) melted unsalted butter**

1. Place the potatoes in a large saucepan with water to cover. Bring to a boil and cook until the potatoes are fork-tender, about 20 minutes. Drain and set aside.
2. Preheat the oven to 350°F. Spray a 2-quart casserole dish with nonstick cooking spray.
3. In a large bowl, mash the hot potatoes with the cream cheese, half-and-half, butter, onion powder, salt, and pepper until either coarse and lumpy or light and fluffy, according to your preference. Spoon into the prepared pan. (At this point, you may cover and refrigerate for up to 3 days.)
4. Top the potatoes with the shredded zucchini, yellow squash, and carrot, and sprinkle the parsley over the top. Drizzle with the melted butter. Bake for 30 minutes, or until hot and bubbling. Serve hot.

Deck It Out

You can dress this up or down in any season. In the fall, use a mandoline to shred the yellow summer squash, green zucchini, and orange carrot over the top of the casserole for a look like falling leaves. In the winter, use shredded leeks instead of the squash, coarse black pepper or chopped kalamata olives, and a drizzle of olive oil instead of butter on top. In the spring, garnish the finished dish with a chiffonade of various greens. In the summer, garnish (before or after baking) with a fiesta of finely chopped bell peppers in various colors.

Sweet Potato Salad with Ginger-Lime Vinaigrette

Everybody's got a favorite potato salad recipe, but if you want something a little different that goes well with chicken, pork, or fish, this is it!

Makes 6 servings

- **3 pounds (about 3 large) sweet potatoes, peeled and cut into chunks**
- **½ cup chopped green onions**
- **½ cup chopped fresh Italian parsley**
- **One 2-inch piece fresh ginger, grated**
- **¼ cup extra-virgin olive oil**
- **1 teaspoon grated lime zest**
- **2 tablespoons freshly squeezed lime juice**
- **Kosher or sea salt and freshly ground black pepper to taste**

1. Place the sweet potatoes in a large pot with water to cover and bring to a boil over high heat. Reduce the heat to medium and boil until cooked through but not too soft, about 15 minutes. Drain and transfer the potatoes to a large bowl.
2. Toss the potatoes with the green onions and parsley. In a small bowl, whisk together the ginger, olive oil, lime zest, and lime juice. Season with salt and pepper. Pour the dressing over the potatoes and toss to blend. Serve warm or at room temperature.

Take It Easy

If you're pressed for time, use three 15-ounce cans of sweet potatoes, rinsed well under running water and patted dry between paper towels.

Smoke-Roasted Root Vegetables with Garlic and Rosemary

This is delicious winter fare, and the touch of smoke makes it perfect for a black-tie barbecue buffet table. This is a splendid way to update regular roasted potatoes with a kiss of smoke.

Makes 8 servings

Suggested wood: Apple, cherry, hickory, or pecan

- **2 large baking potatoes, peeled and quartered**
- **2 large sweet potatoes, peeled and quartered**
- **2 parsnips, peeled and cut into 2-inch chunks**
- **2 large red onions, quartered**
- **12 large cloves garlic**
- **½ cup olive oil**
- **2 tablespoons fresh rosemary leaves**
- **Fine kosher or sea salt and freshly ground black pepper to taste**

1. Prepare an indirect fire in your smoker to a temperature of 225° to 250°F. In a large disposable aluminum pan, combine the potatoes, sweet potatoes, parsnips, onions, and garlic. Drizzle with the olive oil and toss to blend. Sprinkle with the rosemary, salt, and pepper, and toss again.
2. Smoke, uncovered, for 1 hour. Meanwhile, preheat the oven to 400°F.
3. Toss the potatoes again, then transfer the pan to the oven and roast them for 30 minutes, or until the potatoes are tender when pierced with a knife. Serve hot.

Change It Up

- If you reverse the process (roast first, then smoke second), you will end up with softer rather than crispier vegetables.
- You can entirely roast this dish in a 400°F oven, stirring every 15 minutes, until the potatoes are tender, about 40 minutes.

Asian Noodles

There are so many ways to make a tasty sesame-peanut sauce to not only dress noodles, but also to drizzle over grilled pork or poultry. This recipe includes a Thai spice blend that can be purchased in Asian markets or from sources like Penzeys Spices (www.penzeys.com).

Makes 6 to 8 servings

- ¼ cup soy sauce
- 3 tablespoons peanut butter
- 1½ tablespoons toasted sesame oil
- 1½ tablespoons rice vinegar
- 1 tablespoon Thai spice blend
- 2 teaspoons Chinese chili garlic sauce
- 1 pound thin noodles (linguini, flat Thai noodles, or rice noodles)
- 1 cup green onions sliced on the diagonal
- 2 teaspoons toasted sesame seeds

1. Combine the soy sauce, peanut butter, sesame oil, vinegar, spice blend, and garlic sauce in a small bowl, whisking to blend. Set aside.
2. Cook the noodles according to the package directions. Drain and toss with the sauce. Mound the noodles on a platter and sprinkle with the green onions and toasted sesame seeds. Serve warm or at room temperature.

Deck It Out ·····················

Make a meal instead of a side dish by serving individual portions of the noodles and topping each plate with a grilled chicken breast (that you have basted with the extra peanut sauce) and grilled broccoli or asparagus.

Change It Up ·····················

If you are making the noodles several hours ahead, reserve some of the pasta water to add to the noodles if they become dry. Or if you love the sauce, double the recipe. Then you'll have additional sauce to dress the noodles and to drizzle over grilled meat.

Fideo

When Judith first moved to Kansas City, she took a cooking class in which this tangy, savory pasta casserole was featured. Fideo, a *sopa seca* or "dry soup," has its roots in the Catalan region of Spain, and was brought to Mexico, then Texas and Arizona. One of the steps is browning dry coils of angel hair pasta in oil, which may seem odd, but it gives a depth to the dish you don't get any other way. We love the flavor of this dish, but we also like it because it's a great last-minute meal-stretcher, made mostly from pantry ingredients.

Makes 8 to 10 servings

- **2 tablespoons vegetable oil**
- **One 16-ounce package coiled vermicelli or angel hair pasta**
- **One 28-ounce can diced tomatoes (we like Muir Glen Fire Roasted)**
- **3 large onions, chopped**
- **9 pickled pepperoncini peppers from a jar, chopped (we like Del Cito salad peppers)**
- **½ cup vinegar from the pepperoncini jar**
- **One 10.5-ounce can condensed beef consommé**
- **Kosher or sea salt and freshly ground black pepper to taste**

1. Preheat the oven to 325°F.
2. Heat the vegetable oil in a large skillet over medium-high heat. Add the coils of pasta and brown on both sides, about 5 minutes total.
3. Arrange the tomatoes, onions, and peppers in a large casserole dish. Remove the pasta from the oil and nestle it into the vegetables. Pour the vinegar and consommé over the mixture. Season with salt and pepper, if necessary. (At this point, you may cover and refrigerate the casserole for up to 24 hours before baking.)
4. Bake, covered, for 1 hour or until the pasta is tender and the casserole is bubbling. Serve hot.

Smoked Gouda Grits

Cheese grits have lots of charm and versatility for weekend grilling occasions, from a black-tie barbecue dinner to a relaxed Sunday brunch. Like the little black dress, they're great as they are or can be accessorized appropriately to go uptown or downtown. We love these cheese grits with the flavor of the hearth, achieved by using a smoked cheese, whether you've smoked it yourself or bought it that way. If you can't find smoked cheese, you can cheat a little bit by using regular Gouda along with a teaspoon or so of bottled liquid smoke flavoring or smoked paprika.

Makes 4 to 6 servings

- **2 cups water**
- **1 cup chicken broth or stock**
- **1 tablespoon chopped garlic**
- **1 cup stone-ground white or yellow grits**
- **1 cup heavy cream**
- **1 cup cubed smoked Gouda cheese**
- **Fine kosher or sea salt and freshly ground white pepper to taste**

1. Combine the water, chicken broth, and garlic in a large, heavy saucepan. Bring to boil and slowly whisk in the grits. Cook over low heat, stirring frequently, until the grits thicken to a porridge consistency, about 15 minutes.
2. Remove from the heat and stir in the cream and the cheese, stirring until the cheese melts. Season with the salt and pepper. Serve hot.

Change It Up

Substitute other artisanal smoked cheeses for the Gouda. You'll find the most variety by visiting and purchasing from an upscale grocery or gourmet cheese shop.

Yay-Rah-Rah: Tailgate Grilling

There's a good reason why people take all the trouble to tailgate—it's fun! Some people keep it simple and bring a small grill, a couple of paper plates and cups, a few hot dogs, and that's it. Others pack the candelabra and the filet mignon. We BBQ Queens are somewhere in the middle. Small portable grills like camp-size gas grills and little Weber Smoky Joes are the norm for tailgating. And now—news flash!—there are portable gas grills and charcoal smokers that attach to the trailer hitch on the back of your vehicle. Their retractable arms let the grill sit over to the side of the vehicle, allowing easy access to the back of the vehicle and providing a grill that's literally ready to go.

Plan ahead for easy cleanup and pack the food in plastic containers that will fit into each other when the party is over. Bring a container for the dirty dishes and/or several trash bags for all of the disposables.

Top 10 Tailgate Grilling Rules

1. Choose a menu of dishes that require at most a fork or a spoon to eat.
2. Think thin! Flattened chicken breasts, sausages, burgers, thin steaks, and pork tenderloin grill quickly and make great sandwiches.
3. Skewered foods win.
4. Prepare simple, make-ahead side dishes and desserts.
5. Keep hot food hot.
6. Keep cold food cold.
7. Use oil and vinegar dressings instead of mayonnaise for pasta, potato, or vegetable salads.
8. Offer an array of different toppings for make-your-own grilled pizzas.
9. Don't forget to bring the grill and its fuel!
10. Clean up after yourself.

Setting the Scene

For a big bash in a parking lot or field, we're in favor of throwaway plates and cups. For small group tailgating, why not invest in some fun reusable plastic plates and matching cups in your team's colors? Stay with the color theme and bring the Queen of Sugar Cookies iced or frosted in the team colors.

Making Beautiful Music

Anything peppy is the ticket in the music department: Try some lively zydeco or rock 'n' roll your heart out with the Stones. Naturally, you get extra points for playing music from a hometown band.

Perfect Partners

Whether it's Bloody Marys for brunch before a noon game, cold beer or root beer before an afternoon game, or hot chocolate laced with schnapps on a cold day, your beverage options are plentiful.

Choose from This Mix of Make-Ahead and Make-on-Site Dishes

Wood-Grilled Country Bread with Four Seasons Toppings (page 45)

Grilled Mini Tuna Burgers with Rémoulade (page 74)

Grilled Mini Lamb Burgers with Cilantro-Mint Butter (page 60)

Grilled Siciliano (page 69)

Rioja-Style Grilled Pork Tenderloin Tapas (page 61)

Bistro Salads (pages 189, 191, and 192)

Blue Cheese Coleslaw (page 173) or Cilantro Slaw (page 167)

Queen of Sugar Cookies (page 214)

Grilled Chocolate Crostini (page 216)

Oven-Baked Herbed Risotto

When you're focusing on the grill festivities during the weekend, the last thing you want is a fiddly side dish, sauce, or dessert that requires competing indoor kitchen time. You either prepare those things ahead, or find a low-maintenance recipe that can take care of itself while you're busy outdoors. Hence, this risotto that just bakes in the oven—there is no stirring, no careful watching, no stress! We love the flavor and texture of this risotto as it is, but as women who welcome change, we can't resist the temptation to gussy this up on occasion, as you'll see below.

Makes 8 servings

- **4 cups chicken broth or stock**
- **½ cup water**
- **2 tablespoons unsalted butter**
- **½ cup chopped onion**
- **2 tablespoons mixed chopped fresh herbs (such as chives, tarragon, Italian parsley, oregano, dill) or 2 teaspoons mixed dried herbs**
- **1½ cups Arborio rice**
- **½ teaspoon freshly ground white pepper**
- **1 cup grated Parmesan, Asiago, or Gruyère cheese**

1. Preheat the oven to 350°F.
2. In a large saucepan, bring the chicken broth and water to a boil over high heat. While the broth mixture is heating, place the butter, onion, herbs, rice, and pepper in a 2-quart casserole dish. Pour the boiling broth mixture over the rice mixture. Carefully transfer the casserole to the oven.
3. Bake for 40 minutes, or until the rice is tender. Stir in the cheese and serve hot.

Deck It Out

Serve buffet-style in the casserole dish, garnished with a central "bouquet" of fresh herb sprigs and a few shavings of Parmesan cheese.

Change It Up

- Instead of the herbs, add ½ teaspoon saffron threads.
- When you stir in the cheese, also stir in ½ teaspoon white truffle oil.
- Top the finished risotto with grilled asparagus spears, grilled pepper slices, or grilled mushrooms.

Italian Sausage, Pine Nut, and Wild Mushroom Stuffing

We love this recipe as a gently flavored stuffing for the holiday bird or as a side dish for grilled poultry! Use your favorite artisanal bread.

Makes 10 servings

- **8 cups diced rustic bread, such as rustic French, rosemary olive, or ciabatta**
- **½ cup pine nuts**
- **1 pound bulk Italian sausage, sweet or hot**
- **1 cup (2 sticks) unsalted butter**
- **1 large onion, diced**
- **4 stalks celery, diced**
- **8 ounces assorted fresh wild mushrooms (morels, chanterelles, oyster, shiitakes, and/or black trumpets), cleaned and roughly chopped if large**
- **¼ cup minced fresh tarragon**
- **¼ cup minced fresh sage**
- **4 cups chicken broth or stock**
- **Fine kosher or sea salt to taste**
- **1 teaspoon freshly ground white pepper**

1. Preheat the oven to 350°F. Butter a 3-quart casserole.
2. Scatter the diced bread and the pine nuts on a baking sheet and toast in the oven for 10 to 15 minutes, or until the pine nuts are just lightly browned. Set aside to cool.
3. In a large skillet over medium-high heat, brown the sausage. Drain off and discard the fat. Transfer the sausage to a large mixing bowl and set aside. Wipe out the skillet with a paper towel.
4. Melt the butter in the skillet and sauté the onion and celery until softened, about 10 minutes. Add the mushrooms and sauté for 8 to 10 minutes more, or until the mushrooms have softened. Transfer the onion-mushroom mixture to the sausage bowl. Stir in the diced bread, pine nuts, tarragon, and sage, and blend well. Spoon the bread mixture into the prepared casserole.
5. Pour the chicken broth into a medium-size bowl and stir in the salt and white pepper. Pour the seasoned broth over the bread mixture. Cover with aluminum foil and bake for 45 minutes; then remove the foil and bake for 15 minutes more, or until the stuffing holds together in a mass. Serve hot or warm.

Decadent Desserts to Keep the Party Going

Every barbecue bash deserves a memorably sweet ending. In this chapter, we present a simple, versatile array of entertaining-worthy desserts: grilled and planked fruits, bake-ahead cakes that can serve as "frozen assets," a mix-and-match tart, crispy cookies, and dessert sauces that all share one characteristic: they're irresistible! You'll find plenty of easy recipes to add to your dessert repertoire without an iota of anxiety.

Since your main food focus will be on the grill or smoker, these desserts have the added benefit of being able to be made ahead, either all or in part. So you'll have plenty of time to freshen up and don your party outfit before your guests arrive.

Some of our desserts are simply sublime. You can't get much easier or more delicious than wine-splashed fruit. And if you've never tried Grilled Chocolate Crostini (page 216), you're in for a treat. Who knew that grilled baguette slices, good dark chocolate, and a sprinkle of sea salt could be so good? Move over, s'mores!

Summer Fruit in Chambord

Ripe, sweet, juicy peaches are our favorite in this recipe. Use the measurements as a guideline, but it is most important to choose fruit and berries that are luscious and ripe, so let that first and foremost be your guide. Serve this with Kir Royales (a glass of Champagne with a splash of Chambord).

Makes 6 to 8 servings

- **3 ripe peaches or nectarines, peeled and sliced**
- **12 large strawberries, cored and halved**
- **1½ cups blackberries**
- **1½ cups Chambord**
- **¼ cup Grand Marnier or other orange-flavored liqueur (optional)**

Place the fruit in a large glass bowl. Pour the Chambord and the Grand Marnier, if using, over the fruit. Let sit for 1 to 2 hours, stirring gently a couple of times. Serve at room temperature or chilled.

Change It Up

- If a sweeter dessert is desired, add a spoonful or two of sugar.
- Does the fruit need a flavor lift? Then add a tablespoon or two of lemon, lime, or orange juice.

Razzle-Dazzle: Table Toppers

Dress up your table settings with all kinds of different toppers. Your linen closet holds sheets, bedspreads, coverlets, and quilts that will make interesting tablecloths, we promise. For napkins, use colorful fingertip towels that are easy to wash, dry, and fold (no ironing!).

Wine-Splashed Peaches, Plums, and Berries

Splish-splash! This is another delectable concoction focusing on farm-fresh fruits and berries. The combination of the wine with an almond-flavored liqueur is marvelous. For a grilled variation, cut the peaches and plums in half, grill them, and then place them in the bowl with the other ingredients.

Makes 6 to 8 servings

- **4 ripe peaches, peeled and diced**
- **4 ripe plums, peeled and diced**
- **1 cup sweet white or red wine**
- **¼ cup amaretto or other almond-flavored liqueur**
- **2 tablespoons sugar**
- **2 teaspoons freshly squeezed lemon or lime juice**
- **1 cup raspberries**
- **3 tablespoons sliced almonds**

1. Place the peaches and plums in a pretty glass bowl. Combine the wine, amaretto, sugar, and lemon juice and mix well. Pour over the fruit and stir. Cover and chill for 1 hour.
2. Just before serving, add the raspberries and almonds, gently folding them into the mixture.

Change It Up

Red and green grapes make a nice addition or substitution in this dish. If you want to make it even more like a sangria, also add slices of peeled orange, lemon, lime, and grapefruit.

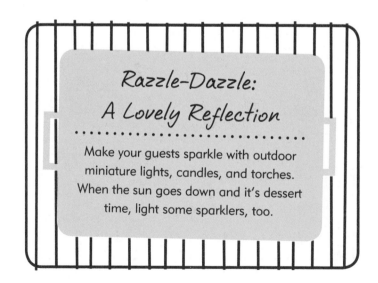

Razzle-Dazzle: A Lovely Reflection

Make your guests sparkle with outdoor miniature lights, candles, and torches. When the sun goes down and it's dessert time, light some sparklers, too.

Wine- and Liquor-Splashed Fruits

A beautiful glass bowl filled with fresh slices of peaches, strawberries, pears, nectarines, apples, plums, apricots, or figs, or whole cherries, blueberries, or raspberries is a delight to all the senses. When the fruit is macerated or poached in wine, liquor, or liqueur, it becomes a divine dessert fit for royalty—so say us BBQ Queens!

The fruits and berries may be served over luscious Almond Bundt Pound Cake (page 224) or alongside our Queen of Sugar Cookies (page 214). White and angel food cake are good go-withs, too, and are available ready made at the grocery store. Try any of the fruits spooned over a scoop of ice cream or sherbet, or serve the fruit on its own, in pretty bowls with plenty of the syrup and a garnish of fresh snipped mint, lemon balm, or rosemary.

Prepare the fruit 1 to 8 hours prior to serving. A drizzle of citrus juice keeps peaches, pears, and apples from browning. Delicate raspberries, blackberries, and the like need an hour or less to macerate in any of the syrups and don't need to be poached.

Here are some additional fruit and liquor pairings to experiment with.

- Peaches and apricot brandy
- Pineapple and golden rum
- Blackberries and brandy
- Golden raisins and grappa
- Strawberries and Lambrusco
- Oranges and dark rum
- Pears, raisins, and port
- Cherries and fruit-flavored vodka
- Papayas and Beaujolais

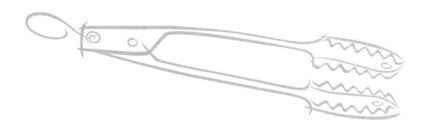

Pears Poached in Moscato del Solo

Sweet sparkling wines hardly need anything added to make a delicious syrup for poached pears. We like the moderately priced Ca' del Solo Muscat from Bonny Doon Vineyards. Bosc or d'Anjou pears are the varieties most commonly poached, but firm and ripe Bartletts are perfect, too. If peaches are your choice instead of pears, try the pretty white-fleshed variety with its contrasting red core.

Makes 8 servings

- **2 cups sparkling sweet white wine**
- **½ cup sugar**
- **2 tablespoons freshly squeezed lemon juice**
- **4 firm, ripe pears, peeled, cored, and halved**
- **Vanilla ice cream (optional)**

1. In a large stainless-steel saucepan, combine the wine, sugar, and lemon juice. Bring to a boil, then lower the heat to a simmer. Add the pears and simmer for about 10 minutes.
2. Place the pears in a pretty, heatproof glass bowl and pour the syrup over them. Place a small china saucer over the pears to keep them submerged in the liquid. This will keep them from oxidizing, which causes the fruit to brown.
3. Serve at room temperature or chilled, with vanilla ice cream if desired. The pears will keep in an airtight container in the refrigerator for up to 2 days.

Deck It Out

Give the pale white pears a splash of color by garnishing with bright edible flowers, such as nasturtiums, pansies, or violets. If serving the pears in a glass bowl, float the edible flowers on top.

Change It Up

Ice wines and sweet red wines—sparkling or not—will also work with this adaptable recipe.

Planked Stone Fruit with Butter-Rum Glaze

This is a great way to serve stone fruits like peaches, apricots, nectarines, or plums. On the plank, they warm up to a luscious fruitiness and take on a hint of wood flavor. While we prefer cedar planks for savory dishes, we like the milder maple or alder for fruit, but any hardwood plank (hickory, oak, etc.) will work. Make sure that you allow an hour to presoak the planks in water so that they stand up to the grilling fire. Serve the fruit with your favorite ice cream.

Makes 4 to 6 servings

Suggested wood: Two 15 x 6½ x ⅜-inch alder or maple planks, soaked in water for 1 hour

Butter-Rum Glaze:
- **1 cup dark rum**
- **1 cup clover or other amber honey**
- **½ cup (1 stick) unsalted butter**
- **2 tablespoons freshly squeezed lemon or lime juice**
- **Freshly grated nutmeg to taste**

- **4 to 6 peaches, apricots, nectarines, or plums, halved, stoned, and peeled**
- **Ice cream of your choice**

1. Prepare an indirect fire in your grill, with a hot fire on one side and no fire on the other. Place the planks on a large baking sheet.
2. To make the glaze, place the rum, honey, and butter in a medium-size saucepan over medium heat until the butter has melted. Whisk to blend, then add the lemon juice and nutmeg and remove from the heat. Place the fruit, cut side up, on the planks and brush with some of the glaze. Reserve the remaining glaze. Bring the baking sheet outside.
3. Place the planks on the no-fire side of the grill. Cover and cook for 10 to 15 minutes, or until the fruit is warm and tender. To serve, place a fruit half on a plate and drizzle with the reserved glaze. Top with a scoop of ice cream.

Deck It Out
Garnish with fresh mint leaves and serve with amaretti cookies or biscotti.

Change It Up
Use mango or papaya halves, but plank them for 20 to 30 minutes.

Queen of Sugar Cookies

Cupcakes and decorated sugar cookies bring out the inner child in all of us, and no one ever turns one down. They're perfect for the weekend, when you have more time for fun projects. This recipe, adapted from one in Judith's *All-American Desserts* (The Harvard Common Press, 2003), can be flavored any way you like—we use lemon here, but you can also try vanilla, almond, or your own special combination of extracts. We especially like crisp sugar cookies, and we even bought special tiara-shaped cookie cutters to do these justice!

Makes about 3 dozen cookies

- ½ **teaspoon baking powder**
- ½ **teaspoon baking soda**
- ½ **teaspoon salt**
- 2½ **cups all-purpose flour**
- ½ **cup (1 stick) unsalted butter, at room temperature**
- ½ **cup granulated sugar, plus more for sprinkling**
- **Grated zest and juice of 1 lemon**
- ⅓ **cup light corn syrup**
- 1 **large egg**

Decorating Icing:
- 2 **cups confectioners' sugar**
- 1 **tablespoon unsalted butter, melted**
- 2 **teaspoons light corn syrup**
- 2½ **tablespoons hot water, or more as necessary (optional)**
- **Food coloring for tinting icing (optional)**

1. To make the cookies, sift together the baking powder, baking soda, salt, and flour into a medium-size mixing bowl and set aside. With an electric mixer, cream together the butter, ½ cup granulated sugar, and the lemon zest in a large mixing bowl until light and fluffy. Beat in the lemon juice, corn syrup, and egg, and continue beating until smooth. Beat in the flour mixture, 1 cup at a time, and continue beating until you have a smooth, soft dough. Turn the dough out onto the counter, cut the dough in half, form each half into a disk, and wrap each disk with plastic wrap. Freeze for at least 30 minutes.

2. Preheat the oven to 400°F. Sprinkle a flat work surface with granulated sugar and roll out half the dough to a thickness of ⅛ inch. (If the dough is too soft, cover and return it to the freezer for a while longer.) Use cookie cutters to cut out the dough and place the cookies 1 inch apart on ungreased baking sheets. Repeat the process with the remaining half of the dough.

3. Bake the cookies until lightly browned at the edges, 6 to 8 minutes. Transfer to wire racks to cool.

4. To make the icing, place the confectioners' sugar, butter, and corn syrup in a medium-size

mixing bowl and beat with an electric mixer on medium speed until thick and well blended. If you wish to color the icing, add the hot water and beat until the icing is smooth and has the consistency of oil paint. Add food coloring to achieve the color you wish and beat again.

5. If you wish to pipe the icing onto the cookies, use a rubber spatula to transfer the icing to a pastry bag fitted with the appropriate tip. If you wish to "paint" the cookies with the icing, add more hot water, if necessary, to achieve the consistency of thin paint, and use a clean soft paintbrush to decorate the cookies. Let the iced cookies dry for several hours before storing. The icing will keep in an airtight container in the refrigerator for up to 2 weeks.

Deck It Out

Arrange the cookies in an overlapping pattern on a doily-lined platter, or arrange them vertically on 3 stacked glass cake stands. Frost a store-bought angel-food cake with whipped cream and arrange the cookies around the perimeter of the cake, pushed into the frosting. Or place each decorated cookie in a cellophane bag and tie with ribbon as a parting gift or party favor.

Change It Up

• For a more lemony cookie, use 1 teaspoon lemon extract in addition to the lemon zest and lemon juice in the recipe.

• For a different flavor, use 1 teaspoon pure almond extract or 1 teaspoon pure vanilla extract instead of the lemon zest and juice.

Grilled Chocolate Crostini

Who says dessert has to be difficult? This one is chic, but oh so easy. Karen remembers a delicious breakfast in Belgium with chocolate sprinkled on homemade buttered bread. Similar to s'mores, but not quite as messy, this is a grown-up version for the grill. Serve with a bowl of juicy ripe strawberries.

Makes 16 crostini

- **One 10-inch baguette**
- **6 to 8 ounces good-quality milk or bittersweet chocolate, in bar or block form**
- **Extra-virgin olive oil for drizzling**
- **Coarse kosher or sea salt for sprinkling**

1. Prepare a medium-hot fire in your grill.
2. Slice off the ends of the bread and then slice the bread on the diagonal ½ inch thick, to get 16 slices. Break or cut the chocolate into 16 pieces. Place the bread, chocolate, oil, and salt on a baking sheet and carry out to the grill.
3. Drizzle the bread with a little bit of olive oil and place over the fire to toast (1 to 2 minutes). Turn the bread over and place on the indirect-heat side of the grill. Place a piece of chocolate on each slice of bread. Close the grill lid and let heat for a couple of minutes. Remove the crostini from the grill and set on a serving dish. Sprinkle with a tiny bit of salt and devour while warm.

Warm Chocolate Truffle Cupcakes

The truffles for this recipe must be made ahead and placed in the freezer for at least 1 hour prior to baking the cupcakes. That being said, these are divine and are worth making and eating every single crumb and gooey bit of chocolate. The baked cupcakes can be refrigerated for several days or frozen in airtight containers for up to 1 month, and warmed in the oven or on the grill prior to serving.

Makes 12 cupcakes

Truffles:
- **¾ cup heavy cream**
- **8 ounces semisweet chocolate chips**

1. To make the truffles, place the cream in a saucepan and bring to a boil. Remove from the heat and add the chocolate chips. Let sit for 5 minutes, then whisk until smooth. This is the ganache. Place the saucepan of ganache in the freezer for about 30 minutes, or until firm. Remove from the freezer and spoon

Cupcakes:

- ¾ cup (1½ sticks) unsalted butter
- 8 ounces semisweet chocolate chips
- 4 large eggs
- ⅔ cup granulated sugar
- 2 teaspoons pure vanilla extract
- ⅔ cup all-purpose flour
- ⅔ cup unsweetened cocoa powder
- Confectioners' sugar for dusting

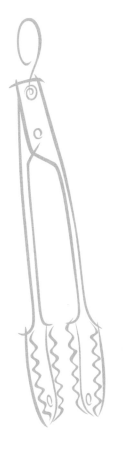

out 12 heaping tablespoonfuls of ganache, forming each spoonful into a ball and placing them on a baking sheet. Freeze the truffles for at least 1 hour.

2. To make the cupcakes, preheat the oven to 325°F. Grease a 12-cup nonstick cupcake tin.

3. Melt the butter in a double boiler. Add the chocolate chips and stir until melted. Remove from the heat and set aside.

4. In a large bowl, beat the eggs, sugar, and vanilla extract until frothy. Add the cooled chocolate mixture and stir to blend. In another bowl, combine the flour and cocoa powder and slowly add to the wet mixture until just blended. Pour the batter evenly into the 12 cupcake wells. Bake for 5 minutes.

5. Remove the truffles from the freezer. Remove the cupcakes from the oven. Quickly place a truffle in the center of each cupcake and press it halfway down into the batter. Immediately return the cupcakes to the oven and bake for about 16 minutes more, or until a toothpick inserted into the cake portion of the cupcake comes out clean. Remove from the oven to a cooling rack and let sit for 15 minutes.

6. Carefully remove the cupcakes by loosening the outer edges with a knife. Gently jiggle and lift the cupcakes out onto individual serving plates. Serve warm, with a dusting of confectioners' sugar for garnish.

Deck It Out

For an over-the-top dessert, spoon a pool of White Chocolate Cappuccino Ganache (page 237) onto each dessert plate. Place the cupcake on the sauce. Add a scoop of vanilla ice cream and drizzle with Dark Chocolate Ganache (page 237).

Vanilla Cupcakes with White Chocolate–Cream Cheese Frosting

Cupcakes bring out the inner child in all of us. And homemade cupcakes are the best of all. Garnish these with sweetened flaked coconut, fresh berries, or colored sprinkles.

Makes 12 cupcakes

Cupcakes:
- **5 tablespoons unsalted butter, at room temperature**
- **⅔ cup sugar**
- **1 teaspoon pure vanilla extract**
- **2 large eggs**
- **2 cups all-purpose flour**
- **1½ teaspoons baking powder**
- **⅛ teaspoon salt**
- **½ cup buttermilk**

Frosting:
- **¾ cup heavy cream**
- **3 ounces white chocolate, finely chopped**
- **8 ounces cream cheese, at room temperature**

1. Preheat the oven to 350°F. Line 12 cupcake wells with cupcake liners.
2. In a large mixing bowl with an electric mixer, beat the butter and sugar together on medium speed until light and fluffy, about 3 minutes. Add the vanilla extract and eggs, beating well to blend.
3. In a small bowl, combine the flour, baking powder, and salt. Beat the dry mixture into the butter mixture, 1 cup at a time, alternating with the buttermilk. Pour the batter into the cupcake liners.
4. Bake for 18 to 20 minutes, or until dark around the edges, golden brown in the center, and springy to the touch. Remove to a wire rack and let cool completely.
5. To make the frosting, place the cream in a large glass bowl. Microwave the cream until it just begins to boil, 2 to 3 minutes on High, or bring the cream to a boil in a small heavy saucepan on the stovetop. Remove the cream from the microwave or the heat. Add the white chocolate and let sit for 5 minutes (do not stir). Then gently stir the melted chocolate until it blends to a shiny white mixture. Cover and chill until cold, about 30 minutes. Place the cooled white chocolate mixture in a large mixing bowl. Add the cream cheese and beat on high with an electric mixer until soft peaks form. Frost the cupcakes shortly before serving.

Deck It Out

Garnish the cupcakes with unsprayed edible flowers, such as violets, linden, honeysuckle, or rosebuds. Go cute and quirky with a metal cupcake "tree" that holds all the cupcakes, or serve them arranged on graduated and stacked glass cake stands.

Change It Up

Instead of vanilla extract, add 2 teaspoons freshly grated orange zest to the cupcake batter. Spread the top of each cooled cupcake with orange marmalade, then frost.

Razzle-Dazzle: Floral Containers

Beautiful clear or cut-glass vases are simple and elegant. For a more casual gathering outdoors, use old jars, especially Mason jars. Any summer barbecue is made more festive by Mason jars overflowing with violets or miniature daisies. Tie a bow of raffia around the neck of the jar for an extra touch. For an autumn holiday event, carve out small vertical gourds or miniature pumpkins and fill them with assorted mums or carnations in the color of your choice.

Home for the Holidays

A holiday dinner is about giving thanks for life's abundance: family, friends, and food. The celebratory food takes center stage, especially when it's served on sumptuous platters or in your best serving bowls. For Thanksgiving, just imagine a burnished mahogany smoked turkey on a large platter, surrounded by bunches of fresh sage, thyme, and rosemary, or a crown roast of pork filled with dried fruit stuffing and surrounded by Seckel pears and lady apples. During Hanukkah, serve a fragrant leg of lamb, carved into rosy slices at the table. For Christmas Eve, create a platter of grilled seafood and citrus fruits. And for Christmas or New Year's Day, offer a festive grilled beef tenderloin or smoked standing rib roast, garnished with "holly" made from fresh rosemary branches and fresh cranberries. With a big meal to prepare, you'll be glad you're using your outdoor kitchen for the main course and maybe a side dish or two.

Setting the Scene

Keep your table simple but meaningful. This is the time, however, to bring out your best china, silver, and linens. For Thanksgiving, a low, flat centerpiece of miniature Jack Be Nimble pumpkins, bittersweet or wild grapevines, or greenery and nuts in their shells underscores the harvest theme. For Hanukkah, emphasize the special significance of candles glowing in a silvery menorah, and dress the table in white linens with cobalt blue water glasses and accents. For Christmas or New Year's, fill a glass bowl or compote dish with clove-studded oranges or seasonal fruits, and place pots of amaryllis, paperwhites, or white poinsettias amidst lots of fresh greenery. Filling glass bowls with bright globe ornaments in complementary colors is another easy way to get instant style. For any holiday, stack glass cake stands in graduated sizes to display homemade cookies, seasonal citrus fruits, or other goodies.

Making Beautiful Music

For Thanksgiving or Hanukkah, play your favorite classical music. For New Year's Day, some jazz will perk everybody up. And for Christmas, play carols, of course.

Perfect Partners

With turkey or seafood, choose a dry white wine. Perhaps a good German Riesling for the turkey, and a Soave, an unoaked Chardonnay, or a Fumé Blanc for the seafood. For ham or crown roast of pork, a young red like a Cabernet Sauvignon with berry-like flavors or a fruity white like Viognier would be good. For beef entrées, bring out those big, expensive reds you've been saving for just such an occasion: Brunello di Montalcino, Burgundy from Romanee-Conti, a great Australian Shiraz, or a peppery Côte-Rotie. You can never go wrong with a great Champagne or sparkling wine, either.

For this menu, we're suggesting only the big, celebratory entrées that will be the centerpiece of your dinner. The side dishes that go particularly well with each entrée are suggested within each recipe.

Choose from Among These Dishes

Big Easy Grilled Beef Tenderloin (page 96)
Smoked Rib Roast with Horseradish Crème Fraîche (page 98)
Persian Grilled Leg of Lamb with Tabbouleh Stuffing and Pomegranate
    Sauce (page 104)
Latin-Style Barbecued Pork Loin with *Aji-li-Mojili* (page 116)
Cherry-Smoked Rack of Pork with Cider-Mustard-Bourbon Sauce (page 120)
Double-Smoked Ham with Whiskey-Cider Sauce (page 124)
Herb-Smoked Turkey with Pinot-Tarragon Butter Baste (page 140)
Stuffed Prosciutto-Wrapped Turkey Breast (page 136)
Herb-Grilled Seafood Platter (page 150)

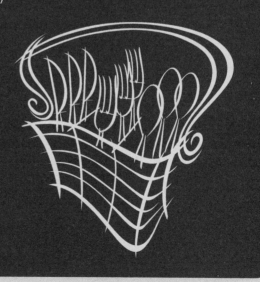

Fresh Apple Spice Cake

This recipe has been around for many years, and we have made it dozens of different ways. We've added varying spices such as allspice, cloves, nutmeg, pumpkin pie spice, and more. Golden and dark raisins, dates, and dried apricots have found their way into the batter. Black walnuts, English walnuts, and Missouri pecans have given it a different taste, and the nuts can be toasted, grilled, or smoked if you like (see page 232). It can be baked in a sheet pan, cake pan, Bundt pan, or springform. It just depends how you plan to serve it. Besides being a great dessert, it is also delicious for breakfast or brunch as a coffeecake. What's known as a "keeping cake," this has a crunchy exterior when served the same day you make it. If you cover it with foil and store it, it softens and tastes even better the next day.

Makes 8 to 10 servings

- **3 cups all-purpose flour**
- **2 cups sugar**
- **1 teaspoon baking soda**
- **2 teaspoons ground cinnamon**
- **1 teaspoon ground cloves**
- **1 teaspoon ground allspice**
- **1 teaspoon kosher or sea salt**
- **1¼ cups vegetable or canola oil**
- **3 large eggs, beaten**
- **2 teaspoons pure vanilla extract**
- **5 to 6 medium-size tart apples, peeled, cored, and chopped**
- **1 cup golden raisins soaked in ¼ cup brandy**
- **1 cup chopped nuts, such as English walnuts, black walnuts, or pecans**

1. Preheat the oven to 375°F. Spray a 9-inch springform pan with nonstick cooking spray.
2. In a large bowl, combine the flour, sugar, baking soda, cinnamon, cloves, allspice, and salt. Make a well in the middle of the dry ingredients. Add the oil, eggs, and vanilla extract. Stir until just blended (the mixture will be dense). Add the apples, raisins (with the brandy), and the nuts.
3. Pour the batter into the prepared pan and bake for 70 to 75 minutes, until the top is a dark crispy brown. Serve warm, at room temperature, or chilled. The cake will keep at room temperature for 2 to 3 days or can be refrigerated for up to 1 week.

Deck It Out

Bake this in a fancy Bundt pan and serve slices with vanilla, black walnut, or butter pecan ice cream and Dulce de Leche Sauce (page 236).

Change It Up ··················
- Bake in a Bundt pan for 75 to 80 minutes at 375°F.
- Bake in a rectangular sheet cake pan for 60 to 70 minutes at 375°F.

Choco-licious Sheet Cake

When you've just ended a stressful week or you're entertaining a crowd that contains all ages, make this cake. It's easy, sure to cheer you right up (with all that chocolate), and pleases everyone from your preschooler to your great-grandma.

Makes 12 servings

Cake:
- **2 cups granulated sugar**
- **2 cups all-purpose flour**
- **¼ teaspoon salt**
- **1 teaspoon baking soda**
- **½ cup buttermilk**
- **1 cup (2 sticks) unsalted butter**
- **¼ cup unsweetened cocoa powder**
- **1 teaspoon ground cinnamon**
- **1 cup freshly brewed dark roast coffee**
- **2 large eggs**
- **1 teaspoon pure vanilla extract**

Chocolate Icing:
- **½ cup (1 stick) unsalted butter**
- **¼ cup plus 2 tablespoons milk**
- **3 tablespoons unsweetened cocoa powder**
- **One 1-pound box confectioners' sugar**
- **1 teaspoon pure vanilla extract**

1. Preheat the oven to 400°F. Grease a 17 x 12-inch jellyroll pan.

2. In a large, heatproof mixing bowl, stir together the granulated sugar, flour, and salt. In a small mixing bowl, stir the baking soda into the buttermilk. In a medium-size heavy saucepan over medium-high heat, combine the butter, cocoa powder, cinnamon, and coffee and bring to a boil. Pour the cocoa mixture over the flour mixture and stir to blend. In a small bowl, beat the eggs with a fork and add to the batter. Stir in the vanilla extract and the buttermilk mixture and blend well. Spoon the batter into the prepared pan.

3. Bake the cake until it has pulled away from the sides of the pan and a cake tester inserted in the center comes out clean, 15 to 20 minutes.

4. While the cake is baking, prepare the icing. In a medium-size heavy saucepan over medium-high heat, combine the butter, milk, and cocoa powder, and bring to a boil. Remove from the heat and stir in the confectioners' sugar and vanilla extract. Spread over the cake and serve warm or at room temperature.

Change It Up · · · · · · · · · · · · · · · · · · ·

This simple sheet cake is so good as is, but we BBQ Queens always love to take a great recipe and make additions. It's our "recipe as a blueprint" theory. You get the architect's plans for your house, then you always make changes (enhancements) as you build. So Karen adds 1 cup of chopped nuts, like pecans or walnuts, to the batter. Macadamias, anyone? Go for it. Judith loves shredded coconut, so she likes to add 1 cup to the icing.

Almond Bundt Pound Cake

How do we love thee, pound cake? Let us count the ways. A moist pound cake can be baked days ahead of time, and it actually tastes better when left to "ripen." It looks great on a cake stand. And you can do so many different things with it. Of course, the better quality ingredients you use, the better flavor you'll have. That's why we prefer to use almond paste we mail-order from American Almond Products Company (www.lovenbake.com). They also have a hazelnut praline paste that's wonderful in the variation below, and other nut pastes including pistachio. We also like almond paste by Odense, usually available in a tube at the grocery store. You can wrap and freeze the pound cake for up to 3 months, to have on hand as a "frozen asset."

Makes 10 to 12 servings

- 2¾ cups granulated sugar
- 1 cup (2 sticks) unsalted butter, softened
- 4 ounces almond paste, at room temperature
- 6 large eggs, at room temperature
- 3 cups all-purpose flour
- ½ teaspoon salt
- ¼ teaspoon baking soda
- ¾ cup sour cream
- 1 teaspoon pure almond extract

1. Preheat the oven to 350°F. Grease and flour a 10-cup Bundt pan.
2. In the bowl of an electric mixer, cream together the sugar, butter, and almond paste until light and fluffy. (If the almond paste is not soft, cream this first, then add the butter and sugar.) Beat in the eggs, one at a time.
3. Sift the flour, salt, and baking soda together in a medium-size bowl. Beat the flour mixture into the butter-egg mixture, 1 cup at a time, alternating with the sour cream. Beat in the almond and vanilla extracts until you have a smooth batter. Spoon the batter into the prepared pan.

- **1 teaspoon pure vanilla extract**
- **Confectioners' sugar for dusting**

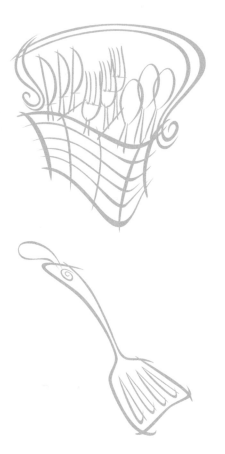

4. Bake for 1½ hours, or until a knife inserted near the center comes out clean. Cool for 15 minutes in the pan, then invert on a wire rack to remove from pan and cool completely. Dust with confectioners' sugar before serving.

Deck It Out

Place the cake on a pretty cake stand, dust with confectioners' sugar, then drizzle it with hot Dark Chocolate Ganache (page 237) or a simple confectioners' sugar glaze. Arrange seasonal berries and fruits around the bottom of the cake and in the center. For an autumn dessert, sauté apples, pears, or bananas in equal parts melted butter and brown sugar until bubbly. Spoon over slices of cake that have been topped with cinnamon or vanilla bean ice cream.

Take It Easy

Buy a good-quality pound cake and serve slices with warmed Dark Chocolate Ganache (page 237) or Nutella, Butter-Rum Glaze (page 213), or White Chocolate–Cream Cheese Frosting (page 218).

Change It Up

- To make Hazelnut Praline Pound Cake, use hazelnut praline paste instead of almond paste, and instead of almond and vanilla extracts, use McCormick Vanilla Butter and Nut Flavor. Drizzle the finished pound cake with Dark Chocolate Ganache (page 237) or warmed Nutella.
- To make Lemon Poppy Seed Pound Cake, use 3 tablespoons poppy seeds instead of almond paste, and instead of the almond and vanilla extracts, use the grated zest of 4 lemons.

Panettone Bread Pudding with Eggnog Custard

We love a tender, luscious bread pudding for dessert. It's comfort food at its finest. You can assemble a bread pudding ahead of time and bake it at the last minute. This version is one you can make from Thanksgiving through the Super Bowl. Just buy a packaged panettone (an Italian Christmas sweet bread available at this time of year) and ready-made bottled eggnog, and you're halfway there. There are other variations to this recipe for when it's not panettone season, as you'll see below.

Makes 8 servings

- **2 tablespoons unsalted butter, softened**
- **6 cups cubed panettone or other fruited sweet yeast bread**
- **¾ cup chopped dried apricots**
- **2 cups bottled eggnog**
- **3 large eggs**
- **1 teaspoon pure vanilla extract**
- **½ teaspoon ground cinnamon**

1. Preheat the oven to 350°F. Grease the inside of a 13 x 9-inch baking dish with the butter.
2. Scatter the bread cubes on a baking sheet and toast for 15 minutes in the oven.
3. Combine the toasted bread cubes with the apricots in the prepared pan. In a large bowl, whisk together the eggnog, eggs, vanilla extract, and cinnamon. Pour over the bread and fruit. (At this point, you may cover and refrigerate for up to 24 hours.)
4. Bake the bread pudding, uncovered, for 45 to 50 minutes, or until a knife inserted in the center comes out clean. Remove to a wire rack to cool, then spoon the bread pudding onto plates or into bowls.

Deck It Out

Serve this dessert restaurant style by using a biscuit cutter to cut out individual portions. Drizzle with warm Dulce de Leche Sauce (page 236) and top with sautéed apples or pears or poached dried apricots. Or, for people who love eggnog, top the portions with Eggnog Whipped Cream: In the bowl of an electric mixer, whip 2 cups heavy

cream until stiff peaks form. Lightly stir in ½ cup eggnog. If you wish, add 2 to 4 tablespoons brandy. The whipped cream will be the consistency of a thick sauce. It is also a drinkable potion. (Maybe thin it with a little more brandy for that!)

Change It Up

- Instead of panettone, use challah, brioche, or other light, rich bread.
- Instead of eggnog, use 2 cups half-and-half and 1 additional large egg, along with a pinch of freshly grated nutmeg, 1 tablespoon rum, and 1 tablespoon sugar.
- Instead of apricots, use currants or golden or dark raisins.

Razzle-Dazzle: Confectionery Sprinkles

A dusting of powdered sugar or cocoa over a plated dessert is so simple, yet so chic. Some other confectioneries for sprinkling on desserts include colored sugar crystals, snowflake-like sugar crystals, candy sprinkles, and little barbecue-themed candy sprinkles shaped like pink pigs, black and white cows, and more. Sprinkle these on sugar cookies or cakes.

Chocolate Ice Cream Cakes

Here's another dessert than can change to fit your whim, your guests, or the ice cream in your freezer. Judith grew up in a great ice cream town—Cincinnati, Ohio—and was spoiled for choice between the ice creams offered at Graeter's and Aglamesi's. But wherever you live, search out the best quality ice cream for this dessert and you'll be happy with the result. Make and assemble one pound cake to serve 6 to 8 people and freeze the other cake to have handy as a "frozen asset" for future weekend entertaining.

Makes 2 cakes, each to serve 6 to 8

- ¾ cup semisweet chocolate chips
- 1 cup boiling water
- 2 cups all-purpose flour
- 1 teaspoon baking soda
- ¼ teaspoon salt
- 1½ cups packed light brown sugar
- ½ cup (1 stick) unsalted butter, softened
- 2 teaspoons pure vanilla extract
- 2 large eggs, at room temperature
- ½ cup sour cream
- ½ cup confectioners' sugar for dusting
- 2 pints softened ice cream, such as coffee, chocolate chip, pistachio, or coconut

1. Preheat the oven to 325°F. Grease two 9 x 5 x 3-inch loaf pans.
2. Place the chocolate chips in a medium-size bowl and pour the boiling water over them. Set aside. In another medium-size bowl, combine the flour, baking soda, and salt.
3. Beat the brown sugar, butter, and vanilla extract in a large mixing bowl with an electric mixer until creamy. Add the eggs one at a time, beating well after each addition. Beat in the chocolate mixture and the sour cream. Gradually beat in the flour mixture. Spoon into the prepared loaf pans.
4. Bake for 55 to 65 minutes, or until a cake tester inserted in the center comes out clean. Cool in the pan for 30 minutes, then invert the cakes onto a wire rack and remove to cool completely. (At this point, the cooled pound cakes may be wrapped in plastic wrap, then placed in a freezer bag and frozen for up to 3 months. Thaw at room temperature before continuing.)
5. Using a serrated knife, cut each pound cake horizontally into 3 layers. Lay the bottom layer of each cake on a flat surface. Using a rubber spatula or a large metal spoon, spread half a pint of ice cream over each layer and top each with the middle layer of cake. Spread the

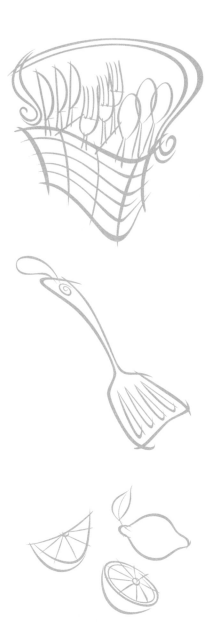

remaining ice cream on top of the middle layers, then place the top pound cake layers over the ice cream. Gently press down on the top with your hands, then wrap each cake in heavy-duty aluminum foil and place in the freezer. Freeze for at least 1 hour and up to 3 months.

6. Remove the cakes from the freezer 30 minutes before serving. Dust the tops of the cakes with confectioners' sugar, and cut each cake into 6 to 8 slices.

Deck It Out

Serve each slice in a pool of one of the Trio of Dessert Sauces (pages 236 to 237) and/or crowned with whipped cream and fresh berries.

Take It Easy

Buy chocolate pound cake from a local bakery or use thawed frozen golden pound cake.

Change It Up

Mix 2 pints of softened vanilla ice cream with your favorite crushed candies or mix-ins, such as peppermint sticks, chocolate-covered toffee, peanut brittle, or chopped cherries, then fill the cake with your own signature ice cream.

Iced Berries 'n' Cream

An easy ice cream? Yes! The secret is in the Philadelphia-style preparation, with just cream, fruit, and flavorings—no egg custard to make first! Its consistency falls somewhere between a sorbet and an ice cream. Garnish this rosy confection with fresh mint in summer or rosemary sprigs and a few fresh cranberries in winter.

Makes 1 generous quart

- **2 cups sugar**
- **2 cups water**
- **4 cups (about 3 pints) hulled fresh or frozen strawberries, raspberries, blackberries, or black raspberries**
- **Juice of 2 lemons, strained**
- **½ cup heavy cream**

1. Bring the sugar and water to a boil in a large, heavy saucepan. Remove from the heat and let the simple syrup cool, then refrigerate for at least 1 hour.
2. In a blender or food processor, puree the berries and pass the mixture through a fine-mesh sieve to remove any seeds. In a medium-size bowl, mix the berry puree with the simple syrup and lemon juice. In a small bowl, mix ½ cup of the pureed mixture with the cream and set aside.
3. Pour the berry puree mixture into an ice cream maker and freeze according to the manufacturer's directions. When the ice cream is almost frozen, pour in the cream mixture and continue processing until the ice cream is frozen. Serve immediately, or remove to an airtight container and freeze for up to 4 hours.

Deck It Out

This frozen confection is heavenly served with Almond Bundt Pound Cake (page 224), a dollop of whipped cream, and a sprinkling of fresh berries.

Change It Up

Here's an even easier adaptation. Puree one 16-ounce bag or 15-ounce can of berries in syrup, frozen solid, in a blender or food processor. Add the strained juice of 2 lemons,

½ cup heavy cream, and the puree to a slightly softened store-bought ice cream, mixing to combine. Refreeze briefly before serving. We also like this using one 15-ounce can of pears or pineapple in syrup, frozen solid, and proceeding as above, adding 2 tablespoons of pear brandy or rum along with the lemon juice to make Iced Brandied Pears 'n' Cream or Iced Pineapple Rum 'n' Cream.

Bumbleberry Crumble

An easy, delicious, homey dessert like this one is just what you want to celebrate a lazy weekend—when fresh berries are in season or when you just want to pretend they are. Because the filling is a jumble of berries, we had a little fun with the name of this recipe. We really like the touch of lemon and the flaked almonds in the topping.

Makes 6 to 8 servings

- **6 cups fresh or frozen mixed berries, such as blackberries, blueberries, and raspberries**
- **1 tablespoon instant tapioca**
- **Juice of 1 lemon**
- **1 cup sugar**

Topping:
- **Grated zest of 1 lemon**
- **¾ cup sugar**
- **1 cup all-purpose flour**
- **½ cup (1 stick) unsalted butter, at room temperature**
- **½ cup sliced almonds**

1. Preheat the oven to 375°F. Lightly butter a 13 x 9-inch baking dish.
2. Combine the berries, tapioca, lemon juice, and sugar in a large mixing bowl. Stir gently to blend well. Transfer the mixture to the prepared baking dish.
3. To make the topping, combine the lemon zest, sugar, and flour in a small bowl. Using your fingers, rub the butter into the flour mixture to form large crumbs. Sprinkle the crumbs on top of the fruit. Scatter the almonds over the topping and bake for 35 minutes, or until the top is browned and crispy. Serve hot or warm.

Deck It Out

Serve the warm crumble with a scoop of your favorite ice cream. It's especially good with butter almond. Ohhh, and don't forget that a pour of whipping cream is darn good, too.

Toasted, Roasted, and Smoked Nuts

Sometimes we get a little nutty. We both like the enhanced richness of nuts that have been toasted in the oven or in a skillet. When bags of pecans, English walnuts, pine nuts, or almonds arrive in our kitchens, we toast the shelled nuts over medium heat in a dry skillet for about 10 minutes, stirring several times. Or we place the nuts in a single layer on a baking sheet and set them in a preheated 350°F oven for 10 to 12 minutes. They're done when you just begin to smell them. Let the nuts cool and pour them back into the original bag. Set the bag in a zipper-top plastic freezer bag and label and date. Now you have toasted nuts ready to pull out of the freezer to enhance your baked goods or to add to a salad or side dish.

The metaphorically nutty part is that we also like to roast them on our grills and in the stovetop smoker. For either the grill or the stovetop smoker, have the temperature at 350° to 375°F. For a charcoal or gas grill, add 1 cup dry wood chips or ⅓ cup dry wood pellets in a foil packet poked with holes and placed over the heat. Close the lid to the grill and let the wood begin to smolder. This takes about 15 minutes. Then set the nuts, in a disposable aluminum pan, on the indirect side of the grill, close the lid, and cook for 10 minutes.

Prepare a stovetop smoker by placing 1½ tablespoons of your favorite fine wood chips in the bottom of the pan. Set the heat deflector and the grill grate in the pan. Set 2 to 3 cups of nuts in an aluminum pan or sheet of heavy-duty aluminum foil crimped around the edges to fit in the smoker. Partially close the lid and turn the heat to medium. When the first wisps of smoke appear, close the lid completely and smoke the nuts for 10 minutes.

Here's our recipe for Spicy Nuts, which make a great cocktail hors d'oeuvre. You can cook them in the oven, on the grill, or in the stovetop smoker. Place 3 cups of nuts (almonds, pecans, or walnuts) in a bowl. In another bowl, combine 2 tablespoons Worcestershire sauce, 2 tablespoons olive oil, 2 teaspoons sugar, 2 minced garlic cloves, ½ teaspoon ground cloves, ½ teaspoon red pepper flakes, and ½ teaspoon coarse kosher salt. Pour over the nuts and stir until well coated. Pour off any excess liquid and bake, grill, or toast as above.

Golden Raspberry Meringues with Pistachios

Now that meringue cookies are everywhere, it's time to make an old idea new again. An English dessert called Eton Mess blends crumbled meringues, fresh strawberries, and whipped cream into a delightful confection. We've changed it up a bit here, and we encourage you to do the same (remember our "recipe is a blueprint" philosophy). Use whatever berries are in season and whatever flavor meringue cookie you like, and come up with your own quick, unique dessert. During the week, we'd just slurp this up in a bowl. But on the weekends, we like to serve it in parfait glasses.

Makes 8 servings

- **4 cups golden or red raspberries**
- **1 cup heavy cream**
- **2 cups crumbled meringue cookies**
- **2 tablespoons finely chopped pistachios**

1. Place ½ cup of the berries in each of eight parfait glasses.
2. In the bowl of an electric mixer, whip the heavy cream until stiff peaks form. Fold the crumbled meringues into the whipped cream. Spoon the whipped cream mixture on top of the fruit and dust each parfait with the chopped pistachios. Serve immediately.

Razzle-Dazzle: Flavored Sugars

We love the delicious flavors of sugar created by Golden Fig Epicurean Delights (available at specialty food stores and SuperTargets). Our favorites include Lemon Rosebud Sugar, Lemon Lime Sugar, and Hibiscus Sugar. They are wonderful sprinkled on sugar cookies, shortbreads, biscotti, and pie pastry. Try mixing these into tea and homemade lemonade, too.

After-Dinner Favorites

Queen Bee

Is a queen bee like a black widow? Love 'em and leave 'em (or rather kill them)? Anyway, this drink is deadly good, and we can't be held responsible for what you might do after drinking this. We like it as an after-dinner drink. Then go to bed and stay out of trouble!

Makes 4 servings

- **Ice cubes**
- **½ cup coffee brandy**
- **¾ cup lemon- or lime-flavored vodka**
- **¼ cup cream sherry**

Fill four cocktail glasses with ice cubes. Combine the brandy, vodka, and sherry in a pitcher and stir well. Divide the mixture evenly between the glasses and serve.

Silk Stocking

We found this after-dinner drink fit for a lady, princess, baroness, or BBQ Queen in A. J. Rathbun's *Party Drinks!* (The Harvard Common Press, 2004).

Makes 4 servings

- **Ice cubes**
- **¾ cup white (silver) tequila**
- **¾ cup crème de cacao**
- **½ cup heavy cream**
- **Freshly ground cinnamon for garnish**

1. Fill a pitcher with ice cubes and add the tequila, crème de cacao, and heavy cream. Stir to blend.
2. Divide equally among four stemmed glasses, without allowing any ice cubes to slip in. Garnish with a sprinkle of cinnamon.

Queen of Tarts

Let's start with one yummy, easy, can't-mess-it-up crust that you pat into the pan and can make in advance. Then the filling can change with whatever you have in your cupboard, or whatever you decide to pick up at the store. The tart can go uptown with chi-chi garnishes like pomegranate seeds and mint leaves—or downtown, garnished with chocolate cookie crumbs or drizzled chocolate sauce. That's versatility, BBQ Queen style.

Makes 8 servings

Cookie Crust Pastry:
- ½ cup (1 stick) unsalted butter, at room temperature
- 1 large egg yolk
- 1 cup all-purpose flour
- ¼ teaspoon salt
- ½ teaspoon pure vanilla or almond extract
- ¼ cup sugar

Filling:
- 2 cups store-bought lemon or lime curd; 1 cup good-quality jam or preserves such as apricot, peach, raspberry, or strawberry; 1 cup good-quality almond paste, pistachio paste, or hazelnut praline paste (see page 224); or 2 cups whipped cream or crème fraîche

Garnish:
- Whole berries, sliced fruit, or chopped nuts of your choice

1. To make the crust, place all the ingredients in a food processor and process until the dough forms a ball, about 10 seconds.

2. Pat the dough into the bottom and up the sides of an 8-inch round or a 13 x 4-inch rectangular tart pan with a removable bottom. Prick the pastry all over with a fork. Cover and refrigerate for at least 30 minutes (or wrap with plastic wrap and freeze in the pan for up to 3 months).

3. Preheat the oven to 350°F.

4. Bake until the pastry is pale brown, 15 to 20 minutes. Cool completely. Release the sides of the pan and place the tart crust on a serving plate.

5. To assemble the tart, spoon the filling of your choice into the prebaked tart crust and smooth with a spatula. Garnish the top with fruits, nuts, or whatever you like. Serve immediately.

Deck It Out ························

Fill the tart shell with Golden Raspberry Meringues with Pistachios (page 233). Garnish with additional golden and red raspberries and serve with Gold and Silver Champagne Cocktails (page 33). Simply divine!

Change It Up ························

- Fill the crust with orange curd and top with candied ginger and crushed gingersnaps.
- Fill with Dark Chocolate Ganache (page 237) and top with shaved chocolate.
- Try White Chocolate Cappuccino Ganache (page 237) topped with chocolate-covered coffee beans.

A Trio of Dessert Sauces

These easy, toothsome sauces taste wonderful with a variety of desserts, from homemade or store-bought pound cake or angel food cake to ice cream–stuffed cream puffs to sliced fresh fruit. As BBQ Queens, we just love that whole mix-and-match approach.

Dulce de Leche Sauce

Dulce de leche is a Mexican caramel sauce now available at many grocery stores, placed near the sweetened condensed milk. Nestlé's "La Lechera" is available in cans, Smuckers has a jarred version, and Hershey sells one in a squeeze bottle. If you can't find dulce de leche at your grocery store, spoon a can of sweetened condensed milk into a saucepan or the slow cooker and cook over medium-low heat until it caramelizes and turns a golden brown, then remove from the heat and stir in the lemon juice and the rum, if using. The final touch of sea salt gives this sauce a fabulous flavor lift.

Makes about 1 cup

- One 14-ounce can dulce de leche
- 1 tablespoon freshly squeezed lemon juice, or to your taste
- 2 tablespoons dark rum (optional)
- Sea salt (we like *fleur de sel* in this) to taste

Spoon the dulce de leche into a saucepan and warm over low-medium heat until heated through. Stir in the lemon juice and the rum, if using. Add a pinch of sea salt, then taste and add more if desired. Serve warm. The sauce will keep, covered, in the refrigerator for up to 1 month. Reheat before serving.

Dark Chocolate Ganache

The higher the proportion of cacao in the chocolate you use, the better and richer the sauce will be, although even ganache made with packaged chocolate chips tastes mighty fine.

Makes about 2 cups

- 1 cup heavy cream
- 8 ounces good-quality semisweet chocolate, chopped

Place the cream in a large glass bowl. Microwave the cream on High until it just begins to boil, 2 to 3 minutes. Or bring the cream to a boil in a small, heavy saucepan on the stovetop. Remove the cream from the microwave or the heat. Add the chopped chocolate and let sit for 5 minutes (do not stir). Then gently stir the melted chocolate until it blends to a shiny dark chocolate sauce. Serve warm, or let cool, then refrigerate for up to 3 weeks; reheat before serving.

White Chocolate Cappuccino Ganache

The variations on the classic chocolate ganache are endless, but this is an especially yummy one, especially if you like your daily latte or cappuccino.

Makes about 2 cups

- 1 cup heavy cream
- 2 teaspoons instant espresso powder
- 8 ounces good-quality white chocolate, chopped
- ½ teaspoon ground cinnamon

Place the cream and espresso powder in a large glass bowl. Microwave the cream mixture on High until it just begins to boil, 2 to 3 minutes. Or bring the cream mixture to a boil in a small, heavy saucepan on the stovetop. Remove the cream mixture from the microwave or the heat. Add the chopped chocolate and let sit for 5 minutes (do not stir). Add the cinnamon and gently stir the melted chocolate until it blends to a shiny ivory-colored sauce. Serve warm, or let cool, then refrigerate for up to 3 weeks; reheat before serving.

Measurement Equivalents

Please note that all conversions are approximate.

LIQUID CONVERSIONS

U.S.	Metric
1 tsp	5 ml
1 tbs	15 ml
2 tbs	30 ml
3 tbs	45 ml
¼ cup	60 ml
⅓ cup	75 ml
⅓ cup + 1 tbs	90 ml
⅓ cup + 2 tbs	100 ml
½ cup	120 ml
⅔ cup	150 ml
¾ cup	180 ml
¾ cup + 2 tbs	200 ml
1 cup	240 ml
1 cup + 2 tbs	275 ml
1¼ cups	300 ml
1⅓ cups	325 ml
1½ cups	350 ml
1⅔ cups	375 ml
1¾ cups	400 ml
1¾ cups + 2 tbs	450 ml
2 cups (1 pint)	475 ml
2½ cups	600 ml
3 cups	720 ml
4 cups (1 quart)	945 ml (1,000 ml is 1 liter)

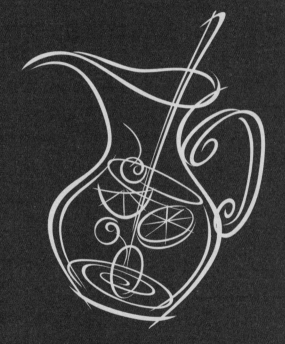

WEIGHT CONVERSIONS

U.S./U.K.	Metric
½ oz	14 g
1 oz	28 g
1½ oz	43 g
2 oz	57 g
2½ oz	71 g
3 oz	85 g
3½ oz	100 g
4 oz	113 g
5 oz	142 g
6 oz	170 g
7 oz	200 g
8 oz	227 g
9 oz	255 g
10 oz	284 g
11 oz	312 g
12 oz	340 g
13 oz	368 g
14 oz	400 g
15 oz	425 g
1 lb	454 g

OVEN TEMPERATURE CONVERSIONS

°F	Gas Mark	°C
250	½	120
275	1	140
300	2	150
325	3	165
350	4	180
375	5	190
400	6	200
425	7	220
450	8	230
475	9	240
500	10	260
550	Broil	290

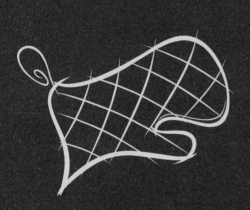

Index